THE CAMBRIDGE COMPANION TO
W. E. B. DU BOIS

As the pre-eminent African American intellectual of the twentieth century, W. E. B. Du Bois was one of the figures who most clearly saw the problem of race in the United States within global and economic perspectives. Today he remains a central figure in American history. His literary masterwork *The Souls of Black Folk* (1903) is among the most widely read and most often quoted works of African American literature. Du Bois was also a pioneering historian, sociologist, and civil rights activist, and a novelist and autobiographer. This *Companion* presents ten specially commissioned essays by an international team of scholars which explore key aspects of Du Bois's work. The book offers students a critical introduction to Du Bois, as well as opening new pathways into the further study of his remarkable career. It will be of interest to all those working in African American studies, American literature, and American studies generally.

SHAMOON ZAMIR is Reader in American Studies at King's College London. He is the author of *Dark Voices: W. E. B. Du Bois and American Thought, 1888–1903* (1995).

CAMBRIDGE COMPANIONS TO AMERICAN STUDIES

This series of Companions to key figures in American history and culture is aimed at students of American studies, history and literature. Each volume features newly commissioned essays by experts in the field, with a chronology and a guide to further reading.

Volumes published:

The Cambridge Companion to Benjamin Franklin ed. Carla Mulford
The Cambridge Companion to Thomas Jefferson ed. Frank Shuffelton
The Cambridge Companion to W. E. B. Du Bois ed. Shamoon Zamir

Volumes in preparation:

The Cambridge Companion to Bob Dylan ed. Kevin Dettmar
The Cambridge Companion to Frederick Douglass ed. Maurice Lee
The Cambridge Companion to Malcolm X ed. Robert Terrill

THE CAMBRIDGE
COMPANION TO

W.E.B. DU BOIS

EDITED BY
SHAMOON ZAMIR

CAMBRIDGE
UNIVERSITY PRESS

CAMBRIDGE UNIVERSITY PRESS
Cambridge, New York, Melbourne, Madrid, Cape Town, Singapore, São Paulo

Cambridge University Press
The Edinburgh Building, Cambridge CB2 8RU, UK

Published in the United States of America by Cambridge University Press, New York

www.cambridge.org
Information on this title: www.cambridge.org/9780521692052

First published 2008

Printed in the United Kingdom at the University Press, Cambridge

A catalogue record for this publication is available from the British Library

ISBN 978-0-521-87151-8 hardback
ISBN 978-0-521-69205-2 paperback

CONTENTS

CONTENTS

NOTES ON CONTRIBUTORS

ANGE-MARIE HANCOCK is Assistant Professor of Political Science and African American Studies at Yale University. Her research interests stand at the crossroads of American politics and political theory, with an emphasis on intersectional identities of race, gender, and class and their influence upon public policy. *The Politics of Disgust: The Public Identity of the "Welfare Queen"* (2004) won the W. E. B. Du Bois Award for Best Book from the National Conference of Black Political Scientists. Her past and forthcoming work appears in *Law and Policy*, *SOULS*, *Women, Politics and Policy*, and *Perspectives on Politics*.

RICHARD H. KING is Professor in the Department of American and Candian Studies at Nottingham University. He has published very widely in the fields of US and European intellectual history and the history and literature of the US South. His publications include *The Party of Eros: Radical Social Thought and the Realm of Freedom* (1972), *A Southern Renaissance: The Cultural Awakening of the American South, 1930–1955* (1980), *Civil Rights and the Idea of Freedom* (1992) and most recently *Race, Culture and the Intellectuals, 1940–1970* (2004).

SIEGLINDE LEMKE taught at the John F. Kennedy Institute, Free University Berlin, for fifteen years and recently became a Professor at the Albert-Ludwigs-University, Freiburg, Germany. Her publications include *Vernacular Matters: A Comparativist Approach to American Literature* (forthcoming from Duke University) and *Primitivist Modernism: Black Culture and the Origins of Transatlantic Modernism* (1998). She also co-edited Zora Neale Hurston's *The Complete Stories* (1995). Her article on Du Bois, "Berlin and Boundaries: Sollen vs. Geschehen" appeared in *boundary* 2, vol 27/3 (2000): 45–78.

WILSON JEREMIAH MOSES is Ferree Professor of American History at Pennsylvania State University. His research has emphasized the intellectual culture of African American elites in the nineteenth and early twentieth centuries and has consistently integrated political and economic with artistic and literary interests. His many publications include *The Golden Age of Black Nationalism, 1850–1925* (1978); *Black Messiahs & Uncle Toms* (1982); *Alexander Crummell: A Study in*

Civilization and Discontent (1989); *The Wings of Ethiopia: Studies in African American Life and Letters* (1990); *Afrotopia: Roots of African-American Popular History* (Cambridge University Press, 1998); and *Creative Conflict in African American Thought* (Cambridge University Press, 2004). He is currently working on *Enlightened Despotism and the Early Republic: Studies of Our Great White Fathers*.

AXEL R. SCHÄFER is Senior Lecturer in US History and Director of the David Bruce Centre for American Studies at Keele University. His main research interests are in US intellectual and political history, with particular focuses on the Progressive Era and on Cold War America. He is the author of *American Progressives and German Social Reform, 1875–1920* (2000) and was awarded the David Thelen Prize of the Organization of American Historians for an article on W. E. B. Du Bois, which was published in the *Journal of American History* (2001). His most recent publications include essays on transatlantic social reform in the Progressive Era and on public funding of religious colleges, hospitals, and welfare agencies in the US after World War II. He is currently completing a book on *The Cold War State, Religion, and the Resurgence of Evangelicalism, 1942–1990*.

KIMBERLY SPRINGER is Lecturer in the Department of American Studies at King's College London. She is the author of *Living for the Revolution: Black Feminist Organisations, 1968–1980* (2005) and editor of *Still Lifting, Still Climbing: African American Women's Contemporary Activism* (1999). Her articles have appeared in numerous scholarly journals and Internet publications.

MICHAEL STONE-RICHARDS teaches comparative literature and critical theory in the Department of Liberal Arts at the College for Creative Studies, Detroit. He is also a member of the Program Committee of MOCAD (Museum of Contemporary Art, Detroit). His book of essays, *Logics of Separation: Exile and Transcendence in Aesthetic Modernity*, is forthcoming. He has published widely (in English and French) in critical theory as well as the intellectual history of the avant-garde. He is also a founding editor of *CHAMBERWORKS*, the journal of the Detroit Humanities Group@CCS.

JENNIFER TERRY is Lecturer in English Studies at the University of Durham. Her research interests lie in American literature, postcolonial studies, and writings of the black diaspora. Her doctoral thesis, completed at the University of Warwick, examined the novels of Toni Morrison. Her current projects include a comparative exploration of African American and Caribbean fiction (forthcoming).

CARMIELE Y. WILKERSON is Assistant Professor of English at Wittenburg University. She teaches courses in Afro-Caribbean literature and the African diaspora. Her research interests have led her to write on W. E. B. Du Bois and on Afro-Caribbean national identity, including contributions to the *Booker T. Washington*

Encyclopedia and "Hidden Identity: Double Consciousness and The Caribbean Tongue," in a two-volume series on Du Bois.

SHAMOON ZAMIR is Reader in the Department of American Studies at King's College London and author of *Dark Voices: W. E. B. Du Bois and American Thought, 1888–1903* (1995). He has published on African American and Native American literatures and on American poetry, and is the editor of *American Studies: Culture, Society & the Arts*, a new series. He co-founded *Talus*, a journal of creative writing and interdisciplinary criticism, and Talus Editions, a small press. His current research is focused on American photography.

CHRONOLOGY

1868	Born William Edward Burghardt Du Bois, February 23, in Great Barrington, Massachusetts, a small town in the Berkshire Hills. Only child of Alfred Du Bois and Mary Sylvina Burghardt. Father abandons family, never to return, and Du Bois and mother move to family farm owned by maternal grandfather, Othello Burghardt, in Egermont Plain.
1869–1873	Mother works as a domestic servant.
1872	Grandfather Othello Burghardt dies, September 19. Du Bois and his mother move back to Great Barrington.
1874–1878	Attends public school. Proves to be an exceptional student and advances a grade.
1879	Grandmother Sally Burghardt dies. Mother experiences a paralytic stroke but has to continue to work despite disability. Moves with mother to rooms above the railroad station in Great Barrington.
1880–1882	Du Bois and mother live in four rooms at rear of a widow's house while he attends high school. Earns money doing odd jobs, including selling *New York Globe*, a black weekly newspaper. Buys five-volume Macaulay's *History of England*.
1883	Though only 15 years old, becomes an occasional correspondent and reporter for *Springfield Republican*, the most influential regional paper, and for *New York Globe*, a black weekly, and its successor, *Freeman*. Travels to New Bedford, Massachusetts, to meet his paternal grandfather Alexander Du Bois and attends a

West Indian emancipation celebration on August 1, a gathering of 3,000 blacks.

1884   Graduates from high school, the only African American in a class of thirteen. Aspires to attend Harvard, but mother's poverty and other factors prevent this. Works for a year as a timekeeper for a contractor building a granite mansion in Great Barrington.

1885   Mother dies, March 23, aged 54. Local teachers and Congregational churches arrange a scholarship which enables him to attend Fisk University in Nashville, Tennessee. Enters Fisk as a sophomore, seriously ill with typhoid fever in October; edits college newspaper, *Fisk Herald*, studies German, Greek, Latin, classical literature, philosophy, ethics, chemistry, and physics.

1886–1887   Teaches school for two summers in small town of Alexandria, in eastern Tennessee, hears black folk songs and spirituals for the first time. Begins singing Mozart with Fisk Mozart Society.

1888–1889   Graduates with BA from Fisk, gives commencement oration on Bismarck. Enters Harvard College as a junior with aid of Price-Greenleaf grant, rents a room from a black woman in Cambridge, rather than living in dormitory. Studies philosophy with William James and George Santayana, economics with Frank Taussig, and history with Albert Bushnell Hart. Rejected by Harvard Glee Club, develops personal ties with and lectures in the local black community.

1890   Receives BA *cum laude* in philosophy from Harvard. Wins second prize in oratorical competition, delivers one of five commencement orations, "Jefferson Davis as a Representative of Civilization," which receives attention in national press Accepted to graduate school at Harvard.

1891   Receives MA in history, and starts to apply for funding for study in Europe. Begins work on doctorate from which he presents a paper on the suppression of the African slave trade to the American Historical Association in Washington, DC.

1892	Slater Fund for the Education of Negroes provides grant to study at Friedrich Wilhelm University in Berlin, Germany, after rejecting first application.
1893	Studies history, economics, and politics in Berlin. Travels throughout Germany and several European countries, attends opera and symphony, writes a thesis on agricultural economics in the American South. On twenty-fifth birthday, writes a meditation on his destiny.
1894	Denied grant for third year of study. Also denied doctoral degree at Friederich Wilhelm University because of residency requirements. Returns to United States. Accepts teaching job in classics at Wilberforce University, a black college in Xenia, Ohio.
1895	Becomes first African American to receive PhD from Harvard.
1896	Du Bois's doctoral dissertation, *The Suppression of the African Slave-Trade to the United States of America, 1638–1870*, published as a book, the first volume in Harvard Historical Monograph series. Marries Nina Gomer, a student at Wilberforce, from Cedar Rapids, Iowa. University of Pennsylvania hires him to study the black community in Philadelphia's Seventh Ward. He and Nina move to Philadelphia.
1897	Becomes a founding member of the American Negro Academy, along with Alexander Crummell and others. Delivers "The Conservation of Races" before the Academy. Takes professorship in history and economics at Atlanta University, in Atlanta, Georgia, and begins broad study of black social life that will result in the sixteen *Atlanta University Studies* (1898–1914). Burghardt Gomer Du Bois, first child, born October 2.
1899	Son Burghardt dies of diphtheria. A poor black man, Sam Hose, lynched near Atlanta. *The Philadelphia Negro* published by the University of Pennsylvania, and articles published in *Atlantic Monthly* and *Independent*.
1900	Receives grand prize for exhibit on black economic development at the Paris Exposition. Attends Pan-African conference in London where he proposes for the first time

in his speech that "the problem of the twentieth century is the problem of the color-line." Daughter Yolande born October 21 in Great Barrington.

1901   *Atlantic Monthly* publishes "The Freedmen's Bureau," which becomes chapter 2 of *Souls*.

1902   Booker T. Washington offers teaching position at Tuskegee Institutes but Du Bois declines.

1903   *The Souls of Black Folk* appears in April, and goes through six printings by 1905. "The Talented Tenth" published in *The Negro Problem*. Leads opposition to Booker T. Washington's accommodationism.

1904   Carnegie Hall conference of black leadership held. Both Du Bois and Washington speak, and outline their differing social philosophies.

1905   The first conference of the Niagara Movement, a meeting of twenty-nine black leaders in Fort Erie, Ontario; elected general secretary; the organization is dedicated to struggle for black civil and political rights. Founds and edits *Moon Illustrated Weekly*.

1906   Second meeting of Niagara Movement. *Moon* ceases publication. Conducts sociological study of Loundes County, Alabama. White mobs attack and kill blacks in Atlanta; composes the poem "A Litany of Atlanta" in response. After riots wife and daughter move to Great Barrington.

1907   Founds and edits monthly journal *Horizon* (ceases publication in 1910). Niagara Movement fractures due to internal disagreements and debt; final gathering in 1909.

1908   Fourth meeting of Niagara Movement; poor attendance.

1909   Formation of National Negro Committee, forerunner of NAACP, and dominated by white liberals; Du Bois joins. Publishes biography *John Brown*. Final meeting of Niagara Movement.

1910   Founding of National Association for the Advancement of Colored People. Du Bois becomes director of publications and research, elected as sole black member of NAACP board of directors. Moves to New York to edit and write for *Crisis*, the official publication of the NAACP.

1911   Attends Universal Races Congress in London, a meeting devoted to refutation of racial theories. Publishes *The Quest of the Silver Fleece*, his first novel. Joins Socialist Party.

1912   Endorses Woodrow Wilson (Democrat) for president in *Crisis*. Resigns from Socialist Party.

1913   Designs major exposition in New York to commemorate fiftieth anniversary of emancipation; writes and produces *The Star of Ethiopia*, a pageant celebrating black history (performed several times in three other cities in succeeding years). Circulation of *Crisis* reaches 30,000.

1914   Advocates women's suffrage in *Crisis* and also Allied effort in World War I, while acknowledging imperial ambitions and conflicts as cause of conflict.

1915   *The Negro*, a survey of African and African American history, published. Protests against D. W. Griffith's film *The Birth of a Nation*. Death of Booker T. Washington, November 14.

1916   Writes open letter to President Wilson, criticizing segregation policies in federal government. Supports Charles Evans Hughes (Republican) for president.

1917   Unwell; undergoes kidney operations. Active in support of separate training camp for black officers in US military, arguing that this is only way to ensure black participation in war. Urges blacks to seek jobs in war industries. Participates in NAACP silent march against lynching in New York.

1918   Threatened with prosecution by Justice Department if he does not cease open criticism of racism in US military. Offered commission by War Department as special military intelligence adviser on racial problems. In July writes "Close Ranks," controversial editorial in *Crisis*, urging African Americans to support the war, preserve democracy abroad, and delay protesting lack of democracy at home. War Department offer of commission withdrawn. Goes to France to investigate treatment of black troops for NAACP.

1919   Organizer of first Pan-African Congress in Paris and elected executive secretary. Upon return to USA writes editiorial on "Returning Soldiers" which US postmaster tries to suppress; *Crisis* issue sells 106,000 copies, highest sales ever.

1920   *Darkwater: Voices from within the Veil*, collection of essays similar in form to *Souls*, published. Founds and edits *The Brownies' Book*, magazine for black children which ceases publication in 1921.

1921   Second Pan-African Congress in London, Brussels, and Paris. Critical of Marcus Garvey and the Universal Negro Improvement Association.

1922   Works for Dyer Anti-lynching Bill; passes House of Representatives but is blocked in Senate.

1923   Awarded Spingarn Medal by NAACP. Organizes Third Pan-African Congress in London, Paris, and Lisbon. Represents USA at inauguration of president in Liberia.

1924   Travels through Liberia, Sierra Leone, Guinea, and Senegal in Africa. *The Gift of Black Folk: The Negroes in the Making of America* published. Endorses Robert La Follette (Progressive) for president. Continues criticism of Marcus Garvey in *Crisis*.

1925   Alain Locke's *The New Negro: An Interpretation*, the defining text of the Harlem Renaissance, is published and includes Du Bois's "The Negro Mind Reaches Out."

1926   Establishes a Harlem theater group called the Krigwa Players. Returns from visit to Soviet Union impressed with the Bolshevik Revolution.

1927   Fourth Pan-African Congress held in New York.

1928   Daughter Yolande marries poet Countee Cullen in Harlem; wedding attended by 3,000 people; marriage ends within a year. *Dark Princess: A Romance* published.

1929   *Crisis* facing financial failure. Internal dispute within NAACP over debt-ridden magazine continues over next two years.

1930   Awarded honorary Doctor of Laws degree by Howard University, Washington, DC.

1933   Begins to rethink his own position on integration and proposes increased black separatism and economic and social self-reliance. Hands over editorship of *Crisis* to George Streator and Roy Wilkins but retains overall control. Accepts one-year professorship at Atlanta University; teaches seminar on Marx and the Negro.

1934   Advocates voluntary black segregation in editorials. Resigns from *Crisis* and NAACP. Takes up chairmanship in sociology at Atlanta University and attempts to revive *Atlanta Studies*. Travels through segregated South to conduct research. Becomes editor-in-chief of projected multivolume *Encyclopedia of the Negro*.

1935   Publishes *Black Reconstruction in America*, his greatest contribution in the field of historiography.

1936–1937   Becomes weekly columnist for *Pittsburgh Courier*, lasting until January 1938. Travels through Russia, China, and Japan. Five months' stay in Germany in 1936, researching industrial education and reporting on rise of Nazism. Witnesses Hitler's activities and denounces persecution of Jews.

1938   Delivers "A Pageant in Seven Decades, 1868–1938," an autobiographical address at Atlanta University on seventieth birthday. Awarded honorary degrees by Atlanta and Fisk universities.

1939   *Black Folk Then and Now*, revised version of *The Negro*, published.

1940   *Dusk of Dawn: An Essay toward an Autobiography of a Race Concept* published. Founds *Phylon*, an international magazine of black affairs; contributes to it until 1944.

1941–1942   Conducts sociological study of southern blacks.

1943	Organizes First Conference of Negro Land-Grant Colleges at Atlanta. Atlanta University insists he retire by 1944; receives pension for five years.
1944	Offered position with NAACP as director of special research; accepts despite reluctance to return to organization and moves back to New York. Becomes first African American member of the National Institute of Arts and Letters.
1945	Writes weekly column for *Chicago Defender* (until 1948). Participates in San Francisco meeting that drafts United Nations charter; critical of failure to oppose colonialism. Helps organize Fifth Pan-African Congress in Manchester, England, in October; meets Kwame Nkrumah and Jomo Kenyatta, leaders of emergent independence movements in Africa. Wife, Nina, hospitalized for eight months after stroke. Co-authors first volume of *Encyclopedia of the Negro* and also publishes *Color and Democracy: Colonies and Peace*, a critique of colonialism in the post-World War II world order.
1946	Invites twenty organizations to New York to draft petition to United Nations on behalf of African American civil rights; NAACP supports project.
1947	Edits *An Appeal to the World*, an NAACP sponsored volume of essays aimed at garnering world support for the African American struggle for civil rights. Soviet Union supports the initiative in *Appeal* at a UN hearing on human rights but USA opposes it. *The World and Africa* published.
1948	Following publications of memorandum critical of NAACP board of directors in *New York Times*, Du Bois is dismissed from the NAACP. Supports Henry Wallace (Progressive) for president. Along with Paul Robeson, becomes vice chairman (unpaid) of Council of African Affairs, an organization considered 'subversive' by the US attorney general.
1949	Works for and addresses Cultural and Scientific Conference for World Peace in New York. Also attends peace conferences in Paris and Moscow.

1950	Nina Gomer Du Bois dies in Baltimore, July 1. Elected chairman of the Peace Information Center, organization in favour of the banning of nuclear weapons; U.S. Justice Department considers it as being against national interest and organization disbands. Runs for U.S. Senate from New York as the American Labor candidate; receives 4 percent of vote statewide and 15 percent in Harlem.
1951	Marries 45-year-old writer, teacher, and civil rights activist Shirley Graham in secret. Indicted with four other officers of the Peace Information Center, as alleged agents of foreign interests. Fingerprinted and briefly handcuffed at arraignment in Washington, DC. Speaking tour and fundraising campaign for legal expenses raises $35,000. Trial in Washington, DC, November 8–13, ends in acquittal.
1952	Department of State refuses to issue passport on grounds that his foreign travel is not in national interest; later demands a signed statement declaring he is not a member of the Communist Party. Du Bois refuses. Left-wing political stance causes continued division between Du Bois and the black mainstream, especially the NAACP. *In Battle for Peace* offers account of his indictment and trial.
1953	Eulogizes Joseph Stalin in *National Guardian* (New York). Reads Psalm 23 at the funeral of Julius and Ethel Rosenberg, executed as Soviet agents. World Peace Council awards him International Peace Prize.
1954	Joy and surprise at Supreme Court decision in *Brown* v. *Board of Education*, outlawing segregation in schools: "I have seen the impossible happen."
1955	Refused passport to attend World Youth Festival in Poland.
1956	Gives his backing to Martin Luther King, Jr., in Montgomery, Alabama, bus boycott. Invited to lecture in People's Republic of China but again refused passport. Challenges William Faulkner to debate on segregation in Mississippi; Faulkner declines.

1957	Publishes *The Ordeal of Mansart*, first volume of *Black Flame* trilogy of historical novels, intended as a saga of black life in America from Reconstruction to the 1950s. Refused passport to attend independence ceremonies in Ghana.
1958	Ninetieth birthday celebration in New York; 2,000 attend. Begins work on *The Autobiography of W. E. B. Du Bois*. Supreme Court ruling allows him to obtain passport. Begins world tour in August; visits England, France, Belgium, Czechoslovakia, East Germany, and Soviet Union. Receives honorary degree from Humboldt University in East Berlin, previously Freidrich Wilhelm University which Du Bois had attended.
1959	Meets Nikita Khrushchev. Travels to China, meets Mao Zedong and Zhou Enlai. Receives International Lenin Prize. Publishes *Mansart Builds a School*, second volume of *Black Flame* trilogy.
1960	Travels to Ghana and Nigeria to attend celebrations of independence and inaugurations.
1961	Daughter Yolande dies of heart attack in Baltimore in March. *Worlds of Color*, final part of *Black Flame* trilogy, published. Accepts invitation from Kwame Nkrumah to move to Ghana and to revive the *Encyclopedia Africana* project. Applies for membership in the Communist Party of the USA; departs for Ghana in October.
1962	Undergoes prostate surgery in Accra and Bucharest. Travels to China. *Autobiography* published in Soviet Union.
1963	Becomes citizen of Ghana. Turns 95 on February 23. Dies in Accra, August 27, on eve of civil rights march on Washington. Buried with state funeral in Accra, August 29.
1968	*The Autobiography of W. E. B. Du Bois* published in USA.

This chronology is based primarily on the biographical outlines provided in David W. Blight and Robert Gooding-Williams and by Henry Louis Gates, Jr., and Terri Hume Oliver in their respective editions of *The Souls of Black Folk*.

SHAMOON ZAMIR

Introduction

W. E. B. Du Bois has occupied a pre-eminent place in African American literary, social, and political thought for a very long time, and, in recent years, he has been recognized as a figure central to the history of American thought in the twentieth century. His critique of the educational and political policies of Booker T. Washington set the agenda for debates about populism, leadership, and the relative merits of a humanistic education within the black community for much of the century. His role in the founding of the National Association for the Advancement of Colored People (NAACP) placed him at the forefront of the African American civil rights movement. As a key interpreter and disseminator of Pan-Africanism, he became a central figure in postcolonial discourse. As the author of a number of land-mark works in black historiography and sociology, he brought a scholarly rigor to an understanding of the social and historical dimensions of race in the United States which is impressive even today. As a mentor to and supporter of many of the writers of the Harlem Renaissance, he helped shape the literary movement which continues to attract the greatest attention within African American literary studies. Perhaps most importantly of all, in *The Souls of Black Folk* (1903) he produced a work of exceptional literary achievement, among the most widely read and most often quoted works in African American literary history. It is the work by which most readers know Du Bois; it is also the work in which he most thoroughly explores the implications of his famous proposal, made at the first Pan-African confer-ence in London in 1900 and then repeated throughout his career, that "the problem of the Twentieth Century is the problem of the color-line." No other writer has made us understand as clearly and fully as Du Bois that race and modernity are indissolubly linked: to think one is necessarily to think the other.

Du Bois is justly most famous as the author of *Souls*. A collection of fourteen interconnected essays examining the legacies of slavery and the effects of racism from a variety of disciplinary perspectives, it is a text which today is regularly taught on any number of college and university level courses of African American and American literature, as well as those dealing with American cultural and intellectual history and the histories of the American South. For most readers *Souls* provides their primary and most sustained contact with Du Bois, and it is the work which most clearly secures his place within American literary and intellectual history. But as significant an achievement as *Souls* is, it is important to remember that it appeared in the early stages of an extremely productive, varied, and long career. Du Bois worked as a writer, teacher, and activist from the 1890s right up to his death in 1963. During these seventy or so years he produced major and influential work in a number of disciplines and genres.

Though rarely included in standard histories of American historiography and sociology, Du Bois was an early champion in America of positivist methodology in both disciplines and set a remarkably high standard for subsequent studies. *The Suppression of the African Slave-Trade to the United States of America, 1638–1870* (1896) was a meticulously detailed piece of archival research which drew upon Du Bois's encounters with Rankean historiography in both the United States and Germany in order to establish new standards of research for African American historical studies. *Black Reconstruction in America* (1935), Du Bois's other major achievement in black history, was a groundbreaking examination of the African American contribution to the development of the South in the aftermath of the Civil War. Both works continue to hold much of their relevance today. *The Philadelphia Negro: A Social Study* (1899) matched the positivist rigor of *Suppression* and combined extensive fieldwork, conducted largely by Du Bois himself, with an historically informed framework in its account of poverty and social exclusion among the blacks of Philadelphia. *The Philadelphia Negro* established a high standard of research for sociological accounts of African American communities. The famous Atlanta series of sociological and historical studies of African American society, culture, and the past, which Du Bois supervised and edited while a professor at Atlanta University, were a continuation of his early work in historiography and sociology.

In addition to his academic work, Du Bois also wrote poetry, plays, pageants, and a significant body of fiction. These works have not been widely studied, but in recent years the novels in particular have begun to attract considerable critical attention, especially for their attempts to explore race within an international understanding of modernity (e.g. Byerman, Posnock). Du Bois's first novel, *The Quest of the Silver Fleece* (1911), set in the post-Reconstruction South and exploring the problematic of black leadership, shares much with *Souls* but, like much of the subsequent fiction, makes female characters central to the narrative. *Dark Princess* (1928), a peculiar blend of realism and romance, pursues a narrative of an affair between an African American hero and an Indian maharani within a international setting that moves between the United States, Europe, and Asia in its explorations of race, class, and colonialism. *The Black Flame* trilogy consists of *The Ordeal of Mansart* (1957), *Mansart Builds a School* (1959), and *Worlds of Color* (1961), and offers a narrative of black life in America that stretches from 1876 to 1956. Here Du Bois abandons romance, though he revisits the internationalism of *Dark Princess*, and explores an altogether darker vision of the weight of history upon individual lives than in the earlier fictions.

Du Bois made important contributions to African American letters in two other genres: journalism and autobiography. He published widely in newspapers and magazines and founded and edited four journals. The *Moon* and the *Horizon* were early and short-lived attempts to establish journals focused on race, and Du Bois's editorship of the scholarly *Phylon* ran for only four years (1940–4). His major contribution was the founding and editorship of the *Crisis* from 1910 to 1934 (the journal is still in existence). Although it was officially an organ of the NAACP, Du Bois exercised strict and independent editorial control and often found himself in conflict with the views of the parent organization. Nevertheless, under his editorship, the journal became one of the most important national African American periodicals, fostering radical protest and debate as well as the works of creative writers. Through such support and through its literary competitions the *Crisis* came to play an influential role in the shaping of the Harlem Renaissance.

The Autobiography of W. E. B. Du Bois: A Soliloquy on Viewing My Life from the Last Decade of its First Century (1968), published posthumously, was the last major work by Du Bois. As with the earlier *Dusk of Dawn: An Essay Toward an Autobiography of a Race Concept* (1940), it eschewed the self-regard and identity politics that characterize much of the genre and offered instead a more radical subsuming of the self within a collective history. And once again the life was located within international frames, with a movement toward Africa in *Dusk of Dawn* and with an account of a visit to the Soviet Union and communist China in *Autobiography*. These two volumes, however, are not Du Bois's only works of autobiography. Such narratives also play an important role in both *Souls* and *Darkwater: Voices from within the Veil* (1920).

It is perhaps unsurprising that the first phase of serious scholarly interest in Du Bois (from the late 1950s to the end of the 1980s) focused largely on his social and political activism and thought within the ambit of African American Studies, and took the form predominantly of biographical accounts. Over the last fifteen years or so, however, a new and remarkably widespread academic interest in Du Bois has developed. This recent scholarship has not only deepened and consolidated existing approaches to his life and work, it has opened up new avenues of investigation. These assessments have focused above all on Du Bois as a writer and on his place within a cosmopolitan, comparative, and internationally defined intellectual history. This re-evaluation has been the product of but has also very much helped produce a series of significant paradigm shifts in both African American and American Studies.

Three strands of reorientation within contemporary American Studies have been especially formative in the current re-evaluation of Du Bois. First and foremost perhaps has been the broader and deeper engagement with race. Black American culture, history, and the arts have been subject to an unprecedented degree of scrutiny by both African American and non-African American scholars at the same time that race has been recognized as a formative force within "white" and "canonical" cultural histories (e.g. Sundquist; North; Lemke, *Primitist Modernism*; Siemerling). As a result of this, the separation of "margin" and "center" is being replaced by a more dialectical and comparative understanding of African American and European American traditions. It is unsurprising that the man who as early as 1903 prophesied that "the problem of the twentieth century is the problem of the color-line" should be central to this new critical orientation.

Secondly, the revival of interest in Pragmatism as a tradition of philosophical and cultural thought indigenous to the United States has redirected attention to Du Bois and allowed us to see his work in new contexts. Du Bois studied with William James at Harvard and contemporary accounts of his intellectual development have offered widely divergent assessments of his relationship to Pragmatism. A number of critics locate him within a Pragmatist genealogy (e.g. West, Posnock); others have argued that his writings are best understood as a critical reformulation of Pragmatism propelled by the experience of racism in the United States and the influence of European philosophical traditions (e.g. Zamir, *Dark Voices*).

Lastly, and most recently, scholars have argued against the continued usefulness of studying the culture and history of the United States within the confines of a nationalist paradigm. For these writers, to continue to work within such limits is to reproduce potentially the ideology of an American exceptionalism. What is needed instead, it is argued, is a transnational framework. This has led to renewed interest in the mutually formative influence of Europe and America on each other, as well as to a new exploration of hemispheric studies in which continuities and connections between South America, Canada, the Caribbean, and the United States have been brought to the fore (e.g. Rowe, Giles). Within African American studies the move toward transnationalism has taken the form of "black Atlantic" studies, a comparative and mobile understanding of cultural, political, and economic exchanges triangulated between the United States, Africa, and Europe (e.g. Gilroy). Du Bois was engaged by European politics and Marxist thought and activism, he pioneered scholarly interest in African cultural history and was a leading figure in the Pan-African movement, renouncing his American citizenship near the end of his life and accepting residency in Ghana. He has, therefore, become a touchstone for transnational debates within American Studies.

The contributions to the present volume reflect many of the critical orientations and reorientations outlined above, though not in any program-matic way. The *Companion* approaches Du Bois's work through three broad and overlapping frames: literary studies, the theory of race, and national and international intellectual history. Though not divided into separate parts, the *Companion* falls loosely into three sections which mirror these frames. The first four chapters focus on Du Bois primarily as a literary figure. Zamir offers an exploration of both the overall structure of *Souls* and a close reading of its literary strategies. The discussion includes an examination of Du Bois's well-known psychology of "double consciousness" and a consider-ation of the relation of *Souls* to Du Bois's earlier work in history and sociology. Many of the strands in this extended discussion are picked up, amplified, and approached differently in later chapters. Sieglinde Lemke's examination of "Of the Coming of John," the one piece of fiction in *Souls*, continues with close reading through a detailed consideration of Du Bois's use of Wagner and opens out toward the more extensive overview of Du Bois's fiction offered by Jennifer Terry. Finally, Carmiele Wilkerson and Zamir attempt to locate Du Bois as a formative presence within the discourse of the "New Negro" and within the literary history of the Harlem Renais-sance, the most widely studied African American literary movement and also the one with which Du Bois himself was most consistently associated. A second section of sorts is formed by the essays on race, leadership, and civil rights. Ange-Marie Hancock examines the dialectical relationship between race and diversity in Du Bois's thought while Axel Schäfer traces Du Bois's thought on race as it develops through his work as historian and sociologist. Kimberly Springer examines Du Bois's conceptualizations of race leadership and also offers an account of his actual involvement in the history of the civil rights struggle. The last three essays in the volume place Du Bois within broader national and international intellectual histories.

Wilson Jeremiah Moses surveys Du Bois's life-long engagement with the place of Africa in world history, and Richard King suggests different ways in which Du Bois can be sited within American and European traditions of thought. Michael Stone-Richards's detailed comparison of Du Bois and Fanon continues this discussion, and, in its examination of psychology and of *Souls*, also allows the reader to circle back to earlier chapters.

Given the length of Du Bois's life and his incredible productivity as a writer, it is not possible to provide a fully comprehensive account of his achievement in a volume of this size. The editorial approach taken here is certainly not one which might have been taken by a historian, or a sociologist, or a political scientist. But even from the perspective of literary or intellectual history, there are certain aspects of Du Bois's work which have had to be excluded due to limitations of space. So, for example, Du Bois's autobiographical writing and his journalism are touched upon but not considered at length.

The *Companion* also grounds itself first and foremost in considerations of Du Bois's work up to the outbreak of World War II. There are two reasons for this. Though Du Bois continued to write and to produce works of importance throughout his life, his claim upon our attention rests above all on certain key texts which appeared between 1896 and 1940, from *Suppression of the African Slave-Trade* to *Dusk of Dawn*. Secondly, it is also the case that the foundations of Du Bois's philosophical, political, and cultural ideas and attitudes were securely laid through a late-nineteenth-century American and European education, and through the ways in which this education confronted the failure of the promise of Emancipation and Reconstruction which defined and shaped African American social and historical experience during the first fifty years of Du Bois's life.

A Note on Citations

At present the most comprehensive and readily accessible collection of Du Bois's works is *Writings*, ed. N. Huggins (New York: Library of America, 1986). Wherever possible this volume has been used as the common source of citations in the *Companion*. A nineteen-volume edition of Du Bois's works is forthcoming from Oxford University Press under the editorship of Henry Louis Gates, Jr., but was not available at the time of going to press.

I

SHAMOON ZAMIR

The Souls of Black Folk: Thought and Afterthought

> ... a combination of social problems is far more than a matter of mere
> addition; – the combination itself is a problem.
> W. E. B. Du Bois, *The Philadelphia Negro* (1899)

The subtitle of *The Souls of Black Folk* is "*Essays and Sketches.*" Together, the title and subtitle indicate a collection which offers the reader variations upon a theme. The fourteen chapters which comprise the main body of the book were written between 1897 and 1903. Nine had been published previously in various journals and magazines before being revised for inclusion in *Souls*. Taken together, the fourteen chapters range across social, political, and economic history, religion and education, psychology, the sociology of music, autobiography, and fiction. But *Souls* is more than simply a collection of essays and fiction held loosely together by a focus on the broad common ground of African American historical experience and contemporary life. It is a "combination" but one which is more than "mere addition." In bringing together the disparate pieces, in revising the already published ones, and in ordering and framing them in particular ways, Du Bois transfigured them, so that *Souls* became a literary work which is greater than the sum of its parts.

In its opening lines *Souls* announces the problem which is its first subject: "the color-line" as a border which, in its very divisiveness, is constitutive of modernity. The present essay argues that the book's literary achievement lies above all in creating a form in which understanding can only grasp the scope and nature of the problem of race and modernity, its confounding knottiness, by passing through its own undoing and leaving behind the established academic and journalistic conventions of social analysis. In arguing this I do not mean to suggest that Du Bois severs himself from his own pioneering work in historiography and sociology which precedes *Souls*; rather, I am proposing that in developing a model of integrative thought best described as a form of poetic imagination, *Souls* registers a recognition of the limitations of an instrumentalist or specialized shaping of knowledge, a delimiting which Du Bois's own academic work both inherits and innovates. It is because the structural "fact" of "color-prejudice" is always division, both social and psychological, that *Souls* insists upon "the breadth and broadening of human reason" and a "catholicity of taste and culture" as necessary responses.[1] This is why Du Bois's major work is treated here as a comedy. Reflecting on the comic "attitude toward history," Kenneth Burke has written that "the process of processes which this comedy meditates upon" is what he calls the "bureaucratization of the imaginative." By this Burke means to indicate a distrust in "the carrying out of one possibility because it necessarily restricts other possibilities."[2] *Souls* doggedly pursues the plural. Tragically haunted everywhere by social fracture and death, it seeks nevertheless to connect and restore through an imaginative plenitude, even as it acknowledges the limits faced by this endeavor. The mobile line between fragmentation and integration is a structuring principle in *Souls*, and the problem of reading Du Bois's book is the problem of reading this line in its movement. In this sense, "combination itself is a problem."

Although *Souls* has garnered substantial attention from literary scholars and intellectual historians over the last thirty or so years, and especially in the last decade, critical accounts have consistently overlooked the fact that Du Bois himself signaled his awareness of the particular nature of his own form at both the structural level of the whole, and also at the more intimate level of style, image, and metaphor. Du Bois openly acknowledged the demands his work was likely to make on the reader, and in so doing he explicitly invited a reading in which meaning was actively produced rather than passively received. In "The Forethought" and "The After-thought" which frame *Souls*, and in a brief note on the book published in 1904, Du Bois provided what may be taken as guides, provisional and partial to be sure but instructive of general strategies, for a reading of his book. The discussion that follows approaches the problem of form, of multiplicity and coherence in *Souls* through a reading of these reflexive texts. It seeks to address the experience of reading *Souls* as a whole through a reading of some of its smaller parts.

I

About a year and a half after the appearance of *Souls*, Du Bois published a brief note on his own book which seems at first to be an apologia for its failures. Du Bois begins by accepting that his exclusive focus on race, while it allows "clearness of vision" and "intensity of feeling and conviction," inevitably imposes "a certain narrowness of view," and a loss "of that breadth of view which the more cosmopolitan races have." He then offers a backward, and somewhat melancholy, glance over the structure of *Souls* that proposes that the book's heterogeneity is also its undoing:

> *The Souls of Black Folk* is a series of fourteen essays written under various circumstances and for different purposes during a period of seven years. It has, therefore, considerable, perhaps too great, diversity. There are bits of history and biography, some description of scenes and persons, something of controversy and criticism, some statistics and a bit of storytelling. All this leads to rather abrupt transitions of style, tone and viewpoint and, too, without doubt, to a distinct sense of incompleteness and sketchiness.

However, this account of the book as a scrappy anthology in which all the "bits" have failed to transcend the conflicting pulls of their various original purposes quickly turns into the revelation of a unity counterbalancing and underlying the "diversity":

> ... there is a unity in the book, not simply the general unity of the larger topic, but a unity of purpose in the distinctively subjective note that runs in each essay. Through all the book runs a personal and intimate tone of self-revelation. In each essay I sought to speak from within—to depict a world as we see it who dwell therein. In thus giving up the usual impersonal and judicial attitude of the traditional author I have lost in authority but gained in vividness.[3]

The unity promised by autobiography and subjective insight may not entirely harness the volatility of *Souls*'s diverse form, but the unfolding of the personal life *is* one major narrative strand which runs submerged through the whole of the book; it not only helps weave the fourteen chapters together, it is, as will be demonstrated later, an essential element in the distinctive epistemology of the book. *Souls* opens with Du Bois's childhood in Great Barrington, Massachusetts (chapter 1), and concludes with him in his thirties, now a professor at Atlanta University (chapter 14). Along the way Du Bois bears direct witness as both observer and participant to the world of segregation or Jim Crow in which the mass of African Americans lived at the start of the twentieth century. There are many moments in which we see the world through Du Bois's eyes and hear what he himself refers to as the "distinctively subjective note," but most notable are his account of his experiences of teaching the black poor in the hills of rural Tennessee during the summers when he was a student at Fisk University (chapter 4), and his elegy for his dead son (chapter 11). These pieces of a life may not add up to a conventional autobiography, but they are a quiet though firm counterpoint to the larger composition and as such constitute a strong structuring device for the book.

But if in the note from 1904 Du Bois points to autobiography and subjective insight as a source of unity at both the narrative and tonal levels in *Souls*, in the "Forethought" from 1903 he suggests a different structural logic for the design of the book, one which in effect runs parallel to the autobiographical. Here Du Bois divides the book in two parts and describes the progress of the reader from the first (chapters 1 to 9) to the second part (chapters 10 to 14) as a narrative of immersion, a movement towards the inner depths of black spirituality, culture, and psychology usually hidden from or invisible to most whites. In describing the contents of the first nine chapters Du Bois makes it clear that this part of the book deals with aspects of African American life as it is lived within the white world, within, in other words, the constraints and abuses of Jim Crow prohibitions and a system of servitude and poverty that amounts to nothing less than a form of neo-slavery. But in the second half the book shifts its ground: "Leaving, then, the world of the white man, I have stepped within the Veil, raising it that you may view faintly its deeper recesses, – the meaning of its religion, the passion of its human sorrow, and the struggle of its greater souls. All this I have ended with a tale twice told but seldom written" (359).

As a description of the final five chapters of *Souls* this is of course incomplete. Religion is the concern of chapter 10, the "human sorrow" is the personal grief at "the Passing of the First-Born" (chapter 11), "the struggle of its greater souls" refers us to the eulogy on the African American leader Alexander Crummell (chapter 12) and the "tale twice told" is the story of John and his lynching (chapter 13). What is missing from the outline is the final chapter on the Sorrow Songs. When Du Bois prepared the text for a fiftieth-anniversary edition in 1953, he revised the final sentence of his description to read "All this I have ended with a tale twice told but seldom written, and a chapter of song." The original omission was an oversight which allows us to see something of the process of design which went into the making of *Souls*. The book was published on April 18, 1903. The "Forethought" is dated February 1, 1903. At this fairly late stage Du Bois had clearly settled on a plan for the book which included only thirteen chapters. But as Du Bois's correspondence with the publisher, A. C. McClurg of Chicago, makes clear, Francis Fisher Browne, his editor, had urged him to include the chapter on the Sorrow Songs. Du Bois did reconsider his plan but failed to revise the "Forethought." As late as February 21 Du Bois was still working on what would become the well-known final chapter of *Souls*. But the chapter was not Browne's idea; it was part of Du Bois's own original design for the book. This is clear from a letter dated January 21 in which Browne asks Du Bois: "Is it too late to carry out your original intention of having a chapter on 'Sorrow Songs of the Negroes'?" Browne was absolutely right that "it would be a capital addition to the book," and generations of readers owe him a debt of gratitude for his editorial acumen.[4]

The division between the two parts of *Souls* as these are demarcated in Du Bois's "Forethought" is essentially the division between previously published essays and those that were unpublished or written expressly for the volume. The exceptions are "Of the Wings of Atalanta" (chapter 5), which was not previously published and is included in the first part, and "Of the Faith of the Fathers," which had appeared in 1900 and is placed at the beginning of the second part. As David Levering Lewis, Du Bois's most accomplished biographer, has noted, the already published essays were not simply gathered together but "cut, polished, and mounted with a jeweller's precision for the McClurg collection. A good deal of new material was added in some cases, and themes heightened by new endings."[5] The revisions were, then, part of a conscious design which was brought to completion through the inclusion of the new essays. The "Forethought" makes clear that the new essays were more than merely supplements to or a padding-out of what might otherwise have seemed like a fairly slim collection of fugitive pieces; they were intended to give a form that shaped the trajectories of meaning in the already published works beyond their original purposes and contexts.

The deft intertwining in *Souls* of personal life and a broad survey of the lives of the mass of African Americans, on both sides of the veil in both the past and the present, is akin to the blend of individual and collective history which is a characteristic of the Romantic genre of *Bildungsbiographie*.[6] Du Bois maps the autobiographical and the immersion narratives of his collection across a shared geography. As the book moves from the New England North to the South of the Black Belt, it moves along the spatial axis which undergirds African American history and cultural mythology – an axis quite distinct from the East–West one which lies at the heart of much American nationalist historiography and self-fashioning. And this spatial journey is also a journey in time. The deeper South the reader is taken, the deeper the book probes into the African American past.

Critics have noted that the complex spatio-temporal plotting of *Souls* reverses the narrative logic of the traditional slave narrative, the ur-genre of African American literature.[7] The expected movement of the slave narrative is from slavery in the South to freedom in the North, an autobiographical trajectory which is oriented toward the future. In turning back this narrative movement Du Bois registers through his literary form the tragedy of which he writes throughout the book. Exposing the failure of Reconstruction as a whittling away of the promise of Emancipation, *Souls* eschews myths of progress and locates the present as a moment caught in the ebb tide of a regressive history flowing back to a past servitude. The undermining of genre conventions thwarts readerly expectations, and so opens up a space in which the innovation of literary form becomes a means for thinking about the nature of historical and cultural experience outside the blinkered comforts of received opinion.

The object of Du Bois's critique here is not simply the white reader who is pushed to see his nation anew, but also an African American leadership which, in its eagerness to integrate blacks into modernity, has too readily jettisoned the past as an embarrassment and so severed the indissoluble link between memory and action which lies at the heart of Du Bois's writing. As the third chapter of *Souls* makes plain, Du Bois's primary interlocutor here is Booker T. Washington (see Springer in this volume). The founder of the Tuskegee Normal and Industrial Institute, which offered vocational training to artisans, tradespersons, and schoolteachers, Washington was the pre-eminent black American leader on the national stage at the time of the writing and publication of *Souls*. His advocacy of industrial and vocational training over a more humanistic education as the surest path of African American progress, and his tacit acceptance of a seg-regation of the races are the two pillars of his program which are knocked down with exemplary and forceful tact by Du Bois in his third chapter. But *Souls*'s strategic revision of the slave narrative form is also in part a critique of Washington. In his autobiography, *Up from Slavery* (1901), Washington had appropriated the ascent structure of the slave narrative and conflated it with the Horatio Alger narrative of earthly success and with Andrew Carnegie's "gospel of wealth." Du Bois argues repeatedly in *Souls* that Washington in fact has confused means and ends, that his program has left the true human purposes of progress behind and substituted in their stead an empty materialism. Du Bois's use of the slave narrative form refuses the optative mood; *Souls* attempts to embed the reader's consciousness in the human, lived reality of the Black Belt, to unhouse consciousness as it were so that it cannot help but see the full and intractable complexity of being black in America.

If the inversion of the slave narrative structure provides an over-arching frame for the book, individual chapters make use of a diverse range of narra-tives from philosophy, literature, myth, and religion in similar fashion. In other words, the use of authoritative narratives as ironic counterpoints in the construction of its own narratives is a recurrent motif in *Souls*. "Of Our Spiritual Strivings" (chapter 1) is closely modeled on Hegel's *Phenomenology of Mind*, and "The Sorrow Songs" uses Plato's allegory of the cave from his *Republic* as a subtext; Bunyan's *Pilgrim's Progress* lies behind the eulogy to Alexander Crummell in chapter 12; moral lessons derived from the mythical stories of Atalanta and the apples of Hippomenes, and of

Jason's quest for the golden fleece shape the arguments of the fifth and eighth chapters; Wagner's version of the legend of Lohengrin shadows the story of the two Johns throughout chapter 13 (see Lemke in this volume); and Du Bois alludes many times to the biblical tales of the exile of the Israelites and their journey to the promised land in describing the historical fate of African Americans.[8] As with the slave narrative, almost every one of these narratives is powered by a strong teleology, and in every case Du Bois's text works to place in crisis the security generated by the drive to conclusion. This repeated strategy becomes a hallmark of both the cultural criticism and the historical imagination of *Souls*. So, for example, the myths of Atalanta and Jason act as warnings against the pursuit of materialism over ethical and intellectual ends, and the biblical tales of exodus and Bunyan's narrative of Christian's journey to the Heavenly City chime with the use of the slave narrative form because they too highlight the failure to achieve true freedom in post-Reconstruction America.

Priscilla Wald has observed accurately that *Souls* "posits a connection between creating a narrative and struggling with the terms of a cultural identity, a connection that turns aesthetic creation into a political gesture." She locates Du Bois's struggle with narrative in the context of "the proliferation of histories of the United States in the late nineteenth and early twentieth century" which "assumed the task of narrating the nation." The recuperation of a national unity lost in the Civil War was of primary concern to white historians at this time, even as this unity was seen to be under a new threat of heterogeneity posed by the increased migration of African Americans to the North and by the arrival of new immigrants from southern and eastern Europe.[9] Du Bois's breaking and subversion of narrative conventions indicates his refusal to subsume and erase this heterogeneity within a falsely cohesive national story.

Du Bois's resistance to a naive historical progressivism is intimately bound up with his deeply felt sense of the past as a living presence in the here and now. Memory is in *Souls* an active resource, the sign of a radical and critical melancholy rather than the symptom of a debilitating mental paralysis. It is sited and given in its workings through the figures of the grave and song. In the very first line of its "Forethought" *Souls* presents itself as a grave which requires a careful hermeneutics: "Herein lie buried many things which if read with patience may show the strange meaning of being black here in the dawning of the Twentieth Century" (359).[10] Du Bois is indicating something other than the fact that his book will ground itself in a remembering of the historical past; he is alerting the reader that *Souls* itself needs to be understood as a structure of memory, as a book which uses memories of its own unfolding as a principle device to shape this unfolding. I mean that certain moments, images, and words from one part of the book are often recalled, sometimes directly and sometimes in a muted or transformed way, in other parts, and that this is an exceptionally consistent practice in *Souls*. It is perhaps the most consistent device by which *Souls* draws together its disparate parts, and it is a device which requires of the reader an attentive eye and ear, and the interpretive use of an accumulating memory of their subtlest perceptions.

Nowhere does Du Bois better capture the sense of the workings of this memory and of the history of human experience which is its object than in his sense of music as a repository of fragmented meaning which only the imagination can resurrect. At the close of the "Forethought" Du Bois notes that "Before each chapter...stands a bar of the Sorrow Songs, – some echo of haunting melody from the only American music which welled up from black souls in the dark past" (359–60). Each bar is an "echo" not because it is a fragment excerpted from a musical whole, but because the songs as they have come down to Du Bois's time are already far removed from their original versions. This is why later in the book Du Bois is critical of modern "debased imitations of Negro melodies" because they catch "the jingle but not the music, the body but not the soul, of the Jubilee songs" (495). But equally at issue is the interference in communication resulting from cultural separation and from the erosions and transformations wrought by history. The "message" of the songs "is naturally veiled and half-articulate. Words and music have lost each other and new and cant phrases of a dimly understood theology have displaced the older sentiment" (541). Susan Mizruchi has accurately noted of the sorrow songs, following Eric Sundquist's excellent commentary, that "as published *adaptations* of the original slave songs, brought into conformity with Euro-American tastes, they confirm the difficulty of preserving authentic oral culture. As oral inscriptions of the sufferings of slavery, whose own preservation seems tenuous, they embody the dilemma of Black cultural survival." So, in effect, "these songs represent at once an elite language, legible to those who read music, and a secret ethnic code audible only to those who know how the songs 'really' sound."[11]

All this could very well be taken as a description of *Souls* itself. In arguing as he does that the intangible and subjective experience of history which resides behind the "theology" and the modern-day "adaptations" is the real subject of the sorrow songs, Du Bois indicates also the subject of his own writing, and at the same time a problem of reading, because the traces of such experience require the most patient and attentive archaeology before they can be brought to light. But in attempting to undertake such a literary archaeology, Du Bois inevitably repeats the dilemma of the "adaptations." From the perspective of folk culture, *Souls* too is written in "an elite language." It is inaccessible to the very folk whose experience it seeks to voice, and is addressed to a white readership largely ignorant of this experience and of its own entanglement within it. But Du Bois himself is conscious of the pressure placed upon legibility and communication by history's traces and by cross-cultural address. This is why he foregrounds the thematics of reading and writing so often in *Souls*. The guidance Du Bois provides for the reader is again carefully directed. Du Bois's claim in the "Forethought" that he will raise the "Veil" so that the white reader "may view" the "deeper recesses" of the black world is a promise of transparency, consistent with the assertion later in the book that the racial problems of the South require "a plain, unvarnished tale" (476). But this is a view which is revealed only "faintly." When Du Bois comes to speak about his writing at what I referred to earlier as the intimate level of style, image, and metaphor, it is the lack of transparency which he stresses. Earlier in the "Forethought," and following on from the conceptualization of the book as a grave, Du Bois writes that he has "sought...to sketch... the spiritual world" of African Americans "in vague, uncertain outline." That allusiveness and indirection may be a conscious method rather than a failing is more clearly stated in Du Bois's 1904 note on *Souls*, though with a characteristic passing gesture of self-deprecation. He acknowledges that for some readers "the style and the workmanship of the book" may not make "its meaning altogether clear":

> A clear central message it has conveyed to most readers, I think, but around this center there has lain a penumbra of vagueness and half-veiled allusion which has made these and others especially impatient. How far this fault is in me and how far it is in the nature of the message I am not sure. It is difficult, strangely difficult, to translate the finer feelings of men into words. The Thing itself sits before you; but when you have dressed it out in periods it seems fearfully uncouth and inchoate. Nevertheless, as the feeling is deep the greater the impelling force to seek to express it. And here the feeling was deep.[12]

Patience is what Du Bois had asked of the reader in his "Forethought." Here he repeats again the distinction between an obvious content and its "deeper recesses." This hidden world is a world of "feelings" which can be reached only through what appears as "a penumbra of vagueness and half-veiled allusion" rather than the more direct approach which makes the subject "uncouth and inchoate." Frontal lighting flattens the subject; chiaroscuro brings out the subject's contours in all their complexity.

What Du Bois defines here in spatial terms as "center" and surrounding "penumbra," he refers to in temporal terms in *Souls* as "thought" and "afterthought." The movement between the two is negotiated through the thematics of reading and writing. In the discussion which follows, the Du Boisian center examined is education. The arguments for a liberal, humanist education are clearly stated but around them there is a darker psychology of doubt and division. The dialectic of the two is enacted through a complex textual entanglement. The discussion will return to the problem of feeling and history in *Souls* later; the next section reads the book's "After-thought" in detail as an example of what Du Bois calls a "penumbra." This compressed concluding text leads us back to the dialectic of education in earlier sections of the book.

II

The image of *Souls* as a grave, as a book everywhere haunted by the dead, is transfigured in unexpected and startling ways by Du Bois's "After-thought." In its closing moments, *Souls* re-imagines itself as a book of life, or at least as a book finally poised between the threat of an abortive death and the promise of renewal:

> Hear my cry, O God the Reader; vouchsafe that this my book fall not still-born into the world-wilderness. Let there spring, Gentle One, from its leaves vigor of thought and thoughtful deed to reap the harvest wonderful. (Let the ears of a guilty people tingle with truth, and seventy millions sigh for the righteousness which exalteth nations, in this drear day when human brother-hood is mockery and a snare.) Thus in Thy good time may infinite reason turn the tangle straight, and these crooked marks on a fragile leaf be not indeed. (547)

The invocation of the mythos of spring suggests that the spirit of tragedy which has so forcefully and consistently hung over the entire book can finally be converted into a comic resolution, and the oblique insights and probings through which the book has unfolded can be set straight, can be made clear and legible at last. But the brief "After-thought" is among the most compressed passages of writing anywhere in *Souls* and requires careful and patient unpacking. Its few lines gather up important words and images and the arguments they serve from the preceding chapters and meld them together in a confirmation that the second subject of *Souls*, the subject which develops alongside the larger subject of race, is education; it is education conceived as the forms of the life of the mind adequate to an understanding of the color-line within the contexts of modernity, which is to say to an understanding of modernity itself. Leaf, spring, harvest, still-born, book, tangle, afterthought: these words together constitute what Kenneth Burke refers to as a "cluster": "what images *b*, *c*, *d* the poet introduces whenever he talks with engrossment of subject *a*."[13] In the case of *Souls*, the subject is education.

The book has argued throughout that education, in its broadest and truest sense, can be an agent of individual and social transformation, but for this to be so it must be grounded in radical diversity and human purpose rather than in a narrow instrumentalism and insularity. Du Bois states the essence of his ideal in response to the central question of black education in his day, "shall we teach them trades, or train them in liberal arts?": "We are training not isolated men but a living group of men, – nay, a group within a group. And the final product of our training must be neither a psychologist nor a brickmason, but a man. And to make men, we must have ideals, broad, pure, and inspiring ends of living, – not sordid money-getting, not apples of gold" (423). *Souls* attempts at its end to image forth itself as a prophecy of such an education, and also as its living form; to read his book properly, Du Bois seems to suggest, is to bring to life the appropriate forms of intellection. His figure for this final synthesis, and for the thematics of reading and writing through which this synthesis is proposed, is the book of Apocalypse.

The "Forethought" asked the reader to work through the "vague, uncertain outline" of the book, to unearth its "buried" insights, with "patience." But the "After-thought" begins by replacing the "Gentle Reader" of the "Forethought" with "God the Reader." The white bourgeois reader, who is politely invited to accompany Du Bois in a journey behind the veil of the color-line in the "Forethought," is in fact abruptly abandoned before the "After-thought" in the concluding moments of *Souls*'s final chapter. Here, as he expands upon the larger cultural and political implications of his own social and historical account of the African American spirituals, Du Bois suddenly drops the mask of genteel guide he has worn throughout the book and asks curtly, "Your country? How came it yours?," adding that "Before the Pilgrims landed we were here" (545). This may not transgress civility, but it is nevertheless a reminder, unexpected in its forcefulness, that the white reader cannot rest comfortably within the stance of a neutral and concerned observer but must confront his or her own complicity with or ideological interpolation into the American histories of race and empire. This is why the "Gentle Reader" of the "Forethought" is no longer seen as the book's interlocutor in the "After-thought" but in effect as the object of its critical regard. The "After-thought" allows the white reader no rhetorical space in which to distinguish him- or herself from the "guilty people" whose "ears" must "tingle with truth." This displacement or repositioning of the "Gentle Reader" may be taken as the product of right reading, the inevitable result of a proper understanding of the meanings of *Souls*, because a reading of the book not only delivers a revelation of a world external and alien to the white reader, but it seeks also to engender a process of critical introspection. However, it is also the case that the "After-thought" makes the continued illegibility of *Souls* itself a marker of the failure of historical fulfillment (the "righteousness which exalteth nations" remains a wish). Only "God the Reader" can now "vouchsafe" the proper reception of *Souls* which is born into "the world-wilderness" as it comes to completion, and only "infinite reason" can "turn the tangle" of Du Bois's "crooked" writing "straight." In apparently consigning the possibility of a right reading of the allusiveness and indirection which he himself has signaled as hallmarks of his writing to a metaphysical realm, Du Bois is, of course, only ironically underlining the persistence of the historical problem of race, and of reading race.

The last sentence of Du Bois's "After-thought" is ambiguous. Since God is identified as the reader at the start of the "After-thought," it may be obvious to accept that it is his reason which untangles the complexities of the book. But the sentence is so constructed that it is easier to read "infinite reason" as an agency independent of God and working within divine time ("Thy good time"), which is to say time conceived so expansively that history bleeds into eternity. Understood this way, Du Bois's "infinite reason" is more nearly akin to the "reason" or "the Absolute" of Hegelian philosophy, "the unconditioned presupposition of all human account-giving and evaluation, and thereby an understanding of the 'whole' within which the natural world and human deeds [are] 'parts'."[14] So read, the suggestion of the "After-thought" would be that while it is God who safeguards the successful delivery of the newborn book into the world, it is reason, metaphysically conceived, that holds the promise of the book's successful decipherment. Of course, no real choice is either proposed or invited here, and Du Bois's closing ironies should not be taken seriously as a retreat from historical actuality into religious mysticism or philosophical idealism. But what then is the function of the supplication to a supra-human reader who alone can master the book? Is it only a way of pointing out the Gentle Reader's failings as citizen and *littérateur*? Does it signal a grandiose claim to prophetic authority on the part of Du Bois and his book?

The idea of a cryptic or hermetically sealed book which only God or some divine agent can decipher or reveal (and which only the chosen and the wise can understand) is indeed an idea of textuality and interpretation derived from the apocalyptic books of the Bible – it is in fact an image these prophetic books have of themselves as books. In Daniel from the Old Testament, for example, the prophet is commanded to "shut up the words, and seal the book, even to the end of time" (12:4; King James version here and below).

In the Revelation of St. John the Divine, the last book of the New Testament, John is more famously granted a vision of "a book written within and on the backside, sealed with seven seals," and held "in the right hand of him that sat on the throne":

> And I saw a strong angel proclaiming with a loud voice, Who is worthy to open the book, and loose the seals thereof?
> And no man in heaven, nor in earth, neither under the earth, was able to open the book, neither to look thereon.
> And I wept much, because no man was found worthy to open and to read the book, neither to look thereon.
> And one of the elders saith unto me, Weep not: behold, the Lion of the tribe of Juda, the Root of David, hath prevailed to open the book, and to loose the seven seals thereof. (Revelation 5:1–5)

If the association, however oblique, that I am proposing between the imagery of the "After-thought" and that apocalyptic literature is tenable, then in a sense *Souls* could be said everywhere to refer itself to this biblical genre. The word "apocalypse" is derived from a Greek root meaning "to reveal" or "to unveil." *Souls* initiates its narrative with an unveiling, and the veil quickly establishes itself as the book's most common trope, recurring as it does in numerous permutations on almost every other page.

It may reasonably be objected that there is not much of the apocalyptic as this is commonly understood in *Souls*. This is largely true, though there *are* moments, however few, in which the catastrophic visions of the end of days characteristic of the eschatalogies of the books of the Apocalypse are invoked. The epigraph to chapter 8, "Of the Quest of the Golden Fleece," drawn from William Vaughn Moody's *The Brute* (1901), comes closest when it warns that even "the patient and the low /... shall hunger after vanities and still an-hungered go. / Madness shall be on the people, ghastly jealousies arise; / Brother's blood shall cry on brother up the dead and empty skies" (456). Similarly, though less dramatically, the quotation from Arthur Symons's *The Crying of Waters* (1903), which provides the epigraph to the first chapter, prophecies that "there never shall be rest / Till the last moon droop and the last tide fail, / And the fire of the end begin to burn in the west" (363). However, the fact that Du Bois does not construct his own phantasmagoria of judgment day in order to harry the sinful American nation into a realization of its own guilt should not be taken as evidence of the tenuousness of the dialogue being proposed here between *Souls* and apocalyptic literature. The absence of an eschatological dimension in *Souls* is entirely in keeping with the book's resistance to teleology; it is missing not only because the promise of salvation from oppression remains deferred, but also because Du Bois has grasped that the true center of the books of

Apocalypse does not lie in their visions of the end of history. The turbulent dramaturgy through which these books come to conclusion only underlines or confirms what is evident everywhere within them: it may be that, inside Christian belief, history is accepted as progressive and a redemptive future beyond time is received as equally real, but what drives apocalyptic literature first and foremost is its resistance to and denunciation of tyranny and imperial rule in the here and now. This is why this literary and religious tradition has been a sustaining resource for many traditions of Western political nonconformity.[15] It is because *Souls* aligns itself throughout with this aspect of apocalyptic literature that it consistently conceives of itself as a revelation or unveiling – an apocalypse.

It is in the main body of "Of Our Spiritual Strivings," the opening chapter which sets out the historical and investigative scope of the book as well as much of its governing rhetoric, that Du Bois locates his most extended use of judgment day and other motifs from the Apocalypse, interwoven with the related narrative of exodus. Here, as in the final chapter on "The Sorrow Songs," Du Bois recognizes the critical function served by biblical typology within African American folk culture, but he also throws into sharp relief the gulf between historical reality and the religious hopefulness that defines the folk imagination as it attempts to shape its understanding of history through this very typology. In doing so, Du Bois also distinguishes his own use of the apocalypse from its folk uses.

Speaking of the persistent dream of freedom, Du Bois writes that "Away in the days of bondage" African Americans "thought to see in one divine event the end of all doubt and disappointment":

> Emancipation was the key to a promised land of sweeter beauty than ever stretched before the eyes of wearied Israelites. In song and exhortation swelled one refrain – Liberty; in tears and curses the God he implored had Freedom in his right hand. At last it came, – suddenly, fearfully, like a dream. With one wild carnival of blood and passion came the message in his own plaintive cadences:
>
> > "Shout, O Children!
> > Shout, you're free!
> > For God has bought your liberty!" (366)

This is a prefiguring of the more extensive social history of the African American spirituals in the final chapter where Du Bois demonstrates how "biblical phrases" and motifs (the daughters of Zion, the wheel of Ezekiel, the Last Judgment) have been poeticized into the black folk vernacular. For Du Bois, it is "the ten master songs" he identifies that most clearly and purely "tell in word and music of trouble and exile, of strife and hiding; they grope toward some unseen power and sigh for rest in the End" (541). "Such a message is naturally veiled and half articulate," but more so in those other songs in which "Words and music have lost each other and new and cant phrases of a dimly understood theology have displaced the older sentiment" (541). Though Du Bois acknowledges and celebrates the historical experience and the idealism witnessed by the sorrow songs, he remains critical of the potential abdication of historical human agency carried within their theology. In "Of the Faith of the Fathers" (chapter 10), which contains a radical critique of African American religious culture, Du Bois locates this abandonment in the despair of slavery:

> The Negro, losing the joy of this world, eagerly seized upon the offered conceptions of the next; the avenging Spirit of the Lord enjoining patience in this world, under sorrow and tribulation until the Great Day when He should lead His dark children home, – this became his comforting dream. His preacher repeated the prophecy, and his bards sang, –
>
> > "Children, we all shall be free
> > When the Lord shall appear!" (500)

It is because the resilient hopefulness of the folk imagination, in as much as it is also otherworldly, is at the same time a manifestation of a "deep religious fatalism" (500) that Du Bois juxtaposes the optative folk use of biblical typology with a sense of historical realism which itself draws upon this typology, though in less obvious ways. Immediately after describing in the first chapter the folk expectation of a freedom delivered by God through the Emancipation Proclamation, Du Bois writes:

> Years have passed away since then, – ten, twenty, forty; forty years of national life, forty years of renewal and development, and yet the swarthy spectre sits in its accustomed seat at the Nation's feast. In vain do we cry to this our vastest social problem: –
>
> > "Take any shape but that, and my firm nerves
> > Shall never tremble!"
>
> The Nation has not yet found peace from its sins; the freedman has not yet found in freedom his promised land. (366)

The fearful words of Macbeth upon seeing the ghost of the murdered Banquo are a reminder here of a collective rather than individual guilt. The placing of the quotation from *Macbeth* (Act III, scene iv, lines 102–3) after the lines from "Shout, O Children!" repeats the juxtaposition of the bars of music from the spirituals and quotations from white European and American authors at the head of all the chapters (save the final one) in *Souls*. If this juxtaposition is rightly read not as an opposition but as a dialogue intrinsic to the meanings of the book, it is also worth noting that in the present passage Du Bois positions himself, for the moment at least, more closely to the high literary tradition, because he qualifies the historical vision of folk typologies by means of reference to this tradition. But to state it so bluntly may be to lapse into precisely the reductive and simplistic strategies of opposition which *Souls* largely refuses.

The turn to Shakespeare may read as an abrupt shift in register and location from the biblical typologies that precede it, but the turn more properly continues a subdued and silent rhyming with the passage which comes before. Given the invocations of the Apocalypse and of exodus earlier, the "swarthy spectre" at "the Nation's feast" is also a muted recollection of the ghostly "fingers of a man's hand" which write the cryptic prophecy of the fall of Babylon "upon the plaister of the wall's of the king's palace" at Belshazzar's "great feast" in the book of Daniel (5:5) (just as the "right hand" of God in the passage is the very hand which holds the book of the seven seals in Revelation). There is then a continuity which provides an underlying logic for the transitions and turnings in the passage; the difference between Du Bois and the folk tradition is that he does not invest in a millenarian prospect but instead grounds his book in an ongoing and critical revelation of the present, a revelation which is itself presented in a typically hermetic form.

If we turn now from *Souls*'s first chapter back to its "After-thought," we are faced with a problem or impasse of sorts. Given Du Bois's critique of "religious fatalism" in the preceding chapters, it may be worth repeating a question asked earlier: Why is it Du Bois turns to a supra-human agent or agencies at the close of his book? To claim that the turn is ironic in intent may be an answer of sorts. But then is this also true of the imagery of new birth and renewal which pervades the "After-thought"? What are we to make of the irruption of the comic mood which seems to sit uneasily with the sense of historical realism and tragedy which has defined the rest of the book? True, birth is poised on the threshold of death in the "After-thought," and *Souls* is imagined as written on a "fragile" leaf. But, on the surface at least, vitalism is the keynote of the conclusion. The emergence of "vigor of thought and thoughtful deed" from the "leaves" of the book seems imminent, as does the "harvest wonderful." The kinetic energy of the pun in "spring" appears to lift us above skepticism and doubt. It is among the leaves, harvest, and spring of the "After-thought" that we find Du Bois's least conventional appropriations from the books of the Apocalypse, and also his most original transformation of them for his own purposes.

In Revelation one of the visions of the prophetic book is as "the Lamb's book of life" (21:27), which, as soon as it is introduced near the close of the Apocalypse, leads immediately to a vision of "the tree of life, which bare twelve manner of fruits, and yielded her fruit every month: and the leaves of the tree were for the healing of the nations" (22:2). In its final moments, then, the Bible returns to its beginning and to the "the tree of life" which in Genesis grows in the midst of the garden of Eden beside "the tree of knowledge of good and evil" (2:9). In the book of Daniel, it is the interdependence of king and nation which are figured through Nebuchadnezzar's dream of a tree which was "strong" and "reached unto heaven," and the "leaves thereof were fair, and the fruit thereof much, and in it was meat for all" (4:11–12). In the dream, "a watcher and a holy one" commands "Hew down the tree, and cut off his branches, shake off his leaves, and scatter his fruit," but "leave the stump of his roots in the earth" (4:13–15). Daniel interprets the dream to mean that the king will lose his kingdom and wealth until that moment when he recognizes the power of God: "And whereas they commanded to leave the stump of the tree roots; thy kingdom shall be sure unto thee, after that thou shalt have known that the heavens do rule" (4:26). In Isaiah it is the exiled nation itself that blossoms as a tree in its restoration: "And he shall cause them that come of Jacob to take root: Israel shall blossom and bud, and fill the face of the world with fruit" (28:6).

Both the images of the tree of life and of a tree drawing its strength from its roots and not its leaves are used by Du Bois in *Souls*. In chapter 6, "Of the Training of Black Men," Du Bois argues that "no secure civilization can be built in the South with the Negro as an ignorant, turbulent proletariat." Making African Americans "laborers and nothing more" is no solution: "they are not fools, they have tasted of the Tree of Life, and they will not cease to think, will not cease attempting to read the riddle of the world" (435). The fruit of the Tree of Life produces the will to know and understand. The representation of this will as a will to decipherment, as a will to make legible what is at first gnomically illegible, recalls an earlier passage from the first chapter which is more explicit in indicating that Du Bois's subject is education. In the decades after Emancipation, according to Du Bois, "the dream of political power" was replaced by "a new vision": "It was the ideal of 'book-learning'; the curiosity, born of compulsory ignorance, to know and test the power of the cabalistic letters of the white man, the longing to know. Here at last seemed to have been discovered the mountain path to Canaan; longer than the highway of Emancipation and law, steep and rugged, but straight, leading to heights high enough to overlook life" (367). For Du Bois only the university properly conceived can fulfill this promise. Reviewing the establishment of the black universities of Fisk, Howard, and Atlanta after the Civil War, Du Bois acknowledges that the founders "made their mistakes," but insists also that "They were right when they sought to found a new educational system upon the University: where, forsooth, shall we ground knowledge save on the broadest and deepest knowledge? *The roots of the tree, rather than the leaves*, are the sources of its life; and from the dawn of history, from Academus to Cambridge, the culture of the University has been the broad foundation-stone on which is built the kindergarten's A B C" (420–1, emphasis added).

Given Du Bois's deployment of the biblical tropes of Nature's regenerative strength as figures for education, it is fitting that Plato's Academy (the "Academus" in the quote above) was held not in mock-Gothic halls and seminar rooms, but in tree-lined "groves" (420). As if to mark the continuity between ancient and modern academies, between his own work and the larger cultural project, but above all to underline the fact that his book is indissolubly tied to his argument about education, Du Bois describes himself writing *Souls* by again drawing upon an image from nature, one that opens onto the sustaining ancestral presence of the dead: "Through the shining trees that whisper before me as I write, I catch a glimpse of a boulder of New England granite, covering a grave, which graduates of Atlanta University have placed there." The grave is the grave of Edmund S. Ware, the founder of Atlanta University; the stone is from New England because Ware, like many others who took up the challenge of black education after the Civil War, was himself from New England. But in the passage not only is the production of *Souls* woven into the unfolding of the argument about education, so too is Du Bois, because as a graduate from Fisk and the first doctoral graduate from Harvard, he himself is an exemplary product of the university system he proselytizes for, but also because, being from Great Barrington, Massachusetts, he too is from New England. This is a moment illustrative of the *Bildungsbiographie* structure of the book, because in contemplating the grave and the cultural history of which it is a marker, Du Bois own life's narrative is also an available presence. But it is also a moment which *Souls* treats as its own past, a past internal to it as it were, when it revises the passage on its final page and so makes of it a site for self-reflection. The inscription on Ware's grave reads:

IN GRATEFUL MEMORY OF THEIR FORMER TEACHER AND FRIEND AND OF THE UNSELFISH LIFE HE LIVED, AND THE NOBLE WORK HE WROUGHT; THAT THEY, THEIR CHILDREN, AND THEIR CHILDREN'S CHILDREN MIGHT BE BLESSED.

(432)

The heartfelt sentiment enshrines Du Bois's program of the Talented Tenth, of an educated and trained upper social echelon which can provide enlightened leadership for the black masses. The university is, of course, the rock upon which, for Du Bois, this program must be built. But, as I have argued elsewhere, *Souls* repeatedly tests, challenges, and qualifies Du Bois's confident faith in his own program.[16] It is this dialectical process which is signaled at the end when Du Bois presents himself as a "weary traveller" cheered on his way by "My children, my little children" who are the students of Atlanta singing the spirituals (546). Ware stands for a selfless and paternal pedagogy delivered to generation after generation of "children," but at the book's end (which, as already indicated, can be read as a reworking of Plato's exploration of knowledge and action in his allegory of the cave), it is these very "children" who urge their teacher into the "world-wilderness" of the "After-thought", clutching his newborn book.

If my reading has digressed it has done so for a reason. My intention was to demonstrate how the "After-thought" draws upon and draws together imagery of an organic vitalism from earlier sections of the book, and how in this regard *Souls* could be said to be conscious of certain antecedents in the biblical books of Apocalypse and prophecy. However, the reading has progressively become enmeshed in other strands and movements besides education, which was my original concern. But this is how *Souls* works; this is what it does to the reader attentive to its subtle connections. For the moment I want to withdraw from these larger creative entanglements at work in *Souls* and to retrace my steps; I want to return to the vocabulary of the "After-Thought" and to the subject of education because almost every word of Du Bois's conclusion, and not just those associated with Nature's vitality, help gather up Du Bois's argument about this subject as a way of sealing the book.

The very word "afterthought" is used repeatedly earlier in *Souls* to help elaborate a global and national context in which Du Bois wishes to locate his arguments about education. At the very beginning of the seventh chapter, "Of the Training of Black Men," Du Bois sketches out three such contexts through a rhythmical point and counterpoint, a play on "thought" and "afterthought." The first of these is a vision of an emergent international inter-connectedness threatened by the persistence of imperial exploitation. Du Bois writes that "the multiplying of human wants in culture-lands calls for the world-wide cooperation of men in satisfying them. Hence arises a new human unity, pulling the ends of earth nearer, and all men, black, yellow, and white." But "behind this thought lurks the afterthought of force and dominion" (424) (just as in the "After-thought" Du Bois is forced to qualify his ethics of sympathy with the acknowledgement that "in this drear day … human brotherhood is mockery and a snare.")

The passage prefigures present-day concerns with globalization (and with transnational perspectives in American Studies), but it also looks back to the account in *The Communist Manifesto* (1848) of the revolutionary transformations of economy and culture wrought by the bourgeoisie. As Marx and Engels argue, "the bourgeoisie has through its exploitation of the world market given a cosmopolitan character to production and consumption of countries" and so has "removed from under the feet of industry the national ground." It is through this process that "the East" is forcibly integrated into "the West" and made to serve its needs.[17] The second context is a national one, "the thought of the older South ... that somewhere between men and cattle, God created a *tertium quid*, and called it a Negro, – a clownish, simple creature ... foreordained to walk within the Veil." But here too "behind the thought lurks the afterthought" that "some of them with favoring chance might become men," even if "in sheer self-defense we dare not let them" (424). The product of the national and global negations of human possibility and potential is a psychology of self-doubt, "the third and darker thought" outlined by Du Bois: "behind the thought" of "Liberty, Freedom, Opportunity" "lurks the afterthought" that perhaps "after all, the World is right and we are less than men" (425).

> So here we stand among thoughts of human unity, even through conquest and slavery; the inferiority of black men, even if forced by fraud; a shriek in the night for the freedom of men who themselves are not yet sure of their right to demand it. This is the *tangle* of thought and afterthought wherein we are called to solve the problem of training men for life. (425, emphasis added)

As my added emphasis on "tangle" signals, while Du Bois reflects on the dilemmas posed by these thoughts and afterthoughts, this dialectical statement of thesis and antithesis, other words from the "After-thought" surface in the writing. It is this "tangle" which is invoked again in the final sentence of the "After-thought" and which is addressed by the "crooked marks" of Du Bois's own writing. For Du Bois, only "Education will set this tangle straight" (426). But this idealism is also tempered by the recognition that "[t]o stimulate wildly weak and untrained minds is to play with mighty fires, to flout their striving idly is to welcome a *harvest* of brutish crime and shameless lethargy in our very laps" (426, emphasis added). It is the threat of this blighted harvest which is transfigured by the hope of a "harvest wonderful" at the close of *Souls*. Similarly, Du Bois's hope in his "After-thought" that his book "fall not still-born into the world-wilderness" marks a continuity with an earlier claim that a educational program for African Americans must proceed "by founding the common school on the university, and the industrial school on the common school; and weaving thus a system, not a distortion, and bringing a birth, not an abortion" (423).

And yet the wished-for birth and transfiguration also remain haunted by the more devastating possibility that the very education which holds the promise of undoing the tangle of the thought and afterthought can become the very source of division and death. In "Of the Coming of John" the tree of life associated with education is transformed into its opposite. The educated African American John returns to his home in the South only to find himself an outsider among both the whites and his own black community. In a narrative that draws upon the symbolism of the story of Cain and Abel and of the Crucifixion, he kills the white John with the limb of the very tree upon which he himself will be lynched. The association between education and the tree of life is severed here; the tree here is the tree of knowledge which in the Bible too is a source of human suffering and death.

Leaf, spring, harvest, still-born, book, tangle, afterthought: these are not exactly what William Empson referred to as complex words, but they are words which nevertheless lead complex lives within *Souls*.[18] Together they form a delicate and elusive figure in the carpet of Du Bois's prose, or what he himself might call a ghostly music. It is a music which resides in the interplay of sound and sense, and in the way our encounter with any one of these words in any given instances is always tied to our encounter with the same word, or words kin to it, in other moments and other semantic fields. Almost anything can lead to everything in *Souls* because the developing interactions of relatively simple words and images weave the book together in such a way that its narrative unfolds not only as a melodic line but also as a chordal or harmonic simultaneity. And for Du Bois, right hearing is synonymous with right reading or understanding. This is why "the ears of a guilty people" which, in their culpability, "tingle with truth" in the "After-thought" recall, from the discussion of black religious culture earlier, those who have created only "debased imitations of Negro melodies" because their "ears … caught the jingle but not the music, the body but not the soul, of the Jubilee songs" (495).

To hear the music or to trace the figure in Du Bois's writing requires the reader to bring into active relationship diverse cultural and intellectual resources. It is in this sense that the "After-thought" has been read here not only as a prophecy of Du Bois's vision of education but also as its living form. This is a form that demands an active reader, even if it figures this reader ironically as suprahuman: "Thus in Thy good time may infinite reason turn the tangle straight, and these crooked marks on a fragile leaf be not indeed." But if the immediate sense of this final sentence seems to be the hope of legibility, it simultaneously proposes the erasure of writing and so the transcendence of reading. "Be not" can be read as a wish that both the "tangle" and the "crooked words" will be set "straight." But words can only *be* "crooked"; if writing is set "straight" it ceases to exist. The "After-thought" has tied the "tangle" which is the problem of race within modernity and within America to the tangles of *Souls* as a text. It is for this reason that the possibility that the social and political problem will be untangled contains within it the potential dissolution of Du Bois's own text by removing the historical necessity for its very existence. "Be not" carries then both the hope of decipherment and understanding, and also of the end of history. Yet, the "After-thought" has its own residual afterthought because the play on "crooked" and "tangle" also makes "knot" sound inside "not," a persistent entanglement within an ultimately postponed disentanglement. The convoluted inversion of the final clause of the last sentence belies the emergence of a transparent legibility by enacting the very textual knottiness which stands also for the problem of race in *Souls*. This is a dark note that troubles the comic ending and calls up again the specter at the feast writing in apocalyptic cipher.

The last sentence of the "After-thought" contains its most direct allusion to the Bible but it refers the reader not to the books of Apocalypse nor to the stories of exodus, but to Ecclesiastes: "That which *is* crooked cannot be made straight: and that which is wanting cannot be numbered" (1:15). The limits of human ability are marked again in the same language a little later: "Consider the work of God: for who can make that straight, which he hath made crooked?" (7:13). In so closing with a direct reference to a biblical text, the "After-thought" mirrors the "Forethought" which concludes by recalling Genesis: "And, finally, need I add that I who speak here am bone of the bone and flesh of the flesh of them that live within the Veil?" This declaration of Du Bois's own African American identity echoes the words of Adam when he sees the newly created Eve: "This is now bone of my bone of my bones, and flesh of my flesh: she shall be called Woman, because she was taken out of Man" (2:23).

These biblical framings at the start and close of *Souls* seem like calculated choices for a text which moves between narrative coherence and its collapse, between an ethical and political idealism and doubt. Genesis is after all a book of origins, full of foundational stories of the nation of Israel, but stories that are also dominated by death, killing, and human division. Ecclesiastes is a very different kind of text. It eschews narrative for a disorienting and challenging proverbial and epigrammatic structure, a dialectical logic which suits the author's subversion of conventional moral wisdom, his skepticism, and his sense of the flux of human life.[19] But if Du Bois's "After-thought" plants the seeds of a persistent uncertainty in the midst of its comic hope for renewal, his "Forethought" sounds its own counter-note. In appropriating Adam's words Du Bois appears to subsume himself within a black collectivity but also signals his separation from the group. Adam acknowledges that Eve is indeed made of the same stuff as he is, but he also marks a division and an otherness. The dialectic of identity and difference between Du Bois as a representative of the Talented Tenth and the black folk underlies the political and cultural psychology at the heart of *Souls* and binds this psychology to the concern with education.

III

The education needed to equip a reader with the challenging range of cultural knowledge and mental skills required for a reading of *Souls* was available to only a very few African Americans at the start of the twentieth century. But, as *Souls* imagines it, such an education led to contradictory ends even for those who had access to it because while it sought to produce a whole and integrated individual, it also simultaneously engendered self-division. "The would-be black *savant* was confronted by the paradox that the knowledge his people needed was a twice-told tale to his white neighbors, while the knowledge which would teach the white world was Greek to his own flesh and blood." Similarly, "[t]he innate love of harmony and beauty that set the ruder souls of his people a-dancing and a-singing raised but confusion and doubt in the souls of the black artist; for the beauty revealed to him was the soul-beauty of a race which his larger audience despised, and he could not articulate the message of another people" (365–6). The prospective teacher or educator and artist become here exemplary embodiments of what Du Bois famously termed "double-consciousness." Familiar as it is, here is the oft-quoted passage in which the doubling of the self becomes a source of a diminishment and fracture of the self rather than of a psychological and spiritual excess and abundance:

> After the Egyptian and Indian, the Greek and Roman, the Teuton and Mongolian, the Negro is a sort of seventh son, born with a veil, and gifted with second-sight in this American world, – a world which yields him no true self-consciousness, but only lets him see himself through the revelation of the other world. It is a peculiar sensation, this double-consciousness, this sense of always looking at one's self through the eyes of others, of measuring one's soul by the tape of a world that looks on in amused contempt and pity. One ever feels his two-ness, – an American, a Negro; two souls, two thoughts, two unreconciled strivings; two warring ideals in one dark body, whose dogged strength alone keeps it from being torn asunder. (364–5)

In associating the psychology of double-consciousness with the *savant* I am making a proposition which may be received as contentious, even as idiosyncratic. What is the basis for reading this psychology as specific to a particular group or class when the ubiquitous use of Du Bois's famous description in African American literary criticism, sociology, and historiography, as well as in post-colonial and race theory, speaks against such a narrow location? I do not contest that this almost universal appropriation is itself evidence of the more general applicability of Du Bois's conceptualization (compare Hancock in this volume), but this appropriation nevertheless does fail to acknowledge the ambiguity of Du Bois's account of double-consciousness and of his varied use of it in *Souls*.[20]

In the paragraphs that follow the description of double-consciousness in the first chapter of *Souls* Du Bois moves systematically from the broadest possible application of his psychological model toward greater historical and social specificity. At first double-consciousness is seen to describe African American experience throughout the whole of American history (accepting for the moment Du Bois's gendered language as a convention): "The history of the American Negro is the history of this strife, – this longing to attain self-conscious manhood, to merge his double self into a better and truer self" (365). This is succeeded by a more precise post-1863 historical placing: "Here in America, in the few days since Emancipation, the black man's turning hither and thither in hesitant and doubtful striving has often made his very strength to lose effectiveness, to seem like absence of power, like weakness. And yet it is not weakness, – it is the contradiction of double aims" (*ibid.*). Du Bois turns now to specific examples of individuals who best embody these "double aims," but in doing this it is notable that he populates his list with social types all of whom belong to the emergent black middle class, the group Du Bois refers to as the Talented Tenth in his work from the period: "the black artisan," "the Negro minister or doctor," the "black *savant*," and "the black artist" (365–6). This list is consistent with Du Bois's survey of the occupational stratification and distribution of urban blacks in his *The Philadelphia Negro* (1899) which demonstrates that about 15 per cent of the population over twenty-one years of age is made up of self-employed businessmen, those "in learned professions" (including clergymen, physicians, and teachers), or "in skilled trades," and those employed as "clerks, semi-professional and responsible workers."[21] These are of course the groups and types which are also the primary subjects of Du Bois's educational program of uplift. The members of the Talented Tenth are indeed bone of the bones and flesh of the flesh of the black masses, but in each example of contradictory and doubled aims that Du Bois offers, it is the simultaneous separation from both white *and* black culture, rather than simply being black in America, which generates self-division. As a university professor and as a writer Du Bois himself embodies the dilemma of the *savant* and the artist, a dilemma that becomes a source of creative energy in the making of *Souls*.

But as I have said, Du Bois's use of double-consciousness remains varied. If it is sometimes applied to black Americans in general and sometimes to a particular social group only, it is also used by Du Bois to distinguish not a class difference, but one between a secular intellectualism and the consolations of religious faith. The difference is apparent in the contrast between his wife's and his own reaction to their baby son's death in "Of the Passing of the First-Born": "She who in simple clearness of vision sees beyond the stars said when he had flown, 'He will be happy There; he ever loved beautiful things.' And I, far more ignorant, and blind by the web of mine own weaving, sit alone winding words and muttering, 'If still he be, and he be There, and there be a There, let him be happy, O Fate!'"(509). Nina Gomer was a student at Wilberforce University, where Du Bois held his first full-time teaching post, when he met and married her. Yet in this somewhat condescending juxtaposition, the confidence of her faith aligns this representative of the Talented Tenth with the black folk of the first chapter whose "innate love of harmony and beauty" protects them from the "confusion and doubt" experienced by the artist. True, when read beside the simple declaration of his wife, the coiled twists of Du Bois's words tip over into bathos; but they also make plain that the entanglements which define the "web of mine own weaving" are the formal embodiment of the psychological and cultural contradictions and double aims investigated by *Souls*.

In a passage of his 1904 note on *Souls* quoted earlier, Du Bois wrote that "it is difficult, strangely difficult, to translate the finer feelings of men into words." The world of feeling, of black souls and spirituality, if of course everywhere the concern of Du Bois's book. But the phrase "the finer feelings of men" carries within it the sense too of "men of finer feelings." Is it their feelings, or *also* their feelings, that Du Bois has in mind? The section from which the quotation is taken follows, after all, Du Bois's acknowledgment that *Souls* is characterized by a "distinctively subjective note" and by "a personal and intimate tone of self-revelation." If criticism fails to examine the ways in which *Souls* embodies both thoughts and feelings of the mass of black Americans and of a group within this group represented by Du Bois himself, it fails to do justice to the specificity of Du Bois's literary address and to the greatness of his achievement.

IV

Before the publication of *Souls* Du Bois had produced two landmark works in historiography and sociology: *The Suppression of the African Slave-Trade to the United States of America, 1638–1870* (1896), based on his Harvard doctoral thesis, and *The Philadelphia Negro: A Social Study* (1899). *Suppression* was a model of meticulous archival research and *Philadelphia Negro* was based on extensive fieldwork and a thorough statistical survey. What the two studies shared was their commitment to the empirical positivism, a scientific method emergent in the human sciences in American academia. This intellectual turn was radical in as much as it helped Du Bois challenge the generalizations and evolutionary or social Darwinist prejudices which he saw as dominant in nineteenth-century historical and sociological treatments of race. But, in attempting to mold the human sciences in the image of the physical sciences, positivism also radically curtailed what was understood as knowledge. Not only did its confusion of knowledge and method take insufficient account of the social and cultural forces shaping knowledge, it also excluded the subjective and the poetic. As Du Bois himself put it at the start of *Philadelphia Negro*, the sociologist "must ever tremble lest some personal bias, some moral conviction or some unconscious trend of thought due to previous training, has to a degree distorted the picture in his view" (2–3). From this perspective *Souls* comes as a surprise. Its "personal and intimate tone of self-revelation" and its "penumbra of vagueness and half-veiled allusion" transgress Du Bois's own pursuit of "cold-blooded scientific research" (*Philadelphia Negro* 3). That I take this transgression as an attempt to expand what is meant by knowledge and what is taken as an appropriate subject of human understanding, rather than as a lapse into sentimental affect, should be obvious by now. It is with reflections on this aspect of *Souls* that the present discussion concludes.

As Blake Stimson observes in a consideration of the transformations of the documentary tradition,

> self-scrutiny and self-doubt conceived of as a motor of inquiry has been a cornerstone of the larger modernist tradition at least since the advent of Kant's critical philosophy. At its best, this self-scrutiny has opened out into dialectical reason and progressively expanding understanding; at its worst, when it has failed to find…means of effective engagement through representation, it has closed in on itself and collapsed into brute cynicism and raw despair for the sensitive, or simple careerism and academicism for the oblivious.

Stimson concerns himself with "the way in which an artistic aim can persist in spite of or even because of that doubt" and "artistic inquiry" can return "to scrutinize itself in the mirror again and again and again in order to find a cleavage or fissure in its own limit condition that turns mirror into window opening onto a sense of adequately comprehensive understanding."[22] Du Bois's "Forethought" conceives of *Souls* as a window because the book opens out onto a revelation of the black world in both its most obvious aspects and also in its "deeper recesses." His note from 1904 proposes that it is also a mirror, an act of self-scrutiny in the midst of looking out. Du Bois's dense and complex writing negotiates these two perspectives, and charts his hesitations and doubts, his doubled consciousness, with admirable honesty and without abandoning the project of political and cultural understanding to solipsism.

In its dialectical effort and success *Souls* belongs to an impressive tradition of American nonfictional or documentary prose works which includes *Walden* (1854), *The Education of Henry Adams* (1907), Henry James's *The American Scene* (1907), and James Agee and Walker Evans's *Let Us Now Praise Famous Men* (1941). Agee's rich anti-documentary documentary provides an especially apt affiliation in its concern with the Southern poor, white but also black, in its refusal to reduce these men, women, and children to social problems, in its deep suspicion of the instrumentalist logic and political agendas of social documentary and sociology, and in its remarkable effort both to plot these resistances and doubts and to develop alternative representations through innovative literary form. Such a form, suggests Agee with a less restrained and more provocative catholicity than Du Bois,

> would be an art and a way of seeing existence based, let us say, on an intersection of astronomical physics, geology, biology, and (including psychology) anthropology, known and spoken of not in scientific but in human terms. Nothing that springs from this intersection can conceivably be insignificant: everything is most significant in proportion as it approaches in our perception, simultaneously, its own singular terms and its ramified kinship and probable hidden identification with everything else.

Agee, like Du Bois, repeatedly reaches for musical metaphors to describe both reality and the structure of understanding he seeks, because in "orchestral complex" all elements "interlock, interform one another"; but he also proposes "a series of careful but tentative, rudely experimental, and fragmentary renderings of some of the salient aspects of a real experience seen and remembered in its own terms" as the only possible approach to this whole.[23]

It is the challenge of such a multiplicity which Du Bois registers at the conclusion of *Philadelphia Negro* when he writes that "a combination of social problems is far more than a matter of mere addition, – the combination itself is a problem" (385). It is because *Souls* makes the problem of combination its problem that it is led to state eloquently and forcefully the limitations of the sociological imagination, which is also Du Bois's own:

> I have thus far sought to make clear the physical, economic, and political relations of the Negroes and whites in the South, as I have conceived them,

including, for the reasons set forth, crime and education. But after all that has been said on these more tangible matters of human contact, there still remains a part essential to a proper description of the South which it is difficult to describe or fix in terms easily understood by strangers. It is, in fine, the atmosphere of the land, the thought and feeling, the thousand and one little actions which go to make up life. In any community or nation it is these little things which are most elusive to the grasp and yet most essential to any clear conception of the group life taken as a whole. What is thus true of all communities is peculiarly true of the South, where, outside of written history and outside of printed law, there has been going on for a generation as deep a storm and stress of human souls, as intense a ferment of feeling, as intricate a writhing of spirit, as ever a people experienced. (487)

This passage is from the final pages of "Of the Sons of Master and Man," the ninth chapter of *Souls*. It occurs, in other words, at exactly the point at which the "Forethought" divides the book, the point which marks the transition for the reader from one side of the veil to the other. Du Bois is here describing with precision and accuracy what Raymond Williams later came to call "structure of feeling." In attempting to develop a form of cultural criticism more supple than a Marxism which posits an overly deterministic relationship between structure and superstructure, Williams also seeks a more combinatory approach and defines "the theory of culture as the study of relationships between elements in a whole way of life," arguing that we need to move beyond a concern with "character" or "pattern" to "the actual experience through which these [are] lived." Williams's term for this is structure of feeling: "it is as firm and definite as 'structure' suggests, yet it operates in the most delicate and least tangible parts of our activity. In one sense, this structure of feeling is the culture of a period: it is the particular living result of all the elements in the general organization."[24]

For Williams, the arts of a period are especially expressive of the structure of feeling and are therefore privileged repositories for future generations. But Williams also proposes that in certain art works of exceptional achievement, "the creative elements are raised to a wholeness which takes the work right outside the ordinary structure of feeling, and teaches new feeling"[25] *Souls* is such a work. More than a century after publication it certainly affords a glimpse into a past (and yet all too present) American world. But we do not continue to return to *Souls* again and again because it is merely a window on history. *Souls* is a work which has helped create a new historical subject, a consciousness divided and doubled, diminished and enriched in unique and multiple ways in its negotiation of race and modernity.

Notes

1. W. E. B. Du Bois, *The Souls of Black Folk*, in *W. E. B. Du Bois. Writings*, ed. N. Huggins (New York: Library of America, 1986), p. 425. All further page references are given in the text.

2. K. Burke, *Attitudes toward History*, 3rd edn. (Berkeley: University of California Press, 1984), p. 255. The first quotation is from the introduction which is not paginated.

3. W. E. B. Du Bois, "The Souls of Black Folk," *Independent*, November 17, 1904, reprinted in W. E. B. Du Bois, *The Souls of Black Folk*, ed. D. W. Blight and R. Gooding-Williams (Boston: Bedford Books, 1997), pp. 254–5.

4. For the correspondence between Du Bois and his publisher, see the Editors' preface to Du Bois, *The Souls of Black Folk*, ed. H. L. Gates, Jr., and T. H. Oliver (New York: Norton, 1999), p. xxxi.

5. D. L. Lewis, *W. E. B. Du Bois: Biography of a Race, 1868–1919* (New York: Henry Holt, 1993), p. 350.

6. On *Souls* as *Bildungsbiographie*, see S. Zamir, *Dark Voices: W. E. B. Du Bois and American Thought, 1888–1903* (Chicago: University of Chicago Press, 1995), pp. 100, 159–64.

7. On the relation of *Souls* and slave narratives, see especially A. Rampersad, "Slavery and the Literary Imagination: Du Bois's *The Souls of Black Folk*," in *Slavery and the Literary Imagination*, ed. D. McDowell and A. Rampersad (Baltimore: Johns Hopkins University Press, 1989), pp. 104–24, and also the discussion of the book in R. Stepto, *From Behind the Veil: A Study of Afro-American Narrative* (Urbana: University of Illinois Press, 1979).

8. S. Brodwin identifies a number of sources in "The Veil Transcended: Form and Meaning in W. E. B. Du Bois *The Souls of Black Folk*," *Journal of Black Studies*, 2 (March 1972), pp. 303–21; on Du Bois's use of Hegel and Plato, see Zamir, *Dark Voices*, chapters 4 and 5. See also the references in the editions of *Souls* listed in notes 2 and 3 above.

9. P. Wald, *Constituting Americans: Cultural Anxiety and Narrative Form* (Durham, NC: Duke University Press, 1995), pp. 172–4.

10. On *Souls* as "a book of the dead," see S. Mizruchi, "Neighbors, Strangers, Corpses: Death and Sympathy in the Early Writings of W. E. B. Du Bois" (1996), in Gates and Oliver, *Souls*, pp. 286–95.

11. *Ibid.*, p. 288. See also E. J. Sundquist, *To Wake the Nations: Race in the Making of American Literature* (Cambridge: Harvard University Press, 1993), pp. 457–539.

12. Du Bois, "The Souls of Black Folk," p. 255.

13. Burke, *Attitudes toward History*, p. 232.

14. R. B. Pippin, entry on Hegel in *The Cambridge Dictionary of Philosophy*, ed. R. Audi, 2nd edn. (Cambridge: Cambridge University Press, 1999), p. 367.

15. On this aspect of apocalyptic literature, see E. Bloch, *The Principle of Hope* (Oxford: Blackwell, 1986).

16. See Zamir, *Dark Voices*.

17. K. Marx and F. Engels, *The Communist Manifesto*, ed. and trans. L. M. Findlay (Toronto: Broadview, 2004), pp. 65–6.

18. W. Empson, *The Structure of Complex Words* (London: Chatto and Windus, 1951).
19. See R. Gordis, *Koheleth – the Man and His World: A Study of Ecclesiastes* (New York: Schocken Books, 1968)
20. The discussion of double-consciousness which follows draws upon the more extended exploration in chapter 4 of Zamir, *Dark Voices*. There I examine the relationship between Du Bois's "double-consciousness" and Hegel's "unhappy consciousness" in the context of American Pragmatism, especially the thought of William James and Emerson, and of American idealist appropriations of Hegel in the nineteenth century in detail. I do not revisit this intellectual history in the present discussion, but Hancock, King, and Stone-Richards in this volume provide varied perspectives on some of the issues. The literature on the sources and meanings of "double-consciousness" is now substantial, and growing. Useful sources include: A. Rampersad, *The Art and Imagination of W. E. B. Du Bois* (Cambridge: Harvard University Press, 1976), 74; D. D. Bruce, Jr., "W. E. B. Du Bois and the Idea of Double Consciousness," *American Literature*, 64, no. 2 (1992), pp. 299–304; F. M. Kirkland, "Modernity and Intellectual Life in Black," *Philosophical Forum*, 24, nos. 1–3 (1992–3), pp. 136–65; P. Gilroy, *The Black Atlantic: Modernity and Double Consciousness* (London: Verso, 1993), *passim*; S. Adell, *Double Consciousness/Double Bind: Theoretical Issues in Twentieth-Century Black Literature* (Urbana: University of Illinois Press, 1994); and W. Siemerling, *The New North American Studies: Culture, Writing and the Politics of Re/cognition* (London: Routledge, 2005), pp. 31–8.
21. W. E. B. Du Bois, *The Philadelphia Negro: A Social Study* (1899; New York: Schocken Books, 1968), pp. 101–3. Hereafter cited in the text.
22. B. Stimson, *The Pivot of the World: Photography and Its Nation* (Cambridge: MIT Press, 2006), pp. 107–8.
23. J. Agee and W. Evans, *Let Us Now Praise Famous Men* (1941; New York: Ballantine Books, 1966), pp. 221, 98.
24. R. Williams, *The Long Revolution* (London: Chatto & Windus, 1961), pp. 46–8.
25. *Ibid.*, p. 69.

2

SIEGLINDE LEMKE

"Of the Coming of John"

On June 22, 1903, George White of Wilmington, Delaware, was at the workhouse while the pastor of Olivet Presbyterian Church was giving a sermon. Suddenly, several members of the community broke in to abduct Mr. White, who was actually a black man accused of rape and murder.[1] He was tied to a stake, burned, and riddled with bullets. When the Chamber of Commerce of Wilmington met a few days later, it refused to pass a resolution condemning the lynching but instead passed one against forest fires. Their unwillingness to take a public stance against lynching was paralleled on the national level.

In 1899 George Henry White (no relation), a former slave, a Congressman (1897–1901) and the only African American in the House of Representatives, introduced the first anti-lynching bill in Congress. This resolution would have made lynching of a citizen a federal crime.[2] Pointing out that most lynchings were committed by Anglo-Americans against African Americans, White argued that lynching was an extra-legal method used to terrorize them. In spite of his endeavors and passionate plea, the bill was defeated. In fact, 1901 saw the lynching of eighty-six black Americans.[3] In 1902, during the consideration of his "Philippines Bill," President Theodore Roosevelt intimated that lynching was taking place in the Philippines; and in 1903 he publicly commented on the lynching of George White.[4] That year, the same year in which *The Souls of Black Folk* was published, eighty-four African Americans were known to have been lynched in the United States.

In this chapter I examine Du Bois's story about lynching, "Of the Coming of John," and its oblique critical scrutiny of the ideals of black leadership and community, and of a positivistic faith in the progressive amelioration of racial conflicts which Du Bois himself held. "Of the Coming of John" is unusual because it is the only work of fiction among the essays in *Souls*; it has also received less critical attention than some of the other chapters.[5] Read as a fictional text, "Of the Coming of John" is commonly interpreted as disclosing the "tragedy inherent in American racism."[6] Or, it is read as a semi-autobiographical text, pondering "[t]he vise of divided identity in which Du Bois himself was caught: how to balance the acquisition of white, European cultural forms against the preserved beliefs and cultural patterns of black America."[7] I shall argue that it is more than just an allegory of white supremacy and the agony of double-consciousness. This seemingly straightforward story delves into larger human and social concerns deliberating upon questions of trust, faithfulness, and loyalty.

"Of the Coming of John" marks Du Bois's coming out, so to speak, as a writer of fiction because for the first time in his life the scholar presented himself as a creative writer.[8] The author chooses to structure his narrative around a set of dualisms: there are two settings (the North and the South), two major protagonists (the black John and the white John), and two adverse forces (the black community and the white authority-figure Judge Henderson). Accordingly, there is also a dual message expressing a critique of (black) ignorance and (white) violence. Cutting across these dualities are two prominent references to Richard Wagner's opera *Lohengrin* (1850). Since the first is linked to an experience of humiliation and the second occurs at the story's fatal ending, the allusion provides the narrative frame.[9]

"Of the Coming of John" is about John Jones's homecoming after attending seven years of college at the institute in Johnstown. The title, which echoes the folk song by that name, expresses "the voice of exile," about which Du Bois writes in chapter 14, "The Sorrow Songs." This narrative of exile, written from an omniscient point of view, introduces the reader to a peculiar nexus between European art (Wagner's *Lohengrin*) and the most atrocious American social practice. In New York, John attends an opera performance of *Lohengrin* but is forced to leave after a white patron – who turns out to be the white John – complains about his presence. Apparently, the black man is disturbing his female companion. Nevertheless, this brief encounter with *Lohengrin* has a profound impact on John: "[t]he infinite beauty of the wail lingered and swept through every muscle of his frame, and put it all a-tune."[10] The sublime power of art triggers his desire "to rise with that clear music out of the dirt and dust of that low life that held him prisoned and befouled" (527). Wanting to do "some master-work, some life-service," John decides to go back South to "settle the Negro problems there" (527).

John's return to the South, however, ends in a bitter disappointment. Not only are his efforts of racial uplift not appreciated by his own people, his homecoming ends fatally. At the close of the story, after he kills the white John while trying to avenge the harassment of his sister, he is about to be lynched. At that very moment he hears "the faint sweet music of the swan.

Hark! was it music, or the hurry and shouting of men?" (537). When the mob approaches to revenge the murder of the white John, the black John is "softly humming the 'Song of the Bride,' – 'Freudig geführt, ziehet dahin' [Joyously led, move on]" (535).

This citation of Wagner is rather perplexing. At that moment John can hardly be feeling joy. Why would Du Bois choose this particular opera and this particular line that refers to Lohengrin and Elsa approaching the wedding chamber? And why would he misquote the famous line, '*Treulich geführt ziehet dahin*' (Faithfully led, move on), thereby eliding the difference between being joyously (*freudig*) and faithfully (*treulich*) led?[11]

The misquotation could be attributed to an "acoustic error on Du Bois's part," as Russell Berman maintains, or to a confusion with "the Schiller text from Beethoven's Ninth."[12] Being the first critic who has noticed this error and pondered this enigma, Berman suggests that the substitution of "joyously" for "faithfully" was not intentional but "can be understood to have made good sense to the author." Although he does not expound on this statement, there is reason to argue that Du Bois did not simply forget the original line (which he could have easily looked up), nor is it likely that he would have mindlessly substituted a bilabial fricative sound (f) for a palatal plosive (t). This substitution, I argue, was intentional. First, we need to remember that Du Bois was fluent in German.[13] Secondly, he later explicitly commented on the significance of "*Treue*" and "*treulich*." In the 1930s Du Bois said about Wagner's *Lohengrin*:

> It is a hymn of Faith. Something in this world man must trust. Not everything – but Something. One cannot live and doubt everybody and everything. Some-where in this world, and not beyond it, there is Trust, and somehow Trust leads to Joy. It is this theme that a great artist seeks to treat for the thought and enlightenment of mankind. He uses myth, he uses poetry, he uses sound and sight, music and color. And he uses actors on a stage. The result is beautiful, as in the bride-song, but it is more than that: it rises to a great and glorious drama which at times reaches the sublime.[14]

So important is the notion of "*Treue*" to that opera that Du Bois would later explicitly comment on it. Linking joy to trust, he implicitly refers back to the *Treue*/*Freude* nexus. Do trust, loyalty, and faithfulness necessarily lead to joy? Should artists always aim to enlighten mankind? Does Du Bois imply that artistic creations with their potential to reach the sublime are more effective than works produced by sociologists or politicians?

According to this critical assessment of *Lohengrin*, we might infer that what is at stake in the seemingly simple story "Of the Coming of John" are such universal values as faith and art. In that light, the reference to Wagner makes a great deal of sense because most of his works were about the notion and problem of loyalty, *Treue*. Friedrich Nietzsche even claims that all of Wagner's protagonists are entangled in the problem of trust and devotion. And Nietzsche rhetorically asks: "Why does it [faithfulness between brother and sister, friend to friend, slave to master, ... Elsa to Lohengrin] illuminate him [Wagner] brighter and purer than anything else? What secret entails the word faithfulness [*Treue*] for his entire being?"[15] Accordingly, the slippage of *treulich/freulich* at the heart of "Of the Coming of John" assumes a larger significance.

Du Bois seems to suggest that the glorious Lohengrin is the fictional equivalent of John Jones. While John is a self-elected race man who aspires to improve the lot of black people in Altamaha, Lohengrin, the son of Parzival, was sent by the gods to become the *Schützer von Brabant* (protector of the Brabant people). Sent to earth by the Holy Grail, the immortal Lohengrin falls in love with the beautiful but all-too-human Elsa, the daughter of the Herzog von Brabant. Elsa has been wrongly accused of having murdered her brother, but when the king requests that she proves her innocence, she refuses to defend herself. Instead, Elsa claims that a knight will appear to affirm her innocence. This shining knight, who comes floating along the river on a boat pulled by a swan, is Lohengrin. After fighting and defeating Friedrich, Lohengrin marries her on the condition that she should never inquire about his name or background. Under this rule or taboo (*Frageverbot*), he demands that Elsa love him regardless of his name and race. To which she responds: "*so halt in Treu ich dein Gebot!*" (so I will faithfully commit to your rule!) (*Lohengrin* 51).

Friedrich's wife, Ortrud, then drives the prong of distrust into Elsa by suggesting that Lohengrin might not be of noble background. Fighting against this Elsa's faith in Lohengrin wins out again and they marry. When bride and groom enter the bridal chamber, the chorus sings: "*Treulich geführt ziehet dahin, wo euch in Frieden die Liebe bewahr! Siegreicher Mut, Minnegewinn eint euch in Treue zum seligsten Paar.*" (Faithfully guided, draw near to where the blessing of love shall preserve you! Triumphant courage, the reward of love, joins you in faith as the happiest of couples!) (*Lohengrin* 72). At that moment, they are faithful to one another as well as deliriously happy. Both are jointly singing: "*Fühl ich zu dir so süß mein Herz entbrennen, atme ich Wonnen, die nur Gott verleiht*" (As I feel my heart go out to you, I breathe delights that only God alone bestows) (*Lohengrin* 74). But at that delightful climax, Elsa feels the burning desire to know who her husband is, and she asks the forbidden question: "*Den Namen sag mir an*" (Tell me your name) (*Lohengrin* 74), thus forcing him to tell the secret that will end their romantic relationship.

The consequence, Lohengrin realizes, is tragic: "*Weh, nun ist all unser Glück dahin*" (Now all our happiness is gone) (*Lohengrin* 77). Having been summoned to the king, Lohengrin reveals that he was sent by the Grail; appointed as a champion of virtue, he was sent to fight for justice.

After this revelation Lohengrin is about to leave Brabant, and as he steps on his boat pulled by the swan, which is actually the bewitched Gottfried, he prays to the Grail for the spell to be broken. Suddenly, the swan loosens the iron chain and metamorphoses into Elsa's brother, the legitimate successor to the throne. Elsa rushes to embrace him. Gottfried is freed from bondage and justice is secured. The audience's faith in the power of goodness and (brotherly) love is restored.

Berman argues that Du Bois (thinking about his German girlfriend Dora) identified with Lohengrin, but Du Bois might have just as well aligned the black John and Gottfried who, trapped in the wrong body, was doomed to serve his master as a swan. Berman's assumption that in "the montage of bridal march and lynching... Wagner and Lohengrin are standing in as sites of a life without prejudice," reduces the message of this short story to its critique of race prejudice. Du Bois, however, reveals more than "the tragedy of egalitarianism," as Berman has it.[16] Apart from grappling with the impossibility of justice and the atrocity of prejudice, Du Bois offers a cautionary tale about the devastating effects of distrust. This salient nexus of lynching and Lohengrin, art and terror, invites us to read "Of the Coming of John" as a hymn of faith.

The substitution of "joyously" for "faithfully" makes sense only if we assume that the protagonist John sang this line with a sarcastic or fatalistic tone. Confronting his impending death, John notices the grim visage of the "haggard white-haired man" as he holds on to the "coiling twisted rope" (535). The respected judge turns into a vigilante, joining the crowd of vicious unruly men who seem to *enjoy* killing another. Joyously, they pursue their heinous ritual. While the mob is declaring the triumph of (their) civilization through John's murder, John, in turn, chooses to meet their savagery not only with sarcasm but also with sublime condescension. Perhaps humming Wagner's well-known line helps him face his doom more easily because this invocation of an arcane bit of European high art makes him morally superior to his murderers. In fact, not only would they have remained blissfully ignorant of the fact that John was quoting Wagner, they would also have been unaware, obviously, that John was *misquoting* Wagner.

Du Bois was imputing to John sentiments that he himself felt about his sojourn in Europe: "standing against American narrowness and color prejudice, with the greater, finer world at my back urging me on."[17]

Facing the dramatic effect of American color prejudice and, literally, standing with his back against the lynching tree, John hums the bridal march because it puts him on the side of the ("greater, finer") world of European high art.

Moreover, humming Wagner's music transposed John into an imaginary world that seemed far removed from the desperate reality in which he was trapped. The dream-like vision of the "faint sweet music of the swan" seems to be the prelude to a life after death when John might live happily, or joyously, ever after. The substitution, then, serves a symbolic function in a narrative that deals with human cruelty, and more generally, the lack of faith. Given that the sexual harassment of his sister is the cause for John's fate, the story suggests that a black man or woman cannot trust a white man. But the notion of trust was at issue in the story even prior to the scene in the forest, in which he witnesses the harassment of his sister.

When the black John returns to town and the initial fascination with the college-educated young man vanishes, people in Altamaha become suspicious of his progressive ideas. Before John had initially left his community, his fellow townspeople were convinced that getting an education would "spoil" him. Upon his return from college, the blacks think him "silent, cold" and "full o' fool notions" (529). When he lays out his plans to start an Industrial School and to organize philanthropic work, "[a] painful hush seized that crowded mass" (530). He gives this speech in the church, and the congregation feels offended. The religious faithful are appalled by his freethinking. And when the church elder speaks out against his progressive ideas, John "felt himself held up to scorn and scathing denunciation for trampling on the true Religion" (530). John, the veritable New Negro, who committed his education to help deliver his people, becomes increasingly alienated from his community. His people, in other words, do not *trust* him. Rather, they dismiss his education and "queer thought-world" (525). Paradoxically, Du Bois seems to be saying that the educated self-elected race man must, by definition, break trust with his own people, unwittingly but inevitably. Precisely because the cosmopolitan figure of John aspired through education to facilitate his people's liberation, he commited a form of community betrayal – a certain peculiar betrayal of the intimacy of community – because he must reject their "narrow life" (525).

Likewise, as we might expect, white people distrust him. The Judge even withdraws his funding for the school when John is reported for expressing radical ideas "on the French Revolution, equality, and such like" (532). Judge Henderson reminds John that "the Negro must remain subordinate" (532). Foreshadowing John's tragic ending, Henderson admonishes him that "we have to lynch every Nigger in the land" who wants to reverse this hierarchy. "Now, John," the Judge asks, "are you, with your education and Northern notions, going to accept the situation and teach the darkies to be faithful servants and laborers?" (531). Du Bois seems to be arguing that white folks, like the Judge, think John "a dangerous Nigger" (532), primarily because of economic reasons, and that black people think him "queer" because of his atheist and intellectual ideas. Whereas the white people distrust John's "Northern notions," the black ones call John a "damn Nigger," distrusting his "fool notions" (529).

This short story and fictive elaboration on the significance of faithfulness and *Treue* can also be read as an allegory of Du Bois's concept in "The Talented Tenth." In contrast to the optimistic tone of the essay, also published in 1903, "Of the Coming of John" highlights the tragic flip side to the concept of the talented tenth – that of alienation. The fictional account of an exceptional man with *Bildung* (education) trying to uplift the masses exposes the idealist, utopian, and tragic dimension inherent in Du Bois's vision of the promise and perils of black higher education and black political leadership.

Lohengrin and John are both exceptional men. While Lohengrin is an immortal sent by the gods, John is a member of an educated elite who embarks on a self-chosen mission. Lohengrin's tragic separation from his lover reconfirms the incompatibility of the mortal and the immortal spheres; John's tragic end reconfirms the incompatibility of the racial spheres. Both heroes suffer from a dual identity, a "double-consciousness," as Du Bois called it. While Lohengrin tries to conceal his true identity, John struggles to reconcile his old rural identity (Altamaha) with his new educated self (his Johnstown identity). Both have to confront antagonistic evil forces. Whereas the figures of Friedrich and Ortrud represent the reactionary *ancien régime*, the reactionary forces in "Of the Coming of John" are symbolized by the Judge and the lynch mob. Both narratives suggest that one cannot trust characters like Ortrud, with her perfidious lies and dishonest character, or like the paternalistic and ruthlessly racist Henderson.

Du Bois is arguing, novelly, that race relations, like all human relations, are about trust. Trust became such an important concept at the turn of the century that sociologists and philosophers explicitly addressed its significance. Georg Simmel, for example, insisted in his pathbreaking volume *Soziologie* (1908) that "without the phenomenon of faithfulness [*Treue*], society would not exist."[18] Simmel, a founding figure of modern sociology, was appointed lecturer in 1885 at the Friedrich Wilhelm University in Berlin (where Du Bois studied a few years later), and had already written an essay "On Collective Responsibility" as early as 1890. In *Soziologie* Simmel devoted a lengthy excursus to the concept of faith (*Treue*), defining it as the "soul's ability to prevail."[19] When he maintains that the notion of faith and soul (*Treue* and *Seele*) are closely related, Simmel signifies, unintentionally, on the title of Du Bois's book.[20] In a rather mechanistic understanding, Simmel claims that *Treue* is based on a sense of bonding (*Verbundenheit*), which keeps relationships alive even after they lose their initial momentum. Thus, faith is quintessential to both personal and collective relationships because it creates a sense of unity (*Einheitsbildung*), and its binding element is mostly that of gratitude (*Dankbarkeit*) instead of obligation.[21] Whereas Simmel was unable to imagine an absolutely faithless human being, Wagner did so in the figures of Ortrud and Elsa. The tragedy of "Of the Coming of John" presents Du Bois's nightmare of a life without trust. The lack of solidarity, be it racial or human, brings about the hero's demise and puts an end to racial uplift in Altamaha.

Since Du Bois never explicitly extrapolated on the significance of faith or solidarity on a programmatic or conceptual level, a look at passing remarks in his autobiographical texts may be instructive. His life's goal was linked to "his dream of racial solidarity," as he wrote in *Darkwater*.[22] In "The Concept of Race," he delineated that a race-man's "loyalty to this group idea tends to be almost unending and balks at almost no sacrifice."[23] Du Bois's unwavering commitment to notions of trust notwithstanding, there were times, as he recalled in his autobiography, "when these loyalties diverge[d]."[24] While Du Bois experienced conflicting loyalties as agonizing, it is exactly the space of tension spanned between such loyalties where the cosmopolitan dimension unfolds.

In his discussion of Du Bois's cosmopolitanism, Anthony Appiah reminds us that "[t]he one thought cosmopolitans share is that no local loyalty can ever justify forgetting that each human being has responsibilities to every other...Du Bois's cosmopolitanism is displayed in his openness to the achievements of other civilizations; his celebration of European culture, high and low, is always evident."[25] Appiah explicitly mentions "Of the Coming of John" in order to show Du Bois's loyalty to and his appreciation of a culture that is not his "own." Perhaps his essay "Opera and the Negro problem" is an even better example of the argument for his cosmopolitanism. He praises the Wagnerian opera especially because it represents the "ever-unanswered tragedy of pain and death...the suffering and triumphs and defeats of a people." Highlighting its universal appeal, Du Bois recommends that Wagner's operas in particular and classical music in general "should be part of the education of every man of culture." Of course, Du Bois had very particular and precise views about the nature of what he called "real education." In that same article, he proposes that "those who seek real education – who wish in truth to know Life" should consult poets, artists, and musicians.[26] His trust in the liberal arts is well known and it is what set him apart from Booker T. Washington's strategy of promoting vocational education. Du Bois, in "Of Our Spiritual Strivings," argues for training "the broader, deeper, higher culture of gifted minds and pure hearts" (*Souls* 370). His cosmopolitan worldview enabled him to choose Wagner and Herder as allies in his overall agenda to enlighten and elevate the hearts and minds of African Americans. In his insistence upon a broader "real" education focusing on the liberal arts and high culture, he was much closer to Humboldt's idea of *Bildung* than to Washington's embrace of masonry and bricklaying. Du Bois's trust in the elevating and edifying effect of the arts is perhaps best captured in the confession: "I hated to see the fine soul of a poet and littérateur thus dulled and frayed in the rough work of actual propaganda and agitation."[27]

In conclusion, W. E. B. Du Bois, the pioneering sociologist of the African American experience, desperate to employ the tools of social scientific analysis to ameliorate the plight of his people, articulates in "The Talented Tenth" a mandate, a platform, for intra-racial responsibility of an educated elite. It turns out, however, that his simultaneously published short story not only problematizes that very commitment to trust and responsibility but also suggests that such a form of leadership might well-nigh be impossible to fulfill. Du Bois used two different discursive realms – the short story and the polemical essay – to define the thesis and antithesis of the dialectic of the educated 10 percent and the remainder of the black community. Perhaps, despairing at the pessimism inherent in "Of the Coming of John," Du Bois attempted to critique or eliminate its inevitably tragic ending with a rousing call to arms to his fellow college-educated black women and men. Nevertheless, these two statements will stand forever in an oscillating relation as embodying the bipolar moment of trust and alienation between the elite and the masses within the black community, a paradox that obtains to this day.

Notes

1. J. E. Newton, 'Black Americans in Delaware: An Overview,' in *A History of African Americans of Delaware and Maryland's Eastern Shore*, ed. C. Marks (Wilmington: University of Delaware, 1997).
2. G. W. Reid, "North Carolina's Black Congressman: 1874–1901," *Journal of Negro History*, 64, no. 3 (1979), p. 238.
3. *Ibid.*
4. Moreover, in a letter to Governor Winfield T. Durbin of Indiana, President Roosevelt wrote that "[a]ll thoughtful men…must feel the gravest alarm over the growth of lynching in this country, and especially over the peculiarly hideous forms so often taken by mob violence when colored men are the victims," and he congratulated Governor Durbin for using the National Guard

to disperse the lynch mob (Theodore Roosevelt, "My Dear Governor Durbin," August 6, 1903), in *Addresses and Presidential Messages of Theodore Roosevelt 1902–1904* (1904; New York: G. P. Putnam's Sons, 1971) p. 277. As a consequence, Roosevelt lost a lot of political support among white people in the South and received threats so that he needed protection from the Secret Service.

5. Among the scholars who have tried to interpret this story are Appiah, "Ethics in a World of Strangers"; Berman; Fontenot; Rampersad, *Art and Imagination*; Sundquist; Walker; Wald; and Williams: see Further Reading.

6. A. Rampersad, *The Art and Imagination of W. E. B. Du Bois* (Cambridge: Harvard University Press, 1976), p. 76.

7. E. J. Sundquist, *To Wake the Nations: Race in the Making of American Literature* (Cambridge: Harvard University Press, 1993), p. 524.

8. Prior to 1903 Du Bois had never published his poems and literary texts, and many of his exercises in creative writing were limited to his notebooks. See also S. Zamir's discussion of the unpublished short story 'A Vacation Unique' in his *Dark Voices: W. E. B. Du Bois and American Thought, 1888–1903* (Chicago: University of Chicago Press, 1995), pp. 46–50, 217–25.

9. Most likely Du Bois's interest in Wagner and his appetite for high culture in general originated during his two-year stay in Europe when Du Bois visited a number of distinguished museums (e.g. the Louvre, the Uffizi, the Neue Pinakothek, the National Gallery in London) and encountered the sublime beauty of the arts in a European setting. He also attended concerts of classical music and opera performances, for example at the Berliner Staatsoper. Returning to Berlin in the 1930s, Du Bois saw more than ten operas: "I am bathing myself in music," he wrote in 1936 (quoted in *Newspaper Columns by W. E. B. Du Bois*, ed. H. Aptheker [White Plains, NY: Kraus-Thomson Organization, 1986], p. 156).

10. W. E. B. Du Bois, *The Souls of Black Folk*, in W. E. B. Du Bois, *Writings*, ed. N. Huggins (New York: Library of America, 1986), pp. 526–7. All further page references are given in the text.

11. *Richard Wagner, Lohengrin: Texte, Materialien, Kommentare*, ed. A. Csampai and D. Holland (Reinbek bei Hamburg: Rowohlt, 1989), p. 72. Hereafter cited in the text as *Lohengrin*.

12. R. A. Berman, 'Du Bois and Wagner: Race, Nation and Culture between the United States and Germany', *German Quarterly*, 70, no. 2 (1997), p. 134.

13. Du Bois was fluent in German when he submitted his Ph.D. thesis to his German supervisor at the Friedrich Wilhelm University.

14. W. E. B. Du Bois, "Opera and the Negro Problem," *Pittsburgh Courier* (31 October 1936), reprinted in *Newspaper Columns*, ed. Aptheker, p. 130.

15. F. Nietzsche, *Unzeitgemäße Betrachtungen, Viertes Stück* (Munich: Reclam, 1969), p. 12 (my translation.)

16. Berman, "Du Bois and Wagner," pp. 128, 130.

17. Quoted in Sundquist, *To Wake the Nations*, p. 491.

18. G. Simmel, *Soziologie – Untersuchungen über die Formen der Vergesellschaftung* (Berlin: Duncker & Humblot, 1908), p. 439 (my translation).

19. *Ibid.*

20. There is reason to speculate that Du Bois's title was inspired by the German interest in matters of the soul (*Seele*). Starting with Herder's treatise *Vom Erkennen und Empfinden der Menschlichen Seele* (1774) and including Simmel's investigation "Das Heil der Seele" (1902), many Germans have pondered on the human soul (*Seele*). In fact, Simmel's wife Gertrude is the author of *Vom Sein und Haben der Seele*.

21. Simmel says: "[I]t is impossible to underestimate the sociological importance of gratitude" (Die soziologische Bedeutung der Dankbarkeit indes ist eine kaum zu überschätzende), in *Soziologie*, p. 440.

22. Quoted in Sundquist, *To Wake the Nations*, p. 494.

23. *Ibid.*, p. 96.

24. *The Autobiography of W. E. B. Du Bois: A Soliloquy on Viewing My Life from the Last Decade of its First Century*, ed. H. Aptheker (New York: International Publishers, 1968), p. 169.

25. K. A. Appiah, "Ethics in a World of Strangers: W. E. B. Du Bois and the Spirit of Cosmopolitanism," *Berlin Journal*, 11 (2005), p. 24.

26. Du Bois, "Opera and the Negro Problem," pp. 130, 156, 131.

27. Rampersad, *Art and Imagination*, p. 170.

3

JENNIFER TERRY

The Fiction of W. E. B. Du Bois

Introduction

Within the body of work of W. E. B. Du Bois, a figure described by the editors of the *Norton Anthology of African American Literature* as "the most multi-faceted, prolific, and influential writer that black America has ever produced," his fiction has long been overshadowed by other contributions and modes of writing.[1] None of his five novels received a great amount of attention or acclaim at the time of publication and only relatively recently have the first two, *The Quest of the Silver Fleece* (1911) and *Dark Princess* (1928), started to be the subjects of critical analysis and debate. In much of Du Bois's writing there are distinctive intersections between sociological, historical, autobiographical, philosophical, and psychological inquiries and interventions. Elements of creative writing, too, can be found in the nonfiction work; the short story "Of the Coming of John" plays its part in *The Souls of Black Folk* (1903), and *Darkwater: Voices from within the Veil* (1920) combines the lyrical with other forms of commentary. This fact, along with the author's case, as laid out in the essay "Criteria of Negro Art" (1926), for art as political, offers a sense of Du Bois's own understanding of the value, place, and purpose of imaginative writing. It positions his fictional and poetic compositions as a part of the same investigative, elucidatory, and highly committed project as the rest of his oeuvre and is suggestive in terms of approaching the novels which themselves traverse the genres of romance, historical fiction, life writing, and social realism.[2] This chapter will focus on Du Bois's novels, exploring their attempts to give voice and weight to experiences that have been "stripped and silent," pushed beyond the veil within American letters.[3]

Du Bois's first novel was written during the first decade of the twentieth century, a period of social upheaval, change in his own life, and reflection on the achievements and failures of *The Souls of Black Folk*. The narrative charts a romance involving Bles Alwyn, a young African American scholar and later politician and race man, and Zora, an heroic black woman who transforms from wild child of the swamp to educator and community leader, yet it also coheres around the symbol of the silver fleece, that is cotton and its appropriation. Indeed, the organization of Southern agriculture and post-slavery society is at the heart of Du Bois's concerns as he portrays turn of the century injustice but, in addition, resilient idealism. The predominant setting of the South bears the mark of the Northern author's own time at Fisk and Atlanta Universities and confirms his sense of black American identity as emerging from the Southern plantation system and the experiences of the concomitant enslaved labor force. The central position given to female characters, their trials, and selfhood distinguishes *The Quest* from other contemporary male-authored works, something continued with the later *Dark Princess*. The inextricable combination of the personal and political, of a love story and economic history, of particularity and representativeness is, too, a feature shared by Du Bois's wider fiction.

The Quest begins with the blossoming of Bles and Zora's relationship in childhood within both the protective reaches of Miss Smith's school for blacks and the oppressive shadow of the Cresswell plantation. Detailed at the same time is the balance and tension of various socio-economic forces (the supremacist and "aristocratic" Cresswells, Northern investment as represented by John Taylor, local impoverished whites, and African American sharecroppers) and how such interact, exploiting and exploited. As will be discussed later, Du Bois explores the fraught position of black women within dominant gender ideology as the issue of "impurity" disrupts Bles and Zora's intended union. The departure of Bles for Washington leads to his involvement in party politics and near moral downfall from the cynical maneuvers of self-serving blacks and whites. Meanwhile the abandoned Zora, after broadening her knowledge of the world through travel as a lady's maid, devotes herself to the fulfillment of a communitarian vision, organizing the farming and the education of African Americans back at home in Alabama and even reaching out to disempowered local white mill workers. When a humbled Bles joins her in this work, the pair are finally reunited as a couple, so providing the expected ending for a marriage plot. With its focus on cotton production, processing, control, and profit, *The Quest* establishes itself as concerned with market forces as well as the twists of a romance.

The author's second novel, *Dark Princess*, holds many of the same elements and preoccupations but is far more international in terms of its understanding of political and economic systems, the scope of its plot, and the breadth of its idealistic aspirations. Once more a rather sprawling narrative coheres around a love story, this time involving the disillusioned

African American medical student turned traveler, Pullman porter, and then politician, Matthew Towns, and the Indian maharani, philanthropist, and activist, Princess Kautilya. The Princess follows on from the earlier "colored" heroine, also admired for her fortitude and redemptive influence. This novel, like the essay "Criteria of Negro Art," can be seen as a response to the Harlem Renaissance and those contemporaries who disputed the politicization of art.

Dark Princess follows Towns's experiences in New York, Berlin, and Chicago, and his confrontations with and attempts to escape racial prejudice. His chance encounter with Princess Kautilya in Europe furthers the romance plot but also introduces him to the Great Council of Darker Peoples, a global committee working to combat white supremacy and colonialism. Matthew sets out to prove the worthiness of African Americans to join in this struggle. Yet the deep disillusionment that ensues on his return to the United States, his failure to organize black workers or bring about social change, prompts a turn toward a maverick terrorist plot, averted only by the reappearance of Kautilya. The second half of the novel sees the protagonist, apparently divested of his former ideals, enter into Chicago machine politics, joining forces with the roguish black Republican Sammy Scott and his shrewd aide and soon Towns's wife, Sara Andrews. While Matthew drifts into political compromise, eschewing her hereditary privilege, Kautilya works within an American industrial labor movement. The forces of love and international socialism come back to the fore on the consummation of a passionate relationship between the Princess and Towns. After further delay the couple are finally united in marriage in the South, celebrating at the same time the birth of their son who is to take up the mantle of the worldwide struggle of oppressed against oppressor.

Du Bois's later fiction, *The Black Flame* trilogy, can be seen to arise out of the experiences and thinking of the last twenty years of his life. These three substantial novels detail the story of the Mansart family and other intertwined dynasties, and a great deal of world history, from the 1870s to the 1950s, besides. Preoccupations with race relations, education, economics, and social change survive, but this fiction declines a central romance plot and much of the earlier sense of optimism and potentiality. The somewhat heavy-going texts still combine autobiographical elements, a fictional family saga, and sociological observation. Yet perhaps the isolation from much of establishment America that followed Du Bois's political turn to the left in the 1940s and 50s impacted on his late, more somber, fiction.

The trilogy begins with its most dramatic part, *The Ordeal of Mansart* (1957). This novel establishes the resentments, injustices, and political machinations of the Reconstruction South, drawing out the ways in which those in power, whether Southern landowners or Northern financiers, exploit race hate to play poor whites and ex-slaves off against each other, so reinforcing their own position through a pliant and disunited labor force. Issues of colonialism, rising corporatism, and the veil that hangs between the races are outlined along with the background and education of the trilogy's protagonist, Manuel Mansart. His birth on the same night that his father is lynched for trying to rescue rather than, as accused, ravage a white woman is presented in momentous terms as the ignition of an avenging black flame. *Mansart Builds a School* (1959) picks up the story in the early twentieth century and traces the development of Manuel's career in education, foregrounding the Land Grant Colleges founded to foster black learning in the South. World War I, the Harlem Renaissance, the Wall Street Crash, and the New Deal all feature here and affect the lives of the Mansarts. In taking the narrative through to the 1930s, this volume broadens to encompass the paths of Manuel's four children, Douglass, Revels, Bruce, and Sojourner. It closes, like *The Ordeal*, with imagery of flame and conflict as representative of racial and political struggle.

The trilogy concludes with *Worlds of Color* (1961), published just two years before Du Bois's death. This novel recalls the internationalism of *Dark Princess* as it has Mansart embark on travels through Europe and Asia (taking in England, Germany, France, Russia, China, and Japan) and his college deputy, Jean Du Bignon, visit the Caribbean. These trips allow Du Bois, through his characters, to bear witness to European class systems, wealth founded on the slave trade and colonialism, the rise of fascism, and the ideals of the Russian Revolution. World War II looms large in this volume as does the rising significance of Africa and the Soviet Union, and the Cold War backlash against suspected communists, including Manuel and Jean. Du Bois's preoccupation with education closes with the implications of the desegregation of schooling for future generations of African Americans. Mansart's death in 1954 signals the end of an often thwarted reformer but he is survived by the various aspirations and causes of his several heirs poised to continue the struggle.

"Criteria of Negro Art": Genre, Politics, and Tradition

This section will consider how and where we might situate the fiction of Du Bois in terms of genre, style, literary influences, and the politics of art. The author's own understanding of the value of creative writing is explained in the aforementioned "Criteria of Negro Art." Here he states, "whatever art I have for writing has been used always for propaganda for gaining the right of black folk to love and enjoy....[I] care when propaganda is confined to one side while the other is stripped and silent" ("Criteria" 1000). Du Bois thus sets out a view of art as purposeful beyond aesthetics and does so in the context of a Harlem Renaissance riven by debates about the responsibilities of representation, artistic freedom, tradition, and modernity. His assertion that "all Art is propaganda," however, hardly translates into a steadfast adherence to socialist realism or a partisan political message in his fiction, nor was it meant to ("Criteria" 1000). Indeed, his aim of "gaining the right of black folk to love and enjoy" indicates rather a politicized reclamation of aesthetic pleasure and recognition for a group that has, at least in the field of letters, been denied it, "stripped and silent." Du Bois's position here may seem merely reactionary, and certainly some of his fellow black writers of the early twentieth century disagreed with his insistence on artistic representation as political, yet as the fiction itself reveals, he used a *variety* of approaches to sound out "Truth," "Beauty," and "Right" ("Criteria" 1000). He sought after "a world where men know, where men create, [and] where they realize themselves," and for him part of this is an African American attempt to "face our own past as a people" and self-affirmative response to "the Negro painted by white Americans" ("Criteria" 999). He perceived a continuity, not a divide between art and life and the instrumental power of cultural memory.

His foregrounding of black experience assumes several modes, chief among them being the romance and the historical novel. Du Bois's first two fictions, *The Quest* and *Dark Princess*, both romances, are his strongest. When the author identified the past of blacks in America as "the true and stirring stuff of which Romance is born" he signaled not triviality or escapism but drama and feeling, suffering and triumph ("Criteria" 997). He joined the long rank of American novelists working with this genre and also, perhaps inadvertently, recalled Harriet Beecher Stowe's claim that the "wild and singular relations" arising from slavery "evolve every possible combination of romance." Like Stowe, Du Bois, too, is concerned with "the moral bearings of the subject involved," with "sympathy," and, grounded in a desire for real world change, this factor strains against a simple classification of the early works.[4] *Dark Princess* is subtitled *A Romance* and the dedication to Titania, "Queen of Faerie," frames the narrative with reference to magic and fantasy. An "Envoy" closes the text with the retreat of the "sprites" who have assisted the author weave the story, "that rich and colored gossamer of dream."[5] Yet *Dark Princess* is also a social novel grounded in race and class relations, and Du Bois suggests that perhaps historical truth can be found in the fabric of imagination. This is reinforced by his claim "to tell the truth" in the "Author's Note" to *The Quest* and his closing invocation to the reader: "Lay not these words aside for a moment's phantasy, but lift up thine eyes upon the Horror in this land; – the maiming and mocking and murdering of my people, and the prisonment of their souls."[6] From the happy resolution of the story of Bles and Zora, we are directed not to idle fantasy, but the plight of contemporary African Americans.

This "romance with a message"[7] can be perhaps aligned less with the work of the Harlem Renaissance writers of the 1920s and more with the late-nineteenth-century sensibilities of the African American women novelists Frances Ellen Watkins Harper and Pauline Hopkins. In Harper's *Iola Leroy* (1892) and Hopkins's *Contending Forces* (1900), among other publications, we find both romance plots and pointed observations of cultural and social questions.

Another referent in Du Bois's fiction is gestured toward when he describes *The Quest* as an "economic study."[8] Indeed, *The Quest*'s focus on cotton production, manufacture, and profit in many ways parallels the early-twentieth-century writing of such Naturalist white American authors as Upton Sinclair and Frank Norris (and Rebecca Harding Davis before them). Although this realist association can be seen as jarring with the more sentimental and fanciful strains of Du Bois's early work, it is borne out by his insistent anchoring of narratives in socio-economic struggles. Sinclair's hard-hitting study of the American meat trade, *The Jungle* (1906), like *The Quest*, is centered on laying bare the mechanisms, beneficiaries, and victims of one industry. Norris's grimly realist fictions about mining and wheat production, too, contribute to this turn. *Dark Princess*, despite lacking the single focus of *The Quest*, continues the approach in its engagement with labor movements and through the detailing of Matthew's life as a Pullman porter and later subway-tunnel digger.

In *The Quest* the injustices that have endured in the South since the days of slavery are also explored through the use of the myth of the Golden Fleece. The allusion had been employed by Du Bois earlier in a chapter on the cotton belt entitled "Of the Quest of the Golden Fleece" in *Souls*, but in the novel it becomes a unifying motif and central allegory for exploitation. Bles proffers this interpretation on being told "the story of Jason and the Argonauts" by Mary Taylor: "He pointed...to the quivering mass of green-gold foliage that swept from swamp to horizon, 'Al yon golden fleece is Jason's now'...'Jason was a brave adventurer –' 'I thought he was a thief... The Cresswells are thieves now'...Despite herself Miss Taylor caught the allegory" (*Quest* 25–6). The shimmering crop, produced by the labor of blacks, brings wealth and power to the landowners yet the fleece is also the fragile dream of Zora and Bles when they defiantly nurture their own harvest in the swamp. While the use of classical myth was a tool of several

Modernist writers engaged in re-energizing European letters, Du Bois's incorporation of it here is perhaps better identified as a proto-postcolonial appropriation and revision that remakes the traditional hero as oppressor.

Although both *The Quest* and *Dark Princess* feature "real" historical events and figures, it is the later texts that belong more fully to the genre of the historical novel. Du Bois's thinking on history and writing the past is explained in the "Postscript" to the first part of *The Black Flame* trilogy. Here he states, "I have used fiction to interpret those historical facts which otherwise would not be clear," aspiring to "a fair version of the truth of an era." Imagination can thus play its part in realizing an always "unknown and unknowable history," but especially where there has been "much omitted, much forgotten, much distorted."[9] Du Bois's trilogy encompasses a great deal of world history, spanning over eighty years, but binds to this the experiences, feelings, and thoughts of those living through it, in particular of those on the wrong side of the color-line. A similar, and perhaps less bogged down, endeavor can be found in Margaret Walker's contemporaneous imagining and reclaiming of the history of a family of black women in slavery and beyond, *Jubilee* (1965). The approach even has lines of continuity with the more formally innovative fiction of such African American authors writing today as Toni Morrison.

"The Damnation of Women": Patriarchy, Femininity, and Race

As mentioned earlier, one of the distinguishing characteristics of Du Bois's fiction is the central place occupied by black female identity, gender constraints, and strong-willed women characters. The author's concern can also be gauged from his essay "The Damnation of Women" (1920).[10] Although partial and flawed when viewed from a current perspective, Du Bois's feminism engaged with issues of economic dependence and sexual coercion as well as being attuned to complex intersections of racial and gender oppression. "Damnation" condemns the withholding from women of the right to both be mothers and to work and their confinement to the private sphere. It unpicks the nineteenth-century idealization of womanhood: "women's way was clear: to be beautiful, to be petted, to bear children...In partial compensation for this narrowed destiny the white world has lavished its politeness on its womankind – its chivalry and bows" ("Damnation" 965). But in exploring the construction of femininity, the full strength of Du Bois's critique is felt when it comes to the treatment and perception of black (non) women, forced "to be the breeder[s] of human cattle" under slavery, subject to sexual abuse, and associated with moral degradation and promiscuity, often allotted hard physical labor, and scorned as coarse and ugly ("Damnation" 958). He, too, does a compelling job of reframing the negative legacies of the past by celebrating the emergence of "an efficient [African American] womanhood" ("Damnation" 959). The remarkably self-respecting and capable body of black women to whom he dedicates the essay were enabled by their very exclusion from white "ladyhood," from worship and dependence: "from black women of America, however…this gauze has been withheld…Not being expected to be merely ornamental, they have girded themselves for work" ("Damnation" 965). While Du Bois remains in some ways caught up in patriarchal thinking, much of his fiction, like the essay, attempts to explore and affirm black female identity and worth.[11]

An examination of the fiction in terms of gender relations and depictions of womanhood, primarily focusing on "Of the Coming of John," *The Quest*, and *Dark Princess*, follows. The idealization of a certain form of femininity identified by Du Bois above, was typified by the so-called Southern Belle. The opposite of such female grace and inviolability in American society was the laboring or dark woman, not accorded the protection and pedestal due a lady. Earlier black women writers such as the ex-slave Harriet Jacobs had drawn attention to this double standard, in some cases seeking to undermine it by asserting their own refinement, modesty, and "ladyhood." Others demanded full recognition of their womanhood and motherhood, but celebrated the black woman's traditionally "unfeminine" physical strength, resilience, and independence. Du Bois's negotiation of these questions is of mixed success.

"Of the Coming of John," a chapter of *Souls*, compares the divergent paths of a young black and a young white man, both named John. At the climax of the story, however, is a masculine struggle over control of female sexuality. When the two Southerners by chance coincide at a classical concert in New York, the African American is evicted from his seat, his very presence in their midst supposedly being an affront and threat to the ladies in the audience and, in particular, to white John's companion. The conflict escalates when, back in their hometown, the white man chases after and assumes he has the right to force his attentions on black John's sister, Jennie. Beleaguered in his attempts to improve local black education and confronted with the sight of his sister's assault and possible violation ("to see his dark sister struggling in the arms of a tall and fair-haired man"[12]), he reacts with violence, the outcome of which is his lynching at the close of the story. Du Bois here effectively highlights the difference in attitude toward white and black femininity. He also plays with the expectation of a black male rapist insulting white womanhood and therefore deserving the lynch mob. Yet in this early fiction female identity is marginalized and, as pointed out by Hazel Carby, a woman's sexual victimhood becomes the means by which to explore male experience and a patriarchally informed struggle for control.[13] The engagement with matrices of race and gender grows more sophisticated in later work.

The Quest foregrounds Zora and other female characters such as Miss Smith, Mary Taylor, Carolyn Wynn, and Zora's mother, Elspeth. Each of these, except perhaps Elspeth, is presented as an individual rather than type. Having said this, figures from the popular imagination, for example the New England schoolmistress, are summoned up. In the kindly ministrations of the Puritan headteacher Miss Smith and the sensibilities and strained interactions with her black pupils of Miss Taylor might be identified modified echoes of Stowe's Quaker community leader Rachel Halliday and good-intentioned, if at times misguided, Northern reformer Ophelia St. Clare from *Uncle Tom's Cabin* (1852). Yet where in Stowe's novel the death of Eva leads to a truer bond between Ophelia and her wayward charge Topsy, Mary Taylor's path is toward dissolution not idealized redemption. When she marries into the Cresswell family, attracted to their genteel lifestyle and the son Harry's chivalry, the Northern schoolteacher is set to become, by extension, a Southern Belle. This narrative, however, is thoroughly undercut as, at first politically ambitious, then neglected, betrayed, and abused by her husband, physically ravaged by the loss of a child, and increasingly foolish in her relations with Bles and Zora, Du Bois has her grow an ever more pitiful figure. The feminine ideal is again undone in *The Ordeal of Mansart* when the well-meaning but naive Mrs Breckinridge enters the black part of Charleston alone, thereby endangering Manuel Mansart's father who, in attempting to escort her safely home, is lynched for abducting a white woman. In the later novel Mrs Breckinridge realizes her part in an innocent man's death and, recognizing the fatalism of the gendered and racialized situation, eventually takes her own life too.

The position of Zora herself in relation to issues of sexual control and idealized femininity is effectively illuminated through the use of the marriage plot. By paralleling three wedding unions Du Bois brings attention to the particular difficulties encountered by black women in a post-slavery society. Drawn together as displaced children, Bles and Zora early on plan to share a future and build their hopes on the secret crop of cotton. The promise of this silver fleece is dashed, however, when Bles learns of a former sexual transgression on Zora's part and berates and abandons her. His condemnation of her lack of purity ("All women know! You should have died!" [*Quest* 144]), and rage at the supposed affront to his own masculine authority and ownership devastates Zora and, as her womanly chastity has been, their crop is subsequently appropriated by the Cresswells in a chapter entitled "The Rape of the Fleece." The cotton then provides a symbolic link between the matrimonial union of "respectable" ladies and the shaming of Zora for it is woven into wedding dresses for Mary Taylor and Helen Cresswell. These white cambric gowns thus represent all that has been lost to Zora. Yet *The Quest* goes on to reveal itself a more nuanced engagement with such matters than "Of the Coming of John." Helen Cresswell's marriage to John Taylor proves to be a rather vacuous relationship ("he had something to pet" [*Quest* 195]), and, as already detailed, Mary Taylor's to Harry Cresswell is disastrous. Meanwhile Bles slowly comes to realize the cruelty and injustice of his earlier rejection of Zora. It is her understanding of purity as doing everything within one's power to be faithful, and a view of her girlhood encounter with Harry Cresswell as exploitative, that achieves credence. The black couple's eventual reunion is founded not on Bles's forgiveness of Zora's "sin" or, indeed, acceptance of her "ruined" though she is, but on a recognition of her superior virtues and strengths, of his own failings and rehearsal of the dominant ideology.[14] It is Zora who eventually leads the local community, Zora who at the end of the novel asks Bles to marry her, and Zora who is finally swathed in the luminous glory of the silver fleece: "gleaming...like midnight gowned in mist and stars" (*Quest* 375).

In *Dark Princess* Du Bois again creates a brave and principled heroine. Although the narrative follows, and is predominantly focused through, Matthew Towns rather than Kautilya, she is central to his personal and political development and hence salvation. Flouting standard expectations of a romance plot and of behavior in early-twentieth-century patriarchal society, she is idealized as gentle, refined, and beautiful, yet *also* is politically committed, intelligent, able to withstand menial work, and shares a passionate sexual relationship with Matthew outside of marriage. Her identity as a woman is still framed by gender constraints; to perform her filial and national duty Kautilya should forge a suitable match and line of descent with a maharajah. In addition, although as a princess she has not experienced the extremes of oppression felt by black women under and since slavery, through the incident of her first meeting Towns while subject to the unwanted advances of a white American in Berlin, Du Bois takes care to reveal even her sexual vulnerability as a woman of color, something exacerbated when she takes lowly employment. Yet Du Bois is unconventional in the combination of Kautilya as a moral force and a desiring subject who repeatedly transgresses social boundaries. For an author who felt sullied on reading Claude McKay's *Home to Harlem* (1928) and appeared to call for a more respectable strain of black expression during the Harlem Renaissance, his depiction of the interracial union of the Princess and Matthew is unexpectedly bold and sensual.[15] The contrast between the warmth of Matthew's brief encounter with a Harlem cabaret girl and his sterile marriage to the decent Sara Andrews is, too, a significant rejection of proprieties.

Ambitious and single-minded, Sara parallels the calculating Carolyn Wynn who toys with Bles during his time in Washington in *The Quest*. Although Du Bois asserted the right of women to work in "Damnation," businesslike, sophisticated, and shrewd as well as light-skinned, it might appear that such professional women constitute a negative type in his fiction. This is contradicted, however, by Jean Du Bignon, Manuel's efficient assistant and later his wife who is depicted favorably in *The Black Flame* trilogy. Perhaps another way to consider all three is as reworkings of the Tragic Mulatta figure, conventionally doomed by her mixed race and gendered status, but here invested with considerable agency if not always soul.

The final mode of femininity due critical attention in Du Bois's novels is that of the mother, grandmother, or ancestress. This is usually a positive embodiment who sustains and supports others, as Linda Brent's grandmother does in Jacobs's earlier *Incidents in the Life of a Slave Girl* (1861). In *The Ordeal of Mansart* Manuel's grandmother is a widely respected and powerful woman, and it is she who foretells his calling to serve his people. Matthew's mother in *Dark Princess* is presented as an ancient laborer and giver of life, who shelters Kautilya while she is pregnant, and is named "Kali, the Black One; wife of Siva, Mother of the World" (*Dark Princess* 220). It is at her humble cabin that the novel casts its messianic ending. While we might question the essentialization of such a maternal figure as an all-enduring earth goddess, she forms an important part of Du Bois's attempt to celebrate black womanhood.

Elsewhere, however, the mother is more ambivalent. In *The Quest* Elspeth is so and hence has been viewed as particularly problematic.[16] Physical descriptions render her not monumental like Matthew's mother, but grotesque, a hideous woman whose features fit a racial caricature: "short, broad, black and wrinkled, with fangs and pendulous lips and red, wicked eyes" (*Quest* 11). She is an object of fear for Zora and runs an immoral household for the entertainment of white men. Frequently named witch-like, we could condemn this troubling characterization as an early demonization of femininity and expression of racial self-contempt on the part of Du Bois that is less present in his later fiction. Yet although the mother facilitates sexual exploitation (including of Zora), although she is perceived as evil and portrayed as ugly, her association with ancient powers and legacies links her to the more idealized heritage of the maternal in *Dark Princess* and *The Black Flame* trilogy. It is to Elspeth that Bles and Zora turn for the "wonder seed, sowed…in the old land ten thousand moons ago," to grow their cotton crop and she delivers on this (*Quest* 61). In addition, at her death she is visited by a mysterious yet powerful "conjure man" who later returns to help Zora unite the community (*Quest* 27). Such events complicate the picture of Elspeth as hag, and her connection, like Zora's own, with the natural force of the swamp, wild yet also beyond the control of the plantation, is not wholly negative. In common with Manuel's grandmother in *The Ordeal* who performs "the African Dance of Death," she is a sometimes terrible figure still imbued with enabling pre-slavery knowledge (*Ordeal* 72). While rendered physically repulsive and morally reprehensible, we might view her as at least embodying female power and non-European American culture in interestingly complex ways.

Mobility, Modernity, and Internationalism

This final part of my consideration of Du Bois's fiction will explore the scope of his geographic imaginary and, closely tied up with this, the internationalism of his approach to African American identity and politics. Like the foregrounding of women characters, this is a distinctive aspect of his work. Contemporaneous black authors such as Nella Larsen and James Weldon Johnson do engage with intercultural encounters and travel, as Frederick Douglass had before them, yet, especially in *Dark Princess* and *The Black Flame* trilogy, Du Bois is unusual in the extent to which he situates his characters and their experiences in terms of wider, transnational struggles against oppression, both anti-colonial and socialist. His protagonists may sometimes have parochial origins, but the modernity they confront is frequently a cosmopolitan one, the consciousness they develop diasporic, the politics they adopt outward looking.

Even in *The Quest*, whose action remains within the borders of the United States, we find both Bles and Zora highly mobile in their journeys toward self-realization. The novel's examination of cotton production is alert to a global economy, and the narrative movement is also outward. From Elspeth's cabin and Zora's island retreat in the swamp, the text opens up to Miss Smith's school and later to New York and Washington. The northward trajectories of Bles and Zora can be associated with that of the Great Migration of African Americans during the late nineteenth and early twentieth century. They also fit with the pattern of paths out of restrictive Southern communities toward literacy and liberty charted in earlier slave narratives and labeled by Robert Stepto stories of ascent.[17] For Bles the capital is a place of stimulation, variety, and power: "the kaleidoscopic panorama of a world's doing, the myriad forms and faces" (*Quest* 199). Meanwhile the enormity of New York prompts Zora to broaden her education through diverse and voracious reading: "she walked on worlds, and worlds of worlds" (*Quest* 217). *The Quest* concludes with a reverse journey, the return of both Zora and Bles to their Alabama home, only now ready to realize a vision of black education, economic self-sufficiency, and cooperative living and farming. In the later *Dark Princess* this "Field of Dreams" is reformulated on a far more ambitious scale (*Dark Princess* 73).

Du Bois's fiction was undoubtedly increasingly informed by international themes and global politics. *Dark Princess* appeared at the tail end of the Harlem Renaissance, a period of great creativity associated with the clustering of blacks from all over the diaspora in Manhattan, causing Harlem to be dubbed the "Race Capital of the World." This cosmopolitan cultural force would have fed into the author's growing engagement with Pan-Africanism, anti-colonialism, and Marxism. The rupture of World War I, in which many black soldiers served, in addition, brought African Americans a heightened awareness of their place in a wider world. *Dark Princess*, with its action spread across America, Asia, and Europe, its featuring of a racially composite Great Council of Darker Peoples, and its audacious selection of an Indian maharani as heroine, unquestionably broke new ground in American letters. Perhaps more importantly, like much of Du Bois's nonfiction, it attempts to locate the particular position and perspective of the slave-descended peoples of the United States in relation to others suffering under white supremacy and capitalist expansion.

When Matthew Towns flees to Europe in the face of American prejudice, the voyage prompts him to see himself and his identity anew. Under the heading of "The Exile," his racialized experiences invoke and rework the Modernist expatriate crisis. Although Du Bois is perhaps guilty of exoticization in his portrait of Kautilya, Matthew's subsequent relations with this sophisticated world citizen lie at the heart of *Dark Princess*'s affirmation of decolonized selfhood and transnational alliance. Through the couple's efforts, African Americans and Africans are admitted onto the Great Council which, dedicated to ending all forms of colonial rule, also moves from an elitist to a democratic basis. The status of Matthew and the Princess as cross-cultural mediators is indicated by their mobility in the novel. Matthew traverses the nation, linking the poles of North and South, in his employment as a Pullman porter. Just as on his return to America he worked his passage in the galley of the liner, *Gigantic*, through his labor the train is shown to be a space hierarchized by race and class. Yet it is also a site of potential subversion and connectivity, surpassed only by the protagonist's thrilling airplane flight to the South at the climax of the novel. Here the capacities of modern transportation technology, and the new self-consciousness they engender, contribute in building to the text's utopian resolution. The re-envisioning of the old slave-holding South as a global nexus, ideally placed to maintain links with colonized peoples in Africa, Asia, and the Caribbean, frames the potentially "regressive" return home as an empoweringly internationalist choice. The South then is not resistant to modernity, more usually associated with the industrialized North, nor necessarily constraining, but a place of dawning hope and purpose: "here in Virginia you are at the edge of a black world...I see a mighty synthesis: you can work in Africa and Asia right here in America if you work in the Black Belt" (*Quest* 286). Thus not only does Du Bois draw on wider perspectives to illuminate the African American position, he performs a complete reorientation to reveal it as central to the worldwide struggle against oppression.[18]

While lacking such transcendent optimism, *The Black Flame* trilogy does further the transnational outlook. Indeed, in later life Du Bois developed his involvement with Africa, eventually, at the invitation of President Nkrumah, moving to Ghana. His turn toward communism was also accompanied by increased interest in the Soviet Union, a state visited by Kautilya in *Dark Princess* and Mansart in *Worlds of Color*. The participation of several black characters in World Wars I and II prompts a questioning of national identity; mistreated within the forces and still discriminated against back home, the soldiers and their families protest the contradictions of their citizenship. Here the wars, too, operate as harbingers of a brutal and late capitalist modernity, something not fully accommodated by the earlier romances. Across the trilogy a gradually more "diasporic" view of race is adopted by Mansart and enacted by the increasingly far-flung reaches of plot and character. For example, by the resolution one of Manuel's grandsons has joined forces with a Vietnamese woman freedom fighting in French colonial Africa, while another has been drafted into the US forces engaged in the Korean War. A range of understandings of community and identity are evident and during the course of his travels the protagonist, with some nostalgia, leaves behind what he terms his "racial provincialism."[19] Movements such as this, along with an intensified focus on contemporary global politics, leave the trilogy open-ended, without answers but grounded in an impressively broad and prophetic grasp of the modern world.

Notes

1. 'W. E. B. Du Bois', in *The Norton Anthology of African American Literature*, ed. H. L. Gates and N. Y. McKay (New York: W. W. Norton, 2004), p. 686.

2. An example of Du Bois's attempt at satire can be found in 'A Vacation Unique' (written 1889), an early, fantastical, and incomplete story published in the appendix to S. Zamir, *Dark Voices: W. E. B. Du Bois and American Thought, 1888–1903* (Chicago: University of Chicago Press, 1995).

3. W. E. B. Du Bois, 'Criteria of Negro Art' (1926), in W. E. B. Du Bois, *Writings*, ed. N. Huggins (New York: Library of America, 1986), p. 1000. Hereafter cited in the text as "Criteria."

4. H. B. Stowe, 'Preface', *Dred: A Tale of the Great Dismal Swamp* (1856; Halifax: Ryburn Publishing, 1992), pp. 29–30. For a sustained discussion of canonical American writers and their preoccupation with and dynamic reworking of the genre of romance, see R. Chase, *The American Novel and Its Tradition* (London: G. Bell and Sons, 1957).

5. W. E. B. Du Bois, *Dark Princess: A Romance* (1928; Jackson: University Press of Mississippi, 1995), p. 312. Hereafter cited in the text as *Dark Princess*.

6. W. E. B. Du Bois, *The Quest of the Silver Fleece* (1911; New York: Broadway Books, 2004), p. 378. Hereafter cited in the text as *Quest*.

7. Du Bois's description of *Dark Princess* in a letter to his publisher, in D. L. Lewis, *W. E. B. Du Bois: The Fight for Equality and the American Century 1919–1963* (New York: Henry Holt, 2000), p. 219.

8. W. E. B. Du Bois, *Dusk of Dawn: An Essay toward an Autobiography of a Race Concept* (New York: Harcourt Brace, 1940), p. 269.

9. W. E. B. Du Bois, *The Ordeal of Mansart* (1957; Millwood, NY: Kraus-Thomson, 1976), pp. 315–16.

10. W. E. B. Du Bois, "The Damnation of Women" (1920), in *Writings*, ed. Huggins, pp. 952–68. Hereafter cited in the text as "Damnation."

11. Issues of gender and sexuality, and their meshing with those of race, in the work of Du Bois are increasingly receiving critical attention. Recent, wide-ranging, and provocative treatments can be found in the collection *Next to the Color Line: Gender, Sexuality and W. E. B. Du Bois* ed. S. Gillman and A. E. Weinbaum (Minneapolis: University of Minnesota Press, 2007).

12. W. E. B. Du Bois, "Of the Coming of John," *The Souls of Black Folk*, in *Writings*, ed. Huggins, p. 534. Hereafter cited in the text as "Of the Coming."

13. H. V. Carby examines how Du Bois figures repeatedly "the burden imposed on black men by history because they could not control the sexual reproduction of black women" (*Race Men* [Cambridge: Harvard University Press, 1998], p. 33).

14. My reading thus complicates Carby's argument about figurations of female betrayal in Du Bois's texts (Carby, *Race Men* 33).

15. W. E. B. Du Bois, 'Two Novels' (1928), in *Norton Anthology*, ed. Gates and McKay, p. 784.

16. Arnold Rampersad describes her as "entirely pagan, hideous, and evil" (*The Art and Imagination of W. E. B. Du Bois* [Cambridge: Harvard University Press, 1976], p. 120).

17. R. B. Stepto, *From Behind the Veil: A Study of Afro-American Narrative* (Urbana: University of Illinois Press, 1979).
18. According to E. J. Sundquist, "Du Bois wrote a world literature grounded in a particularly American experience and sensibility...he kept alive the memory of antebellum black struggle whilst opening the way to Pan-African modernity" (*To Wake the Nations: Race in the Making of American Literature* [Cambridge: Harvard University Press, 1993], p. 624).
19. W. E. B. Du Bois, *Worlds of Color* (1961; Millwood, NY: Kraus Thomson, 1976), p. 85.

4

CARMIELE Y. WILKERSON AND SHAMOON ZAMIR

Du Bois and the "New Negro"

During what was an exceptionally long and productive career as a man of letters, Du Bois was closely associated with only one literary and cultural movement: the "New Negro" movement, which is also more narrowly and more commonly referred to as the Harlem Renaissance. It is never easy to date the beginning and end of such a period of creative activity exactly, though there is a clear scholarly consensus that these particular labels refer to an unprecedented literary and cultural productivity by African American artists and intellectuals located largely in the 1920s and 1930s. David Levering Lewis proposes a more precise demarcation between 1917 and 1935, and divides this period into three distinct phases: the "bohemian renaissance" (1917–23), characterized by a growing body of writing on black American culture, society, and history produced mainly by white rather than African American authors; the "era of the Talented Tenth" (1924–6) which Lewis sees as a period in which black and white authors worked in collaboration under the strong leadership of organizations such as the National Association for the Advancement of Colored People (NAACP) and the National Urban League (NUL); and the "Negro Renaissance" (1926–35) in which a new generation of black writers came to the fore to develop new aesthetic and cultural agendas, and to challenge established political programs and attitudes.[1]

If within this time frame we take the New Negro movement to refer to works of art and cultural reflection produced by black Americans, then Du Bois was, by measure of both quantity and quality, among the foremost contributors. Between 1917 and 1935 he published six books (see Further Reading), among them *Dark Princess* (1928), his second novel, and *Black Reconstruction* (1935), his groundbreaking reconsideration of the role of African Americans in the Civil War and post-Civil War period. If we stretch the dates suggested by Lewis at either end just a little, we can include also *The Negro* (1915), Du Bois's first sustained attempt at surveying the contribution made by Africans and African Americans to world history, and *Dusk of Dawn* (1940), an autobiography. Quite apart from his productivity during the years of the New Negro movement, Du Bois had already established himself as the pre-eminent African American writer and intellectual in the two preceding decades with numerous other major publications in a variety of disciplines and genres. As we go on to argue, it may be that the most significant contribution Du Bois made to the New Negro movement was through the shaping influence of these earlier publications, especially *The Souls of Black Folk*, rather than through the work he produced during the years in which the movement was most active.

However, if we understand the New Negro or the Harlem Renaissance as essentially a label for a new generation of black American writers, intellectuals and artists that flourished from the mid 1920s to the mid 1930s, then Du Bois can appear as an elder statesman whose aesthetic and political attitudes were out of step with the new literary and cultural orientations. In comparison with the rawer treatment of black folk and urban cultures, a more transgressive attitude to sexual materials, and the leaning toward left politics in the work of writers such as Zora Neale Hurston, Langston Hughes, and Claude McKay, Du Bois has been easily caricatured as patrician and aloof, bound to an out-of-date genteel literary tradition and to a liberal and integrationist politics signaled by his association with the NAACP.

Surveys of the Harlem Renaissance which have examined generational, individual, and institutional rivalries and conflicts lend credence to this peripheral placement of Du Bois within the core history of the movement but such cultural histories can obscure as much as they reveal. Considered from the perspective of intellectual history, his role in the New Negro movement can be conceived quite differently. His work emerges as absolutely central to the movement. The following discussion proposes that the defining discourses of the New Negro movement, especially as these are formulated by Alain Locke, its foremost theoretician, were shaped by Du Bois's thought at the deepest level; indeed, they are unimaginable without him. Locke's contributions to his justly famous and movement-defining collection *The New Negro* (1925) are everywhere engaged in a dialogue with Du Bois, and in a sometimes unacknowledged reformulation of his ideas; the anthology, effectively a manifesto for the Harlem Renaissance, is shaped substantially by *The Souls of Black Folk*. If this is so, then at least some of the true intellectual and aesthetic origins of the New Negro movement can be found in Du Bois's work from 1903.

The first part of this essay, by Zamir, examines Du Bois's role as Locke's primary interlocutor. The second part, by Wilkerson, considers Du Bois's more evident influence on the New Negro movement in his capacity as editor of the *Crisis*, a widely read and influential black journal. Though it was the official publication of the NAACP, Du Bois exercised considerable independence as editor and used the journal to define and develop many of the political debates and ideas central to the New Negro era. But, in its literary pages, *Crisis* also published and supported many of the younger writers. In this regard, it is impossible to consider the role of the journal without also fully acknowledging the contribution made by Jessie Redmon Fauset as literary editor.

Du Bois and Locke

The New Negro concludes with a contribution by Du Bois. His inclusion was hardly surprising, given his unique standing within the world of African American culture. As Arnold Rampersad has noted:

> Locke's contributors amounted to almost a Who's Who among black American artists, intellectuals, and scholars. Perhaps the only notable absentee was the independent historian Carter G. Woodson ... Among the younger writers Locke missed virtually no one who had published with any distinction thus far ... virtually all of those selected went on to achieve a measure of fame ... Among the older writers he included virtually everyone of the old guard.[2]

What is noteworthy about the inclusion is the type of writing by Du Bois chosen and how its placement shaped a dialogue within Locke's anthology.

Du Bois's "The Negro Mind Reaches Out" had appeared a few months earlier in *Foreign Affairs*, a quarterly review. The essay provides a closing frame by contextualizing the exploration of race and black culture in the United States in the anthology's other contributions within a broad internationalism. Du Bois articulates considerations of race and racism with histories of labor, imperialism, and capitalism. He surveys European colonialism country by country, examining national differences in the treatment of native populations. Whatever the differences, the triumph of the economic motive over ethical and social imperatives provides a common thread to this diverse history. For Du Bois, the promise of the post-World War I world-order is a potential alliance between white labor and colonial and minority struggles for independence and civil rights: "The chief hope lies in the gradual but inevitable spread of the knowledge that the denial of democracy in Asia and Africa hinders its complete realization in Europe. It is this that makes the Color Problem and the Labor Problem to so great an extent two sides of the same human tangle" (*New Negro* 407–8). In its closing pages, Du Bois's essay veers off from this radical hope towards a clichéd primitivism which pits a "spiritually bankrupt" West against "happy" Africa where "masses of its black folk are calmly contented, save where what is called 'European' civilization has touched and uprooted them" (*New Negro* 409). If this is in keeping with the tenor of some of the other contributions to Locke's volume, so is Du Bois's all-too American exceptionalist and arrogant conviction that "the main seat of...leadership" for the "hundred and fifty millions" of black Africans "is today in the United States" (*New Negro* 411).

Locke's own "Foreword" and "Introduction" mirror Du Bois's concluding essay; within the context of the anthology, these two texts seem to prefigure many of the themes and ideas in Du Bois's piece, even while working their changes upon them. The "Foreword," for example (dated November, seven months after the publication of Du Bois's essay), shares a sense of internationalism as a proper context for understanding the development of "race consciousness" in the United States:

> the New Negro must be seen in the perspective of a New World, and especially of a New America. Europe seething in a dozen centers with emergent nationalities, Palestine full of renascent Judaism – these are no more alive with the progressive forces of our era than the quickened centres of the lives of black folk... as in India, in China, in Egypt, Ireland, Russia, Bohemia...and Mexico, we are witnessing the resurgence of a people.
>
> (*New Negro* xv–xvi, xvii)

Locke also shares Du Bois's belief that black Americans are "acting as the advance-guard of the African people in their contact with Twentieth Century civilization": "With the American Negro, his new internationalism is primarily an effort to recapture contact with the scattered people of African derivation ... the possible role of the American Negro in the future development of Africa is one of the most constructive and universally helpful missions that any modern people can lay claim to" (*New Negro* 14, 15). Locke's language may be more muted that Du Bois's balder claim for an African American leadership for Africa, but the hint of a missionary impulse in his formulation of transcontinental collaboration grates equally on contemporary ears.

Locke seals the connection between his own contributions and Du Bois's essay by directly quoting the title of the latter in his "Introduction" in a passage which appears to repeat Du Bois's argument about democracy, namely that the full potential of democracy can only be realized if no race or group is excluded from it:

> The Negro mind reaches out as yet to nothing but American wants, American ideas. But this forced attempt to build his Americanism on race values is a unique social experiment, and its ultimate success is impossible except through the fullest sharing of American culture and institutions. There should be no delusion about this. American nerves in sections unstrung by

race hysteria are often fed the opiate that the trend of Negro advance is wholly separatist, and that the effect of its operation will be to encyst the Negro as a benign foreign body in the body politic. This cannot be – even if it were desirable... Democracy itself is obstructed and stagnated to the extent any of its channels are closed. Indeed they cannot be selectively closed. So the choice is not between one way for the Negro and another way for the rest, but between American institutions frustrated on the one hand and American ideals progressively fulfilled and realized on the other.

(*New Negro* 11–12)

Read in the larger context of Locke's "Introduction" as a whole, this proves to be not so much a simple endorsement and restatement of Du Bois's argument, as a subtle but significant transformation of it. Du Bois's welding together of the labor struggle and the struggles of racial minorities and colonial peoples lends a radical edge to his vision of the emergent new world order (Du Bois, it should be remembered, had joined the Socialist Party, albeit briefly, in 1911). But in the paragraph which precedes the passage quoted above, Locke retreats from precisely this kind of political radicalism. Locke notes that "each generation" has "its creed, and that of the present is the belief in the efficacy of collective effort, in race co-operation." This is the "outcome of the reaction to proscription and prejudice": "It is radical in tone, but not in purpose and only the most stupid forms of opposition, misunderstanding or persecution could make it otherwise." The next sentence could easily be aimed at Du Bois: "Of course, the thinking Negro has shifted a little toward the left with the world-trend, and there is an increasing group who affiliate with radical and liberal movements." For Locke, this shift does not represent the beliefs and desires of the majority of African Americans: "fundamentally for the present the Negro is radical on race matters, conservative on others, in other words, a 'forced radical,' a social protestant rather than a genuine radical" (*New Negro* 11).

Without disputing the validity of Locke's characterization of black Americans, it can be noted that his argument here is in keeping with a displacement of the political by an assertive aestheticism throughout *The New Negro*. A little earlier Locke suggests that the "objectives" of the black American's "outer life are happily already well and finally formulated, for they are none other than the ideals of American institutions and democracy. Those of his inner life [however] are yet in the process of formation, for the new psychology at present is more of a consensus of feeling than of opinion, of attitude rather than of program" (*New Negro* 10). It is of course the aim of *The New Negro* to push these feelings and attitudes toward a more systematic program, and in this the new generation of artists represents a new elite leadership for the black masses, especially for those making the sudden transition through migration from the feudalism of the South to the modernity of Northern cities:

> The migrant masses, shifting from countryside to city, hurdle several generations of experience at a leap, but more important, the same thing happens spiritually in the life-attitudes and self-expression of the Young Negro, in his poetry, his art, his education and his new outlook, with the additional advantage, of course, of the poise and greater certainty of knowing what it is all about. From this comes the warrant of a new leadership.
>
> (*New Negro* 4–5)

This is of course not much more than a narrower restatement, confined as it is to the realm of culture and the arts, of the program for a vanguard black leadership proposed much earlier by Du Bois under the name of the "Talented Tenth."

By including Du Bois *The New Negro* certainly acknowledges his place in African America, even honors him; but by giving the readers a political Du Bois it also strangely displaces him. Du Bois's essay supplements and opens out the aesthetic and cultural discourses which dominate the anthology, but in the process Du Bois's formative presence within these very discourses is either obscured or reduced. The reformulation of Du Bois's idea of the "Talented Tenth," what Locke himself refers to as the "talented few" (*New Negro* 47), is one example of this. Two others should suffice.

First, a comparison of the "Foreword" to *The New Negro* with *The Souls of Black Folk*. Here is the first part of Locke's opening paragraph:

> This volume aims to document the New Negro culturally and socially, – to register the transformations of the inner and outer life of the Negro in America that have so significantly taken place in the last few years. There is ample evidence of a New Negro in the latest phases of social change and progress, but still more in the internal world of the Negro mind and spirit. Here in the very heart of the folk-spirit are the essential forces, and folk interpretation is truly vital and representative only in terms of these. Of all the voluminous literature on the Negro, so much is mere external view and commentary that we may warrantably say that nine-tenths of it is *about* the Negro rather than of him, so that it is the Negro problem rather than the Negro that is known and mooted in the general mind. We turn therefore in the other direction to the elements of truest social portraiture, and discover in the artistic self-expression of the Negro today a new figure on the national canvas and a new force in the foreground of affairs. Whoever wishes to see the Negro in his essential traits, in the full perspective of his achievements and possibilities, must seek the enlightenment of that self-portraiture which the developments of Negro culture are offering.
>
> (*New Negro* xv)

This prospectus for the volume which follows defines the limitations of existing discourses about African Americans, and suggests ways of overcoming these limitations in terms which are essentially the same as those proposed by Du Bois in *Souls*. We will not repeat here the detailed reading of *Souls* provided in the first chapter of this *Companion* which is relevant in many respects to this comparison, except to note that in his own "Foreword" Du Bois also moves the reader from the external view of a sociological and historical survey to the "deeper recesses" of black life; that he too argues for the need to go beyond "the physical, economic, and political relations of the Negroes and whites" to the less tangible level of black "thought and feeling";[3] that in distinguishing between "the Negro problem" and "the Negro" Locke picks up Du Bois's voicing of the "unasked question": "How does it feel to be a problem?" at the start of the first chapter of *Souls* (363); that "self-portraiture" through a subdued autobiographical and reflective literary form, rather than through sociology or historiography, is precisely Du Bois's response to this question; and that Locke's vocabulary of "folk" and "spirit" inherits the defining vocabulary of *Souls*, just as his focus on the spirituals as the most authentic repository of black spirituality and feeling repeats Du Bois's famous commentary on the "Sorrow Songs" in the final chapter of *Souls*.

Locke's essay on "The Negro Spirituals" provides the second and most obvious presence of Du Bois as Locke's primary interlocutor in *The New Negro*. The first paragraph of Locke's essay restates the main arguments of Du Bois's earlier text. For Locke the spirituals "are really the most characteristic product of the race genius as yet in America ... as unique products of American life, they become nationally as well as racially characteristic ... the song of the Negro is America's folk-song." It is because they have survived disregard and numerous historical transformations that they can be said to have attained the status of classics:

> They have outlived the particular generation and the peculiar conditions which produced them; they have survived in turn the contempt of the slave owners, the conventionalizations of formal religion, the repressions of Puritanism, the corruptions of sentimental balladry, and the neglect and disdain of second-generation respectability. They have escaped the lapsing conditions and the fragile vehicle of folk art, and come firmly into the context of formal music. Only classics survive such things.
>
> (*New Negro* 199)

Du Bois too claimed that "the Negro folk-song ... stands today not simply as the sole American music, but as the most beautiful expression of human experience born this side of the seas." And he too stressed the survival of the songs, despite their being "neglected…half despised…persistently mistaken and misunderstood," and despite "debasements and imitations" (*Souls* 536–7, 540).

It isn't that Locke does not acknowledge a certain debt to Du Bois. He is, if anything, initially quite fulsome in his appreciation of "the great service" done by Du Bois "in his unforgettable chapter on the Sorrow Songs" in giving them "a serious and proper social interpretation" (*New Negro* 200). But he goes on to argue that "interesting and intriguing as was Dr. Du Bois's analysis of their emotional themes, modern interpretation must break with that mode of analysis, and relate these songs to the folk activities that they motivated, classifying them by their respective song-types" (*New Negro* 205). What is required is a musicological approach based on "scientific recording" (*New Negro* 206). Du Bois himself had confessed "I know little of music and can say nothing in technical phrase" and had also acknowledged the need for a taxonomy of the songs based on "scientific principles" (*Souls* 538, 540), but Locke hardly does justice to the sophistication and depth of Du Bois's reading of the songs. Du Bois may lack "technical phrase" (though one suspects a degree of false modesty here since he was good enough to sing for the Fisk Mozart Society as a student), but his commentary is always sensitive to a sense of musical form as the true site on which a proper archaeology of history understood as a history of "thought and feeling" can be undertaken. Locke's pitting of an old, fuddy-duddy thematic criticism against a modern musicology disguises the real difference between his approach and Du Bois's: between a cultural criticism which explores the relations of aesthetics, history, and politics, and one which prioritizes technique and formalism.

It is hardly surprising then that Du Bois, while he recognized the achievement of *The New Negro*, feared that Locke could "turn the Negro renaissance into decadence."[4] Du Bois responded to the threat of this potential drift with "Criteria of Negro Art" (1926). This is the essay which has most often been seen to mark the distance between him and the New Negro movement because here Du Bois declared that "all Art is propaganda and ever must be, despite the ailing of the purists."[5] As Ross Posnock has noted in his subtle and careful reading, this is "one of Du Bois's most quoted and yet misunderstood statements… Readers at the time and since isolate this sentence as proof that Du Bois had nervously retreated from the modernism of the Harlem Renaissance toward a politicizing of art inspired by his enthusiastic visit to the Soviet Union in the autumn of 1926."

…Du Bois diverges from Locke's alleged diffidence about what Beauty has "to do with the world." It is "the duty of Black America," he declares, "to begin this great work of the creation of Beauty." Because he finds Locke's Platonic notion of Beauty inadequate to the task of this work, Du Bois turns from it and marries

Beauty to Truth and Freedom, to "the facts of the world and the right actions of men"…While acknowledging that "somewhere eternal and perfect Beauty sits above Truth," Du Bois insists that "here and now and in the world in which I work they are for me unseparated and inseparable."

It is this idea of "art as the practice that creates 'Beauty of Truth and Freedom'" that Du Bois refers to as "propaganda."[6]

The *Crisis*

In the "Foreword" to *The New Negro* Locke acknowledged that the New Negro movement, as a literary movement, "has gradually gathered momentum in the effort and output of such progressive race periodicals as *The Crisis* under the editorship of Dr. Du Bois and more lately, through the quickening encouragement of Charles Johnson, in the brilliant pages of *Opportunity*, a Journal of Negro Life" (*New Negro* xvi). As David Levering Lewis has observed, "Harlem's cultural explosion was not caused by *The Crisis* or *Opportunity*," but nevertheless "the mobilizing role of Du Bois and Johnson and their respective cadres was indispensable."[7]

The *Crisis*, launched in 1910, became a premier publication for black Americans. Although an official publication of the NAACP, *Crisis* also provided Du Bois with an independent editorial platform. While concerned above all with political and social issues, it also brought to the fore many young writers and artists of the Harlem Renaissance. From the pages of the magazine Du Bois directed the aspiring Black American writers he designated the Talented Tenth. Du Bois set out the objectives of the magazine in the first issue (November 1926):

> The object of this publication is to set forth those facts and arguments which show the danger of race prejudice, particularly as manifested today toward colored people. It takes its name from the fact that the editors believe that this is a critical time in the history of the advancement of men. Catholicity and tolerance, reason and forbearance can today make the world-old dream of human brotherhood approach realization: while bigotry and prejudice, emphasized race consciousness and force can repeat the awful history of the contact of nations and groups in the past. We strive for this higher and broader vision of Peace and Good Will.

> The policy of The *Crisis* will be simple and well defined:

>> It will first and foremost be a newspaper: it will record important happenings and movements in the world which bear on the great problem of interracial relations, and especially those which affect the Negro-American.

Secondly, it will be a review of opinion and literature, recording briefly books, articles, and important expressions of opinion in the white and colored press on the race problem.

Thirdly, it will publish a few short articles.

Finally, its editorial page will stand for the rights of men, irrespective of color or race, for the highest ideals of American democracy, and for reasonable but earnest and persistent attempt to gain these rights and realize these ideals. The magazine will be the organ of no clique or party and will avoid personal rancor of all sorts. In the absence of proof to the contrary it will assume honesty of purpose on the part of all men, North and South, white and black.[8]

Du Bois was certainly successful in these objectives since the magazine quickly reached a monthly circulation of 100,000.[9]

As far as the literary influence of the *Crisis* is concerned, Jessie Redmon Fauset's contribution was crucial. A novelist, short-story writer, and poet, Fauset was literary editor of the magazine from 1919 to 1926. Fauset's long-term relationship with Du Bois developed from her appreciation of his work at the NAACP and her sympathy for his cultural and political views. She worked for a year as a freelance editor with him prior to her move to New York to work full-time at the *Crisis*. Without doubt, *Crisis* provided exposure to the younger writers more than any other magazine of the period, and it was Fauset who cultivated and nourished the younger writers and who was a buffer between Du Bois's egotism and their pride. Fauset helped to introduce Du Bois to many of the young writers whom he published in *Crisis*. She was the more social of the two, attending writing salons, parties given by and for the Talented Tenth, and befriending several of the young artists of the period. It was Fauset, and not Du Bois, whom author Langston Hughes named as the midwife of the Renaissance, along with James Weldon Johnson.

Fauset left the *Crisis*, in part due to growing strains in her relationship with Du Bois. He continued publishing literary writing in the magazine, but there is some evidence to suggest that the relationships of contributing authors and the magazine were not as smooth as they had been with Fauset as literary editor. "The Black writers who gained their recognition partially through *The Crisis* and who then in turn lent their prestige to the publication become upset with sloppy office work there after 1926 ... Du Bois and *The Crisis* were more dependent than anyone knew on Fauset's efficiency and ability to relate smoothly to temperamental artists – and to her temperamental editor."[10]

New African American artists and writers such as Langston Hughes, who was discovered and mentored by Fauset, and Claude McKay, continued to gain notoriety for their work independently of the *Crisis* during what

Lewis refers to as the final phase of the Harlem Renaissance. Along with others like Richard Wright and Zora Neale Hurston, they focused their work on the harsh realities of poverty and racism in black America. Du Bois frequently spoke out against their negative depictions while maintaining his support for them. Early in the period Hughes had dedicated his popular poem, "The Negro Speaks of Rivers" (1922) to Du Bois, and had considered Du Bois a major influence. But after 1926 McKay grew disenchanted with what he saw as Du Bois's conservative politics showcased in *Crisis* and with his NAACP affiliation. Contributing to McKay's disillusionment was the fact the Du Bois frequently criticized McKay's work as not meeting high enough standards of writing, and for its violence and overt sexuality. After Fauset's departure, Du Bois supported young artists whose ideals mirrored his own. Those artists who did not support his point of view were censored in *Crisis* directly or indirectly by the absence of their work from its pages.

After 1926 Du Bois continued to contribute to the perpetuation of a positive intellectual foundation for the New Negro, his talented tenth, and he tried to set examples for the writers of the Harlem Renaissance. His earlier publications, *Moon Illustrated Weekly*, a news arm for the Niagara Movement, and *Horizon*, another attempt at publicizing the views of that movement, were both failures. *Crisis*, by comparison, was extremely successful but Du Bois's work with the NAACP became less fulfilling for him as the members became unreceptive to his ideas. He had intended the Niagara Movement, which he had helped found in 1905, to be an aggressive intellectual attempt to organize black Americans who wanted to further the struggle for civil rights through legislative change, and as the movement waned, Du Bois found himself without a platform until the formation of the interracial NAACP in 1909. He had hoped the NAACP would be able to champion some of those same causes but he increasingly found the organizatrion to be too conservative and accommodationist. This is partly why *Crisis* came to represent Du Bois's views more than those of the NAACP.

Though bitterly opposed by several other NAACP board members, Du Bois survived within the organization in part due to the large readership of the *Crisis*, which distinguished it from all other similar black publications. Booker T. Washington, Du Bois's nemesis, controlled the *New York Age*, a weekly magazine edited by James Weldon Johnson before his death in 1916. The literary arm of the National Urban League, *Opportunity*, edited by Charles S. Johnson, competed with Du Bois for literary writers in the 1920s because of its focus on writing contests for budding intellects. Marcus Garvey and the Universal Negro Improvement Association produced the *Negro World* which featured opinions and writers who disagreed with Du Bois's politics.

By 1934 the board members of the NAACP took over the *Crisis* in an attempt to harness Du Bois. In their vote to assume control of the magazine they asserted that "the *Crisis* is the organ of the Association and no salaried officer of the Association shall criticize the policy, work, or officers of the Association in the pages."[11] Du Bois resigned as editor and left the NAACP, and took up the chairmanship in sociology at Atlanta University.

Notes

1. D. L. Lewis, "Introduction," in *The Portable Harlem Renaissance Reader*, ed. D. L. Lewis (New York: Penguin, 1995). Among the many studies of the Harlem Renaissance now available, see especially: N. Huggins, *Harlem Renaissance* (New York: Oxford University Press, 1971); J. Anderson, *This Was Harlem: A Cultural Portrait, 1900–1950* (New York: Farrar, Straus and Giroux, 1981); D. L. Lewis, *When Harlem was in Vogue* (New York: Knopf, 1981); G. Hutchinson, *The Harlem Renaissance in Black and White* (Cambridge: Harvard University Press, 1995); and C. Wall, *Women of the Harlem Renaissance* (Bloomington: Indiana University Press, 1995).

2. A. Locke (ed.), *The New Negro: An Interpretation* (1925), introduction by A. Rampersad (New York: Atheneum, 1992), p. xiii. Hereafter cited in the text as *New Negro*.

3. W. E. B. Du Bois, *The Souls of Black Folk*, in *W. E. B. Du Bois: Writings*, ed. N. Huggins (New York: Library of America, 1986), p. 487. Hereafter cited in the text as *Souls*.

4. Quoted in D. L. Lewis, *W. E. B. Du Bois: The Fight for Equality and the American Century 1919–1963* (New York: Henry Holt, 2000), p. 163.

5. W. E. B. Du Bois, "Criteria for Negro Art" (1926), in *Du Bois: Writings*, ed. Huggins, p. 1000.

6. R. Posnock, *Color and Culture: Black Writers and the Making of the Modern Intellectual* (Cambridge: Harvard University Press, 1998), p. 139. For the quotations from Du Bois, see "Criteria," pp. 995, 1000.

7. Lewis, *Du Bois: The Fight*, p. 163.

8. Du Bois, "The Crisis," in *Du Bois: Writings*, ed. Huggins, p. 1131.

9. Lewis, *Du Bois: The Fight*, p. 2.

10. C. W. Sylvander, *Jessie Redmon Fauset: Black American Writer* (Troy: Whitson Publishing, 1981), pp. 113–14.

11. M. Stafford, "W. E. B. Du Bois: Scholar Activist," in *Black Americans of Achievement*, ed. N. L. Huggins (New York: Chelsea, 1989), p. 99.

5

KIMBERLY SPRINGER

Du Bois, Black Leadership, and Civil Rights

Of foremost importance in defining the Civil Rights Movement in the United States is the question of periodization. When raised as a historical topic, often the term "civil rights movement" conjures images of events such as the Montgomery Bus Boycott and the 1963 March on Washington. Inextricably linked to those events are people such as Reverend Dr. Martin Luther King, Jr. and Rosa Parks. Issues of concern that they are known for advocating include voting rights and desegregation. And while these people, issues, and events all legitimately constitute the *modern-day* Civil Rights Movement, accurately situating the struggle for civil rights along a historical continuum is key. This is particularly the case when examining the role of W. E. B. Du Bois as both a central black leader in the drive for equal rights for blacks, as well as an architect of the later Civil Rights Movement.

This chapter explores two aspects of Du Bois's civil rights activism: his role in forming a concept of black leadership rooted in a "Talented Tenth" and his organizational activism. From 1905 to 1915 Du Bois grappled with the intellectual and strategic problem of the appropriate demands black Americans needed to make of a democratic nation still treating its minorities as second-class citizens. Integration or "separate but equal" accommodation and education? What was best for the future of black Americans: education in vocations, such as blacksmithing and teaching, or a liberal arts education? Who would lead this rising black nation?

During the period from 1910 to 1935 Du Bois served as a founding member and only black board member for many years with the National Association for the Advancement of Colored People (NAACP). Du Bois was also the editor of the NAACP's periodical *Crisis*, which, under his editorship, was a lightning rod for debating the pressing issues facing the NAACP's constituency. His involvement with the NAACP and the *Crisis* marks what some believe to be the height of Du Bois's pre-eminence as spokesman for black America.

Both his intellectual output and his role in forming significant social movement organizations on behalf of racial equality are part of Du Bois's lasting legacy. This chapter examines how Du Bois shaped an ideology of black leadership that remains influential today. Next, both Du Bois's work with the NAACP and with *Crisis* are discussed for their part in what would become the modern-day Civil Rights Movement of formal organizations and agitation. Since, chronologically, Du Bois's life and work preceded the Civil Rights Movement, he overwhelmingly contributed to the parameters of the definition of a civil rights agenda for the 1960s generation that would see the most significant successes realizing that agenda.

Constituting Black Leadership: The Talented Tenth

Du Bois died at age 95. Thus, he lived through crucial periods in the evolution of the black struggle for civil rights. Accordingly, his ideological position also changed with the times to accommodate both advances and setbacks in the quest.

By the time Du Bois was born in 1868, a few key legislative actions were in place to pave the way for full citizenship rights for African Americans: the Thirteenth Amendment to the US Constitution outlawing slavery passed Congress in 1865 and the Fourteenth Amendment in 1868, guaranteeing equal protection under the law to all persons. Despite these laws, Du Bois and his generational cohort were born and came to black consciousness with the failure of Reconstruction as a presence in their lives. Specifically, though the nation hoped to reconcile the North and South in the years following the Civil War, many of the advances blacks made during Reconstruction in political life were quickly eroded as the Supreme Court upheld the "separate but equal doctrine" allowing for racial discrimination at the local, state, and national levels.

Under the cloud of segregation nationwide, Du Bois nonetheless thrived first at Fisk University and later became the first African American to receive a Ph.D. from Harvard University in 1895. Ever the scholar, Du Bois continued in university life, teaching Latin at Wilberforce (the first University owned and operated by African Americans) and also economics and history at Atlanta University.

Du Bois's own educational background and career undoubtedly influenced his strong conviction that an educated black elite would determine black America's future. This belief, both a matter of economics and class, evolved from blacks' collective focus on racial uplift and respectability as guiding ideologies. From free blacks during the antebellum period through to nineteenth-century reformers, literate African Americans assumed responsibility for leading this new nation within a nation. For example, the African American women's club movement advocated education for both men and women as instrumental to African American integration into American society. Additionally, respectability was a tenet that drove civic-minded African Americans to use their educated status to help others adapt to free life. If they respected themselves and their own culture, white society would not have any choice, but to recognize their humanity and place in American society.

Thus, Du Bois's ideas had historical precedence, particularly as represented in his elaboration on Alexander Crummell's idea of a "Talented Tenth." An Episcopalian priest, missionary, and teacher, Crummell first used this phrase in his opening address to the American Negro Academy (ANA) in 1897, in Washington, D.C. In his essay "The Conservation of Races," Du Bois outlined the purpose of the ANA as, "to be the epitome and expression of the intellect of the black-blooded people of America, the exponent of the race ideals of one of the world's great races."[1] Locating the work of the organization in both morals and science, Crummell and Du Bois, as members of the ANA, determined that the future of African Americans in the United States depended on "race organizations" (e.g. "Negro colleges, Negro newspapers, Negro business organizations, a Negro school of literature and art, and an intellectual clearing house, for all these products of the Negro mind, which we may call a Negro Academy"[2]) and an educated elite to lead African Americans to a higher civilization. Du Bois later developed a fuller treatise on his expectations of the Talented Tenth in the 1903 anthology, *The Negro Problem: A Series of Articles by Representative Negroes of Today*.

Perhaps controversially, Du Bois's ideology unequivocally endorsed a select group of people as leaders of the African American masses: "The Negro race, like all races, is going to be saved by its exceptional men. The problem of education, then, among Negroes must first of all deal with the Talented Tenth; it is the problem of developing the Best of this race that they may guide the Mass away from the contamination and death of the Worst, in their own and other races."[3] Compared retroactively to today's historiography of the modern-day Civil Rights Movement, such an assessment appears elitist. Both contemporary historical and sociological Civil Rights Movement studies herald the "footsoldiers" or everyday people who gave the movement its momentum and critical mass. However, at the time of Du Bois's writing he was calling for the establishment of formal black leadership where there had previously been very few individuals whom one would designate as national leaders. As African Americans became geographically removed from the South, moving especially to

Northern industrial cities and towns, leadership that articulated a *national* African American agenda became imperative.

Du Bois was famously at odds with Booker T. Washington over his accommodationist ideas that allowed for the development of a black economy based on vocational skills. Rather than agitate quite vocally and publicly for inclusion in white society, Washington's approach advocated for marshalling skills among the masses, whom Du Bois excluded from his Talented Tenth. Even when Washington died in 1915, Du Bois did not hesitate to excoriate him in the pages of *Crisis* for what he felt was a backward and detrimental approach to black progress. Their ideological disagreements would also manifest at the organizational level with the formation of the Niagara Movement and the NAACP.

Du Bois was unrelenting in his conviction that decisive black leadership of the masses was required. Interestingly, he did not confine his Talented Tenth only to men. Women were just as important to the black nation he envisioned. Du Bois, for example, modelled coalition building in his avocation of woman suffrage as connected to black suffrage:

> Every argument for Negro suffrage is an argument for women's suffrage; every argument for women's suffrage is an argument for Negro suffrage; both are great moments in democracy. There should be on the part of Negroes absolutely no hesitation whenever and wherever responsible human beings are without voice in their government. The man of Negro blood who hesitates to do them justice is false to his race, his ideals and his country.[4]

There was, undoubtedly, a traditionalist aspect to how Du Bois expected black manhood and womanhood to take shape. Both were knowledgeable and cultured, but black men were "talented and unselfish," while black women were "pure and noble-minded" and in need of protection.[5] Like his predecessor, ex-slave and abolitionist, Frederick Douglass, Du Bois articulated a gendered analysis that was unorthodox for the time, but not unheard of.

The second aspect to Du Bois's black leadership was more tactical than ideological. While Washington encouraged an accommodationist position that seemed less militant, Du Bois's position, at his most basic, insisted upon integration into white America *and* separate black development. His ideas for integration were in step with the NAACP, but he saw limits to the efficacy of integration. His consistent calls for separate black institutions would influence later generations' debates over integration versus segregation. How were blacks, as a nation of people, to viably thrive in the nation as citizens? Du Bois insisted that separate was not equal, and until segregation and Jim Crow laws were abolished, African Americans could not productively contribute to the well being of the nation as a whole.[6]

Organizational and Intellectual Foundations of the Civil Rights Movement

Social movements need a number of different actors for success. In addition to the followers, there are leaders that play varying roles. Some are frontline activists in the streets leading demonstrations. Others start insurrections. Still another type of leader might be at the forefront of defining the issues and tactics of a social movement from a theoretical angle. Each type, while they might sometimes seem at odds as to the best course of action, is necessary to the eventual outcomes of social change.

In the case of Du Bois, he is, clearly, an intellectual. Social movement theorists call these people "knowledge workers" because, though usually cast as less productive than manual labor or street-based activism, the generation of knowledge is a specialized skill integral to defining the "presumed facts, assertions, and concepts" of a social movement.[7] Du Bois, as knowledge worker, offered the struggle for civil rights a template for leadership (the Talented Tenth) and a concept for understanding the position of African Americans (double-consciousness). There were, of course, other leaders offering guidance, but Du Bois contributed a lasting legacy that retained its vitality at least through the height of the Civil Rights Movement era.

Social movement theorists also acknowledge the place of the formal educator. Du Bois, as a sociologist, published his research and writing on slavery, reconstruction, black business, leadership, and race relations in general. The formal educator is also a social movement leader through contributing a "corpus of work" that is "considerable and lasting."[8] Finally, this type of leader makes his livelihood from a vocation that encourages sensitivity "to idea and ideals, to conceptions of the way the world is, what is wrong with it, and how it might be and should be changed."[9] Though most well known for his book *The Souls of Black Folks*, Du Bois bequeathed an immense body of work that later black sociologists, such as E. Franklin Frazier (prolific in his own writings on race and class relations in the black community), would credit with pioneering the empirical study of black life in sociology.

In addition to his role as formal educator in institutions of higher education, Du Bois enacted his role as knowledge worker through his founding of the NAACP and editorship of *Crisis*. The NAACP has its roots in a 1905 meeting Du Bois convened in Niagara Falls. Historians note that the twenty-nine participants in the meeting, gathered on the unsegregated Canadian side, were "motivated by their opposition to the conservative leadership of Booker T. Washington," who exerted, "heavy-handed tactics against those who dared to challenge him" and his gradualist approach to racial uplift.[10] Du Bois was elected general secretary. Included in its stated goals, the Niagara Movement, as it came to be called, sought equal opportunities in business and before the law, voting rights, free and compulsory education, abolition of Jim Crow laws, equal treatment in the military, and the general erasure of the color-line. The ultimate demand, though, was public protest and action.

Correspondingly, the Niagara Movement did not leave the entire burden of changing African Americans' situation on the doorstep of the US's social and political systems. They also conferred upon African Americans a number of duties: "the duty to vote; the duty to respect the rights of others; the duty to work; the duty to obey the laws; the duty to be clean and orderly; the duty to send our children to school; and the duty to respect ourselves, even as we respect others."[11] The era's dominant ethos of respectability and racial uplift made the Niagara Movement's statement both a list of demands and a call to responsibility.

In its short existence, approximately four years, the Niagara Movement claimed 150 members with 17 state branches. Their platform of racial justice and ending discrimination presaged the objectives of the interracial NAACP. There was no official connection, but their ideas would carry over into the NAACP's formulation of its objectives with Du Bois as one of the founding board members.

With the establishment of the NAACP in 1909, Du Bois and other black leaders embraced the concept of interracial linkages within organizations. This departure from Du Bois's earlier views on exclusively black organizations was not a dramatic shift, but recognition of the swiftly changing social conditions that demanded new tactics and organizations. The NAACP, in fact, had much in common with the Niagara Movement:

> Like the Niagarans, they sought to improve race relations through agitation, court action, and federal legislation; like them, they envisioned a comprehensive organization with local chapters throughout the United States, including the South, designed to remedy "national wrongs" through agitation. Where the Niagara Movement failed because of the disagreement among its founders, pressure from the accommodationist Booker T. Washington, and the eruption of racial violence in Atlanta, Georgia, the NAACP thrived on its biracial support, northern base, and reform appeal.[12]

Though the Niagara Movement met its demise under pressure from Washington's attempts to disrupt the organization's activities and tensions among its leaders, it offered an alternative vision for organizing the struggle for civil rights.

For the era, the NAACP reflected a new form of radicalism with its legislative approach that many black communities did not immediately appreciate. Growth in the organization's membership numbers was slow with fewer than 200 in the first year; from 1,100 to 8,266 members between 1912 and 1915; and a jump to 91,203 in 310 branches by 1920.[13] In both its membership composition and strategies, the NAACP would become the foremost civil rights organization in the United States working to cross the color-line Du Bois presciently declared the most pressing dilemma of the twentieth century. This was particularly so after the landmark Supreme Court case that desegregated public schools, *Brown* v. *Board of Education Topeka*, Kansas, in 1954.

The growth in the organization's membership was due in no small part to two factors. The first was the Harlem Renaissance that heralded the writers, musicians, and performing artists of the early part of the twentieth century, and marked a dramatic shift in black consciousness. Its proponents, including Du Bois, advocated the role of a distinct African American culture as a vibrant and crucial part of the race's advancement. Though social movements are inherently political, it would be remiss to discount the impact and importance of cultural workers and products that convey the message of the movement. In this case, racial uplift and double-consciousness were persistent themes in Harlem Renaissance poetry, novels, jazz, blues, paintings, photography, and sculpture.

Second, the NAACP had Du Bois as its director of research and publications, and he was also the editor of the *Crisis: A Record of the Darker Races*, the association's official periodical. First published on November 1, 1910, *Crisis* played a central role in the formation of a cohesive civil rights agenda and movement. Through its pages, Du Bois was left to his own devices and continued to push his agenda for black unity despite the NAACP's interracial leadership. In his standing as a black intellectual and formal educator, Du Bois's *Crisis* quickly became the sole shaper of public opinion. His relationship to the association's white board and donors became tense. However, as much as the NAACP might have needed white patronage, it also relied on personal influence and reputation until it found its footing among grassroots membership. Notably, subscriptions to the magazine increased from 10,000 at the end of its first year of publication to 100,000 in 1920.[14]

In its pages, the *Crisis* detailed the NAACP's news and achievements. For example, the organization pursued an anti-lynching crusade in response to the intense racial violence sweeping both the South and the North. In service to Du Bois's goals of black self-determination, the periodical kept its readers informed about the happenings in black higher education, noted the progress of black businesses, and gave opportunities to Harlem Renaissance writers. *Crisis*, for instance, was the first to print Langston Hughes's poem "The Negro Speaks of Rivers" in 1922. When the Great Depression hit the country in the early 1930s, Du Bois used the NAACP magazine's now extensive reach to continue to advocate for black self-sufficiency. "In short, it [*Crisis*] recorded and stimulated, racial pride."[15]

For better or worse, Du Bois employed *Crisis* to challenge the various black leaders staking a claim to the future direction of the burgeoning Civil Rights Movement. He goaded black newspaper editors to use their increasing numbers and editorial space to convey the momentum of the Civil Rights Movement. Du Bois did not hesitate to use the *Crisis* to prod black ministers into using their local influence to sway their congregations into action.

Du Bois also employed its pages to discount other black liberationists who disagreed with him. Marcus Garvey of the Universal Negro Improvement Association (UNIA) accused the NAACP of a number of excesses: it was too white, too gradualist, too bourgeois, too elite, and too focused on adapting to a legal system that he believed never intended to fully recognize black citizenship. With his appeal to the lower classes and recently arrived Southern immigrants to Northern cities, Garvey found a significant audience for his brand of racial separatism. Thus, when he called the organization, "The National Association for the Advancement of (Certain) Colored People," in his characteristic oratorical style, Garvey posed a threat to both white and institutionalized black power-structures. While Garvey "mocked Du Bois as a light-skinned lackey of white men," Du Bois denounced Garvey and his UNIA's philosophy of "Be Black, Buy Black, Build Black," as "spiritually bankrupt and futile."[16] Other black leaders' disdain for Garvey's nationalism and federal efforts to undermine Garvey converged with the *Crisis*'s dim view of his efforts, and culminated in Garvey's eventual imprisonment and deportation back to his native Jamaica.

Du Bois's editorship of *Crisis* lasted until 1934. Though it continued to be successful even when the NAACP's membership numbers dipped, the leadership sought to bring the magazine into closer alignment with the organization's agenda (ending segregation), rather than Du Bois's ever more separatist ideas about an independent black economy. Citing financial constraints, the NAACP's executive secretary at the time, Walter White, forced Du Bois's resignation.

This marked the end of an era for the NAACP and also signalled a change in direction for the Civil Rights Movement. With the success of *Brown*, the organization's membership skyrocketed, reaching a civil rights era peak of close to half a million in the 1960s. Both *Brown* and the increased membership encouraged the NAACP's leadership that their legalistic approach was the way forward. Immediately following Du Bois's departure, the organization formed a dedicated legal department, indicating that forming a wide array of black organizations, as Du Bois wished, was not on the immediate agenda.

Du Bois, never one to stay within institutions with which he did not agree, travelled, lectured, and continued to write as he made his way widely through Europe and marginally in Africa. On his journeys, Du Bois's political philosophy expanded to encompass a more internationalist perspective and his views on Pan-Africanism gained strength. World Wars I and II and anti-colonial revolts throughout Africa were also significant historical events that moved Du Bois both physically and intellectually beyond theorizing solely on black American civil rights issues.

In the modern-day Civil Rights Movement, effectively starting in 1954–5 with *Brown* and the Montgomery Bus Boycott, Du Bois never regained his prominent position as a black civil rights leader after leaving the NAACP. "Even before his eclipse, leadership had passed to functional areas – trade unions, newspapers, businesses, churches, politics, literature – and until Martin Luther King, Jr. no one took Du Bois's charismatic place."[17] Still, this does not diminish Du Bois's role in defining a vision for black leadership that some African Americans today seek to reclaim. Moreover, his radical agenda of limited integration and black self-determination would influence both the 1960s Civil Rights Movement and, to a lesser degree, the late 1960s Black Power Movement. Roy Wilkins, Du Bois's successor on *Crisis*, recalled Du Bois in his speech at the 1963 March on Washington for Jobs and Freedom:

> Remember that this has been a long fight. We were reminded of it by the news of the death yesterday in Africa of Dr. W. E. B. Du Bois. Now, regardless of the fact that in his later years Dr. Du Bois chose another path, it is incontrovertible that at the dawn of the twentieth century his was the voice that was calling to you to gather here today in this cause. If you want to read something that applies to 1963 go back and get a volume of *The Souls of Black Folk* by Du Bois published in 1903.[18]

W. E. B. Du Bois establishes both the historical and sociological necessity of excavating the ideological roots of modern-day social movements.

Notes

1. W. E. B. Du Bois, "The Conservation of Races," in W. E. B. Du Bois, *Writings*, ed. N. Huggins (New York: Library of America, 1986), p. 823.

2. *Ibid.*

3. W. E. B. Du Bois, "The Talented Tenth," in Du Bois, *Writings*, p. 842.

4. G. E. Pauley, "W. E. B. Du Bois on Woman Suffrage: a Critical Analysis of His Writings," *Journal of Black Studies*, 30, no. 3 (January 2000), p. 399.

5. Du Bois, "Conservation of Races," p. 824.

6. Pan-Africanism, an ideology focused on the liberation and unity of Africans on the continent and in the diaspora, played a significant role in Du Bois's thinking from the early 1900s. However, it gained force in the later third of his life in sync with revolutionary African movements throwing off the chains of colonialism.

7. J. Lofland, *Social Movements: a Guide to Insurgent Realities* (New York: Aldine de Gruyter, 1996), p. 134.

8. *Ibid.*

9. *Ibid.*

10. *Let Nobody Turn Us Around: Voices of Resistance, Reform, and Renewal*, ed. M. Marable and L. Mullings (Lanham, MD: Rowman & Littlefield, 1999), p. 227.

11. *Ibid.*, p. 229.

12. J. Moore, "Niagara Movement," in *Organizing Black America: An Encyclopedia of African American Associations*, ed. N. Majagkij (New York: Garland Publishing, 2001), p. 371.

13. *Ibid.*, pp. 371–2.

14. *Ibid.*, p. 372.

15. F. L. Broderick, "W. E. B. Du Bois: History of an Intellectual," in *Black Sociologists: Historical and Contemporary Perspectives*, ed. James E. Blackwell and Morris Janowitz (Chicago: University of Chicago Press, 1974), p. 20.

16. *Ibid.*, D. J. Capeci and J. Knight, "The National Association for the Advancement of Colored People," in *Organizing Black America*, ed. Majagkij p. 373.

17. Broderick, "History of an Intellectual," p. 21.

18. Roy Wilkins, Speech at the March on Washington for Jobs and Freedom, August 28, 1963, in *Speeches by Leaders: The March on Washington for Jobs and Freedom*, ed. The National Association for the Advancement of Colored People (New York: NAACP, 1963).

6

ANGE-MARIE HANCOCK

Du Bois, Race, and Diversity

All who study W. E. B. Du Bois's conceptualization, interrogation, and international activism regarding the sociopolitical significance of race must contend with a foundation built upon his most famous words:

> After the Egyptian and Indian, the Greek and Roman, the Teuton and Mongolian, the Negro is a sort of seventh son, born with a veil, and gifted with second-sight in this American world, – a world which yields him no true self-consciousness, but only lets him see himself through the revelation of the other world. It is a peculiar sensation, this double-consciousness, this sense of always looking at one's self through the eyes of others, of measuring one's soul by the tape of a world that looks on in amused contempt and pity. One ever feels his two-ness – an American, a Negro; two souls, two thoughts, two unreconciled strivings; two warring ideals in one dark body, whose dogged strength alone keeps it from being torn asunder.[1]

Originally published in Du Bois's first nationally circulated article, "Strivings of the Negro People" (from an 1897 issue of *Atlantic Monthly*), these words were then collected into *The Souls of Black Folk*, by far Du Bois's most famous work, in 1903. The "double-consciousness" metaphor often serves as a proxy for Du Boisian racial theory in its entirety. Du Bois, however, was a notoriously complex and prolific thinker whose views continued to evolve for another sixty years until his death in 1963. Thus while any commentary on Du Bois and race begins with the theory of double-consciousness by no means should it end there.

In fact Du Bois's thinking on race presages much work on race as a category of social analysis, and moreover work regarding what are now considered intersecting categories of social analysis: race, gender, class, sexuality, and nation (among many others). Such categories of difference are now theorized as dynamic phenomena that structure power relationships within and between global, intergroup, and interpersonal levels of society. This chapter will first examine the theory of double-consciousness and its related metaphor, the veil of race, then continue with arguments claiming an intellectual space for Du Bois among most contemporary discourses surrounding race today – including the tension between genetic/phenotypic and social constructivist accounts of race; the struggle between structure and agency; the role of race as one explanatory component in a complex web of power relationships along axes of race, gender, class, and nation; and the implications of multiracial coalition politics.

Du Boisian Double Consciousness

Emerging from this first article granting Du Bois national exposure, the "theory of double-consciousness," as it is now called, has been cited as an organizing theme of Du Bois's lifework.[2] Both the article and the revised version that appeared in *Souls* featured Du Bois's use of the veil and double-consciousness to "depict a two-dimensional pattern of estrangement that shaped the lives of black Americans in the age of Jim Crow."[3] The double-consciousness theory has extended its philosophical reach from its base in the United States to politics around the world[4] as an explanation for a certain kind of alienation experienced by marginalized peoples of many ethnicities and nationalities. A later section of this chapter will examine Du Bois's own global expansion of race analysis.

"Strivings of the Negro People" evolved from a presentation Du Bois made to the American Negro Academy in March 1897 entitled, "The Conservation of Races." In that manuscript, Du Bois defined "race" as a concept:

> What, then, is a race? It is a vast family of human beings, generally of common blood and language, always of a common history, traditions, and impulses, who are both voluntarily and involuntarily striving together for the accomplishment of certain more or less vividly concealed ideals of life.[5]

Theorists such as K. Anthony Appiah have focused on the first words of reply to Du Bois's question – "*...a vast family of human beings, generally of common blood and language...*" – in conjunction with other citations from this period to claim that Du Bois's definition of race is irredeemably essentialist. Such scholars claim his definition to be untenably tethered to a notion of biological racial essence that bears all the problems of depending solely on phenotypic markers of race to explain and/or remedy political problems of racial inequality.

While there are scholars who believe that Du Bois thought of race as a biological construct based on the primacy of placement in this excerpt and his adherence to nineteenth-century traditions of nomenclature, evidence abounds across Du Bois's life that for him, race was tied less to blood and instead inextricably bound to the sociopolitical significance attached to race and the material consequences of racial norms that were socially defined and, most importantly, socially enacted at multiple levels of political power.[6] It is critical to note, for example, that Du Bois's definition of race, even as early as the 1897 excerpt cited above, contained a second component, distinguished both by content and relative significance to the definition itself: "...*always of a common history, traditions, and impulses*..." Here Du Bois stated that shared history was a necessary condition of the race concept using the word "*always*" in contrast to the use of "*generally*" for the first less critical component.

Later in *Dusk of Dawn* (1940), Du Bois created a hypothetical conversation with an imagined, presumably non-Negro interlocutor where the subject is again race and how to distinguish among blacks and whites:

> "But what is this group [blacks] and how do you differentiate it, and how can you call it 'black' when you admit it is not black?"
> "I recognize it quite easily and with full legal sanction: the black man is a person who must ride Jim Crow in Georgia."[7]

This notion of race eschews biology and genetics for a pre-constructivist approach to race, presaging contemporary constructivism, an approach now most favored in American and cultural studies. Du Bois successfully gestures toward the critical dilemma facing marginally identified peoples of many categories – the limits of individual agency for self-identification in a context where institutional structures and more powerful groups hold the lion's share of power in defining the racial other. Here Du Bois presaged social theorists such as Charles Taylor, who have articulated theories of identity and racial (mis)recognition grounded in dialogic processes between those in power and those with lesser power. Du Bois's concept of an individual's race identity is dialogically formed through a series of interactions between signal institutions, multiple groups at diverse positions in societal hierarchies, and interactions among people of difference groups. While Du Bois shifted his thinking on many topics, political situations, and ideologies, he remained both prescient and consistent on this vision of how race insinuates itself into society. This process-based notion of racial formation hearkens to a number of debates regarding identity politics and its utility in situations of social stratification or political inequality: (1) the tension between structure and agency; (2) the tension within and between global, intergroup, and interpersonal levels of analysis; and (3) the political anti-inequality program implied by a constructivist approach to race.

Now that we are aware of how Du Bois defined race as a concept, we can turn to what he meant when looking at those who have race – the Negroes in the Jim Crow United States – to whom he referred as having "second-sight" and a sense of "two-ness." As a recently freed people, Du Bois argued, Negroes suffered what Tommie Shelby characterizes as "severe self-alienation," which limited their ability to view themselves independently, producing a "truncated and inauthentic consciousness...suffused with feelings of inferiority and self-doubt, internalized through racist propaganda, material deprivation and violent repression".[8] This precise anomie Du Bois discovered wherever he looked in the black community, whether to Tennessee in *Souls*, or to Farmville, Virginia (1897) or Philadelphia, Pennsylvania (1899) in empirical studies of Negroes in both locations; or in his own life, as he engaged in a struggle for the souls of black America with Booker T. Washington, who capitalized on double-consciousness in a manner that, in Du Bois's opinion, exploited and disenfranchised blacks in unconscionable ways.

From his earliest definition of race as a concept and his identification of double-consciousness as the tragic zeitgeist of black Americans, Du Bois was attentive to the idea that race emerged not simply from biological essences but from social context. Because race and its material outcomes emerged from social institutions and interactions, double-consciousness as an outcome and its socioeconomic manifestations – whether crime, poverty, or unemployment – could not possibly have biological origins, as was argued by social scientists of the time. The Harvard and University of Berlin-trained Du Bois set out to correct decades of false histories and analyses of the Negro condition that had been conducted under racist assumptions.[9] Early on, Du Bois displayed a "scientific optimism"[10] that emanated from his conceptualization of racism as mere ignorance. Applying positivistic approaches, a systematic analysis of the study of natural sciences then emerging as a methodology in the social sciences, would address problems facing the Negro group in a manner that would inspire better social policy.[11]

In this regard Du Bois, in *Souls*, his Atlanta studies, "The Negroes of Farmville, Virginia," *The Philadelphia Negro* (1899), and *Black Reconstruction in America* (1935) produced models of social science that fundamentally preserved Negroes' humanity. Explaining the socioeconomic position of Negroes in America required two necessary factors: rigorous, systematic attention to Negroes as a group and the study of the sociopolitical and economic conditions within which the group operates.[12] Only by recognizing the ways in which groups are socially constituted and interact with other products of human interaction (e.g. political institutions) could an accurate picture emerge. As Du Bois continued to produce this precise form of knowledge, the lack of response to his work and persistency of racial stratification at multiple levels of society led him to recognize factors in racism beyond ignorance, including affective orientation toward racial others. The nagging persistency of this orientation challenged Du Bois throughout his life, ultimately driving his quest for ideologies and policy prescriptions that would produce racial liberation and justice.

Thus quite logically, if on Du Bois's account race is not natural but primarily if not entirely a social construct, we can argue that just as society has changed over the course of history, so have the racial distinctions produced by historical conditions. Du Bois challenged static senses of race as he used black folk and the darker peoples of the world to consider the legacies of the gravest assaults on human communities. In so doing, he acknowledged and examined race as a concept in a much more complicated context than is conventional for the turn of the twentieth century. Du Bois claimed a dynamic sense of racial identity in his work in three controversial ways, which led some to overlook the radical subtext of his work[13] and its impact beyond the black-white global race binary.

Du Bois's Dynamic Racial Context

Du Bois first and perhaps most logically used his interpretations of the political significance of black identity as a construct that shifts dynamically across time. Black identity during slavery for many reasons was emblematic of bondage regardless of whether the Negro person in question was in fact a slave. Following emancipation, he argues that the first ten years "left the bewildered serf with no new watchword beyond the old cry for freedom" (*Souls* 367). Du Bois then claims that the changing religious worship of the Negro community transformed the sociopolitical significance of blackness: "Endowed with a rich tropical imagination and a keen, delicate appreciation of Nature, the transplanted African lived in a world animate with gods and devils, elves and witches; full of strange influences, – of Good to be implored, of Evil to be propitiated. Slavery, then, was to him the dark triumph of Evil over him" (*Souls* 499). This indigenous approach to religion sparked agitation for freedom: "He called up all the resources of heathenism to aid, – exorcism and witchcraft, the mysterious Obi worship with its barbarous rites, spells, and blood-sacrifice even, now and then, of human victims" (*ibid*). While such a spirit of revolt was broken by the mid-eighteenth century (*ibid*), religion as a key constitutive element of black political identity continued: "For fifty years Negro religion thus transformed itself and identified itself with the dream of Abolition, until that which was a radical fad in the white North and an anarchistic plot in the white South had become a religion to the black world" (*Souls* 501). In these passages Du Bois acknowledged the shifting relationship of religion and religious

morals to black political identity. He emphasized how one particular constant – religious faith – has evolved over time as the political meaning of
blackness has changed over time.

Beyond the passage of mere time, however, rests another aspect of black
identity. What it means to be black from a political perspective has never
meant the same thing to all blacks. Du Bois demonstrates the intra-group
diversity of Negroes at any discrete point in time. In this sense he confronted
directly the idea that any single notion of blackness has ever existed, long
before late-twentieth-century support of this position. Du Bois combined
his dynamic sense of black identity over time with this concept of intra-racial
diversity. During slavery, he noted clearly free Negroes as distinct from slaves
in terms of both with whom they identify and their political agenda:

> The free Negroes of the North, inspired by the mulatto immigrants from the
> West Indies, began to change the basis of their demands; they recognized the
> slavery of the slaves, but insisted that they themselves were freemen, and
> sought assimilation and amalgamation with the nation on the same terms
> with other men. (*Souls* 396–7)

Du Bois profiled many blacks he met in his work and through his travels,
post-emancipation, and never did he dictate a single way of conceiving
black identity – even while acknowledging the political need for unity
(*Souls* 394–5). In his chapters on the Freedmen's Bureau, Booker T.
Washington, and the meaning of progress, Du Bois displays three different
dimensions of black identity that vary within and among black people.

In the Freedmen's Bureau chapter and later as he pursued his sociological
inquiries in the Black Belt of Georgia, Du Bois portrayed both the "idler" and
the hard-working Negro (*Souls* 384) as part of a single black community.
While Du Bois left no doubt about his favor of the worker, he acknowledged
the idler as a member of the community nevertheless. Similarly, despite his
vehement disagreements with Washington, Du Bois never challenged his
fundamental right to membership in the black community, nor did he
censor his critique for the sake of public unity. In fact, Du Bois openly
disagrees with that approach:

> But aside from all this, there is among educated and thoughtful colored men in
> all parts of the land a feeling of deep regret, sorrow, and apprehension at the
> wide currency and ascendancy which some of Mr. Washington's theories
> have gained...Honest and earnest criticism from those whose interests are
> most nearly touched – criticism of writers from readers, of government by
> those governed, of leaders by those led – this is the soul of democracy and
> the safeguard of modern society. (*Souls* 395)

This diversity of black public opinion is evident in his many references to multiple strategies in pursuit of black empowerment and formed the foundation of the Niagara Movement's charter. Du Bois's overall goal during the first third of his life was certainly to correct stereotypes and false analyses among his primarily white readers, but another more nuanced approach to identity emerged from this overall effort. Du Bois again did not hide his preferred strategies of education and work to attain empowerment, but was quite content to acknowledge some support for other strategies. He articulated this most lucidly in his description of the community he taught outside of Alexandria, Tennessee:

> I have called my tiny community a world, and so its isolation made it; and yet there was among us but a half-awakened common consciousness, sprung from common joy and grief, at burial, birth, or wedding; from a common hardship in poverty, poor land, and low wages, and above all from the sight of the Veil that hung between us and Opportunity. *"All this caused us to think some thoughts together, but these, when ripe for speech, were spoken in various languages."* (*Souls* 410, emphasis added)

This passage reinforces the notion that the significance of black identity is grounded in key experiences – "*...common hardship in poverty, poor land, and low wages and above all from the sight of the Veil that hung between us and Opportunity...*" – but moreover, the next line indicates that while the experiences of the Veil and lack of opportunity bound this world together, the diverse reactions of Josie, Fat Reuben, Doc Burke, and Uncle Bird, most eloquently conveyed with the rhetorical device of a return visit ten years later, are emblematic of a diversity within the social group known as Negro Americans. In a later chapter Du Bois noted that class diversity exists in all cultures of inequality (*Souls*, chapter 8), going on to identify five distinct economic classes of Negroes – croppers, metayers, wage laborers, fixed renters, and landowners (*Souls* 470–2). His similar actions in *The Philadelphia Negro*[14] and *Black Reconstruction* (see *Reconstruction* 125, 216) indicate that this was not a single act of poetic license.

Complicated conceptualizations of racial identity were not limited to Du Bois's early work in *Souls of Black Folk*. In *Black Reconstruction in America* (1935), Du Bois points to the multivarious interests in cotton and slavery as early as page 6, noting their race, national origin, and economic class: "When we compare these figures with the cotton crop and the increase of black workers, we see how the economic problem increased in intricacy. This intricacy is shown by the persons in the drama and their differing and opposing interests" (*Reconstruction* 6). Later in the book, his writing shows that he has not abandoned the conviction that there is diversity within the Black American community:

> There was no one kind of Negro who was freed from slavery. The freedmen were not an undifferentiated group; there were those among them who were cowed and altogether bitter. There were the cowed who were humble; there were those openly bitter and defiant, but whipped into submission, or ready to run away. There were the debauched and the furtive, petty thieves and licentious scoundrels. There were the few who could read and write, and some even educated beyond that. There were the children and grandchildren of white masters; there were the house servants, trained in manners, and in servile respect for the upper classes. There were the ambitious, who sought by means of slavery to gain favor or even freedom; there were the artisans, who had a certain modicum of freedom in their work, were often hired out, and worked practically as free laborers. The impact of legal freedom upon these various classes differed in all sorts of ways. (*Reconstruction* 125)

In addition to all of the various peoples who exist within the veil of blackness, Du Bois placed himself above the veil due to his advanced classical education (*Souls* 438). Many historians and literary critics have focused upon the role that Du Bois carved for himself as an exceptional black – as one whose outrage existed based on factual knowledge, not mere moral instinct, of his equality with those presumed to be superior. Here it is more important to focus on the degree to which Du Bois in his autobiographies and elsewhere chose not simply to render himself an exception but to write himself into history as an exemplar – in the pursuit of racial justice, international cooperation, and the actual execution, rather than the mere promise, of democracy. While Du Bois clearly recognized – whether through his advocacy work as editor of NAACP's magazine, *Crisis*, or his scholarly work – the necessity of group unity, he did not take group uniformity to be a necessary condition of group unity for mass democratic politics.

The final aspect of Du Bois's dynamic sense of racial identity similarly confronted the democratic dilemma of diversity within in a most controversial way. His keen sense of the tension between structure and agency found him calling for attention to both aspects in pursuit of policy remedies for problems of injustice at the national and international levels. While scholarship on *Souls of Black Folk*, *Black Reconstruction in America*, and *The Philadelphia Negro* has focused on Du Bois as "conservative" in his acknowledgement of black responsibility for some aspects of their position, I want to concentrate less on the ideological underpinnings and instead turn toward the way in which Du Bois challenged the conventional story of pure victimhood, and its impact on his approach to studying race as a category of analysis.

Du Bois and Complex Causality

From the very start of *Souls of Black Folks*, *Black Reconstruction in America*, and *The Philadelphia Negro*, Du Bois refused to strip blacks of all responsibility for the horrors they faced or their current situation. Yet he did so in a way that studied problems faced by a people without stripping them of their humanity and making them the problem itself.[15] In "The Study of the Negro Problems," a presentation made to the near-exclusively white American Academy of Political and Social Sciences in 1897, Du Bois shifted the focus away from Negroes themselves, where blistering attention too often blamed the victim with no regard for the sociopolitical context, toward a more balanced approach. Lewis Gordon characterizes this epistemological shift as one from viewing Negroes as a problem to the study of social problems more generally.[16] In his manuscript, published in the organization's annals in 1898, Du Bois conceptualized Negro Problems as plural rather than singular, and as ever-shifting products of historical development, rather than static over time. He further acknowledged the tension between structure and agency as well as the tension between longstanding, mainstream beliefs in human progress (which he shared) and the Negro's social position in 1897.

In this paper Du Bois outlined the problems associated with research to date that perpetuated the myth that the Negro was less than human. Overall, he argued that Black Americans required rigorous, thorough study in order to advance the cause of racial upliftment. While he remained committed to positivism and the use of Western scientific methods for rigorous examination of these questions, his philosophical questions were driven by his empirical work rather than the reverse. Placing these two claims together joins what Cornel West and Arnold Rampersad have emphasized as Du Bois's pragmatism, with his commitment to untangling the kind of complexity that Robert Gooding-Williams, David Levering Lewis, and Shamoon Zamir have linked to his engagement with Hegel.[17] Failure to appropriately investigate Negroes had resulted in the perpetuation of stereotypes, misdiagnoses of political problems, and, frankly, bad public policy responses following such misapprehensions of the situation.

Perhaps most directly relevant, Du Bois called for investigations to reflect the causal tension between the actions of social groups in pursuit of adaptation to their circumstances and the aspects of social groups' environments which serve as catalysts for such adaptive responses. Not simply content to suggest parallel attention to these distinct components of social problems, Du Bois encouraged through such model works as *The Philadelphia Negro*,

"The Negroes of Farmville, Virginia," and *Black Reconstruction* the critical importance of recognizing the interaction between the two components.

In the first quotation in this chapter, Du Bois clearly recognized the problem faced by Blacks who are prevented from complete self-determination: "...*the Negro is a sort of seventh son, born with a veil, and gifted with second-sight in this American world, – a world which yields him no true self-consciousness, but only lets him see himself through the revelation of the other world.*" In addition to revealing the problem such a double-consciousness poses, Du Bois spent the entire book infusing his black subjects with the capacity, however limited, for self-determination as he sought an explanation and ultimately a solution to the problem of the color-line throughout his lifetime. Most often, Du Bois's discussions of lazy or sexually promiscuous blacks are linked to interpretations that focus on him as Victorian, conservative, or elitist, based on his recommended policy prescriptions of classical education and the talented tenth theory as paths out of poverty, sexual immorality, and racial oppression. Yet another interpretation speaks more directly to Du Bois's concept of race, racial identity, and racial liberation. What follows should not be taken as an argument against the charge of elitism but as a supplemental interpretation.

Two passages in *Souls of Black Folk* particularly demonstrate how Du Bois manages to acknowledge black responsibility in the context of racial oppression without eliding into blaming the victim. While he clearly used a nineteenth-century sociologist's standpoint in analyzing "the Negro problems,"[18] he created a space for action absent in oversimplified stories of pure innocence. His most frequent method of recognizing black individual responsibility in an empowering way was also to acknowledge the macro-level causes for the situation of an aggregated set of individuals, as he did in this passage regarding elite blacks' evaluations of Booker T. Washington's industrial education political agenda:

> ...they know that the low social level of the mass of the race is responsible for much discrimination against it, but they also know, and the nation knows, that relentless color-prejudice is more often a cause than a result of the Negro's degradation; they seek the abatement of this relic of barbarism and not its systematic encouragement and pampering by all agencies of the social power from the Associated Press to the Church of Christ. (*Souls* 400)

While acknowledging the low level of achievement among many blacks, Du Bois also recognizes the tremendous obstacle race prejudice poses to this challenge. Unlike black conservatives, Du Bois does not focus solely on the failure of the individuals; his training in sociology and readings of

Marx encouraged his attention to structural features of the political context in addition to individual-level behavior.

Similarly, as he explained the reasons for poor housing in rural Negro communities, Du Bois recognized that while Negroes themselves could "demand better," they do not because of their previous identity as slaves:

> ...Second, the Negroes, used to such accommodation, do not as a rule demand better; they do not know what better houses mean...Lastly, among such conditions of life there are few incentives to make the laborer become a better farmer. If he is ambitious, he moves to town or tries other labor; as a tenant-farmer his outlook is almost hopeless, and following it as a makeshift, he takes the house that is given him without protest. (*Souls* 459–60)

Du Bois does not encourage or approve of either silence or acceptance among the blacks he discussed above; he simply explains the context for such actions made by large numbers of blacks in the Reconstruction-era south. Further, in both his tribute to Alexander Crummell and his parable "Of the Coming of John," Du Bois clearly lamented the intransigence of backward ways among blacks.

Later, in *Black Reconstruction in America*, Du Bois chronicled structural institutions such as the Freedmen's Bureau and the Black Codes in complementary rather than competing fashion against the picture of black agency he painted at several points. First, in his retrospective chapter, "Looking Backward," Du Bois acknowledged that there were black slave owners: "Negroes in Louisiana owned fifteen million dollars' worth of property. The Ricaud family alone in 1859 owned 4,000 acres of land and 350 slaves, at a total value of $250,000" (*Reconstruction* 154). As well, "As early as 1803, free colored men were admitted to the police force to patrol outside the city limits, to catch runaway slaves and stop looting and crime" (*Reconstruction* 155). In his study of South Carolina, Mississippi, and Louisiana, Du Bois stated: "Without a doubt may of the colored leaders shared in this graft, but from the very nature of the case it was not a large share" (*Reconstruction* 154). Repeatedly Du Bois noted that blacks were a distinct group with a certain amount of agency and neither uniform in status nor economic interest regarding the abolition of slavery or post-war Reconstruction.

Blacks' contributions to their political situation, in conjunction with macro-level factors like the demise of the Freedmen's Bureau and the overthrow of Reconstruction-era state constitutions are all part of the complicated, corrective story Du Bois wished to tell. Portraying blacks as completely innocent victims oversimplifies the story, infantilizes blacks, and prevents black self-determination. But neither did Du Bois blame blacks unilaterally for acting in response to specific sociopolitical contexts.

Establishing a both/and identity – both victim and agent – encourages us to see blacks as a dynamic combination of the two and further reinforces blacks' common humanity.

Du Bois did not simply destabilize the idea of blacks as pure victims; he challenged the very binary of pure black victim/pure white oppressor that characterized much of African American thought during his life (*Souls* 224, 250, 324–5). These kinds of analysis lead Du Bois toward a recognition of complexity within racialized groups that was not limited to black Americans. In *Black Reconstruction in America* Du Bois lauded the examples of Thaddeus Stevens and Charles Sumner in particular in addition to presenting more generally a complicated view of white public opinion (see *Reconstruction* 191–9, 265–6, 573). The extended portraits of Stevens and Sumner further destabilize the binary, permitting another critical aspect of Du Bois's politics to emerge. With no pure white oppressor, he found the political space and courage to form coalitions across national as well as racial boundaries. This hallmark of Du Bois's political work emerged in two particular ways – through his analyses of race, class, and gender as equally important, intersecting components of oppression[19] and through his calls for international action against oppression wherever he was capable of recognizing it.

Du Bois's Coalition Politics

Du Bois's biographers Lewis and Marable both note his international interests – most especially his undying interest in Africa (see chapter 8 of this volume) and limited travel and exploration in the Soviet Union and China. What underlies much of Du Bois's international writing on race was an emphasis on coalition politics, as evidenced through his co-foundership of the NAACP and his editorial stands in solidarity with anti-imperialism and anti-Nazism.

Similarly, Du Bois was sympathetic to the Irish uprising against the British in 1916,[20] and wrote paeans to the "darker peoples of world" in numerous essays on India, African anti-colonial struggles, and China. These principled political stands are usually attributed (and rightly so) to Du Bois's shifting ideologies – from social democracy to socialism to communism – most of which focus on the changing of macro-level factors in order to bring about equality. In *Black Folk Then and Now* (1939) Du Bois moves beyond Marx's international proletariat to a multiracial proletariat:

> The proletariat of the world consists not simply of white European and American workers but overwhelmingly of the dark workers of Asia, Africa,

the islands of the sea, and South and Central America. These are the ones who are supporting a superstructure of wealth, luxury, and extravagance. It is the rise of these people that is the rise of the world. The problem of the twentieth century is the problem of the Color Line.[21]

The use of Marxist nomenclature clearly supports earlier assertions of ideological foundations for Du Bois's coalition politics. Most scholarship focuses on the final words of this passage – "*The problem of the twentieth century is the problem of the Color Line.*" Yet even here, as Du Bois envisioned multiple races and ethnicities sharing common cause, he noted that class relationships matter just as significantly through his attention to the proletariat.

Yet ideology is not the sole foundation. Moving beyond this attribution, two claims are relevant to this chapter: first, from "The Study of the Negro Problems," published during the first third of his career, to *Dusk of Dawn*, published during the last third, Du Bois remained consistent regarding the emphasis on two explanatory factors with regard to race as a category of analysis – structural and individual. Thus despite his commitment to socialism and communism during the later years of his life, Du Bois recognized that group leadership included critique and uplift of the noble masses in order to ensure empowerment:

> The reaction of the educated, ambitious, and financially better off of any group to the condition of the masses is the same: None has more pitilessly castigated Jews than the Jewish prophets, ancient and modern. It is the Irish themselves who rail at "dirty Irish tricks." Nothing could exceed the self-abasement of the Germans during Sturm und Drang. Self-criticism by Blacks is no different.[22]

Second, these stands in solidarity stem from Du Bois's sense of coalition politics, which is most firmly grounded in his ideas about race and the diversity within racial groups in particular. Du Bois continued and completed the earlier thought with this confirmation of his sense of diversity within:

> The culture of the upper-class White is often considered typical of all Whites while Blacks are usually considered "as one undifferentiated low-class mass" and the culture of the lowest-class Blacks is considered typical of all Blacks. Neither Blacks nor Whites are a homogenous group.

By this stage of Du Bois's life, his willingness to philosophically stand in solidarity with like-minded members of different races and nationalities also logically follows from his internationalism, which started with his experiences in Europe as a graduate/doctoral student and his sense of recognition regarding the position of Jewish Germans. Marable notes: "Only after several months of student life did Du Bois recognize another sort of 'veil' within German culture, the poison of anti-Semitism. Intrigued with this unforeseen aspect of intolerance, he concluded that German anti-Semitism had 'much in common with our own race question.'"[23] This position on anti-Semitism remained constant throughout Du Bois's life. In addition to working with several like-minded Jewish Americans in the NAACP, Du Bois's articles frequently noted studies of Jewish people and argued outright for a Black-Jewish coalition.[24] Moreover, his second autobiography, *Dusk of Dawn: An Essay toward an Autobiography of a Race Concept*, was dedicated to NAACP executive Joel Spingarn, longtime ally in the fight for Black American civil rights.

Du Bois's horror regarding the Holocaust found its way into articles published after he returned from a visit to Nazi Germany. In *The World and Africa* (1947), fifty-four years after his initial recognition of "family resemblances" between the two communities Du Bois critiqued the United States by continuing such an analysis:

> Only the Jews among us, as a class, carefully select and support talent and genius among the young; the Negroes are following this example as far as their resources and knowledge allow. It is for this very reason that jealousy of the gifted Jew and ambitious Negro is closing doors of opportunity in their faces. This led to the massacre of Jews in Germany.[25]

While Du Bois was unable to recognize all instances of oppression – the glaring failure to recognize the tragic consequences of Mao Zedong's policies comes to mind – he did use his academic and personal knowledge of the black situation in America as a window for examining race as a category to analyze oppression more broadly. The combination of his expertise and his ideological convictions produced longstanding coalitions with movements often considered unpopular in the west – including women's suffrage in the United States, and anti-colonialism and Pan-Africanism abroad.

Conclusion

Du Bois recognized the lack of homogeneity in racial and ethnic groups. While he was convinced that no group was homogenous, he continued to be daunted by the threat race prejudice presented to the fight for equality and justice. Specifically, Du Bois lamented in both his scholarship and activism the divisive role that structural and individual race prejudice played in making truly egalitarian, multiracial coalitions possible. He explained the reasons for the divide in *Black Reconstruction in America*, and left the socialist movement for its failure to recognize the significant obstacle race oppression presented in preventing the pursuit of a classless world. He frequently demanded and all too rarely received reciprocal solidarity that was both multiracial and egalitarian. Du Bois left us with this unfulfilled legacy at the time of his death in 1963 in Ghana.

Du Bois's recognition of kindred spirits and coalition opportunities occurred in a context that avoided reductionist thinking about race, democracy, or equality. By now it is clear that his racial theory and its relationship to ongoing political struggles for justice around the world presaged much of the contemporary discourse concerning race as a social construction; the interplay between structure and agency in racial identity formation and racial politics, what is loosely called intersectionality theory; and globalization. Du Bois's theory of double-consciousness, and his simultaneously famous and ominous prediction that "the problem of the twentieth century is the problem of the color-line" represent the beginning, not the end of studies of Du Bois and race as a category of social analysis.

Notes

1. W. E. B. Du Bois, *The Souls of Black Folk* (1903), in W. E. B. Du Bois, *Writings*, ed. N. Huggins (New York: Library of America, 1986), pp. 364–5. Hereafter cited in the text as *Souls*.

2. M. Marable, *W. E. B. Du Bois: Black Radical Democrat* (1986; Boulder: Paradigm Publishers, 2005).

3. D. W. Blight and R. Gooding-Williams, "Introduction: The strange meaning of Being Black," in their W. E. B. Du Bois, *The Souls of Black Folk* (Boston: Bedford Books, 1997), p. 11.

4. See, e.g., M. Q. Sawyer, "Du Bois's Double Consciousness versus Latin American Exceptionalism: Joe Arroyo, Salsa, and Negritude," *SOULS: A Critical Journal of Black Politics, Culture and Society*, 7 (2005), pp. 85–95.

5. W. E. B. Du Bois, "The Conservation of Races" (1897), in *Writings*, ed. Huggins, p. 817.

6. J. Olson, "W. E. B. Du Bois and the Race Concept," *SOULS: A Critical Journal of Black Politics, Culture and Society*, 7(2005), pp. 118–128; P. C. Taylor, "Appiah's Uncontested Argument: W. E. B. Du Bois and the Reality of Race," *Social Theory and Practice*, 26, no. 1 (Spring 2000), pp. 103–28; A. Monteiro, "Being an African in the World: The Du Boisian Epistemology," *Annals of the American Academy of Political and Social Science*, 568(2000), pp. 220–34.

7. W. E. B. Du Bois, *Dusk of Dawn: An Essay toward an Autobiography of a Race Concept* (1940), in *Writings*, ed. Huggins, p. 666.

8. T. Shelby, *We Who Are Dark: The Philosophical Foundations of Black Solidarity* (Cambridge: Harvard University Press, 2005), p. 62.

9. W. E. B. Du Bois, *Black Reconstruction in America* (1935; New York: Free Press, 1992), pp. 39, 50, 65–66, 520 (hereafter cited in the text as *Reconstruction*); W. E. B. Du Bois, "The Study of the Negro Problems," *Annals of the American Academy of Political and Social Science* (1898), pp. 1–23.

10. L. T. Outlaw, "W. E. B. Du Bois on the Study of Social Problems," *Annals of the American Academy of Political and Social Science*, 568 (2000), pp. 281–97.
11. Du Bois, "Study of the Negro Problems."
12. *Ibid.*
13. D. L. Lewis, *W. E. B. Du Bois: Biography of a Race, 1868–1919* (New York: Henry Holt, 1993), p. 206.
14. E. Anderson, "The Emerging Philadelphia African American Class Structure," *Annals of the American Academy of Political and Social Science*, 568 (2000), p. 54.
15. See L. R. Gordon, "Du Bois's Humanistic Philosophy of Human Sciences," *Annals of the American Academy of Political and Social Science*, 568 (2000), pp. 265–80, p. 271.
16. *Ibid.*
17. See Monteiro, "Being an African."
18. It is important to note that Du Bois saw the challenge of racial inequality as a set of multiple and interconnected problems rather than a single homogenous challenge, thus the focus on the Negro "problems," rather than "problem."
19. A. M. Hancock, "W. E. B. Du Bois: Intellectual Forefather of Intersectionality?" *SOULS: A Critical Journal of Black Politics, Culture and Society*, 7 (2005), pp. 74–84.
20. Marable, *Black Radical Democrat*, p. 94.
21. W. E. B. Du Bois, *Black Folk Then and Now: An Essay in the History and Sociology of the Negro Race* (New York: Henry Holt, 1939), p. 383.
22. Du Bois, *Dusk of Dawn* (New York: Schocken Books, 1968), p. xix.
23. Marable, *Black Radical Democrat*, pp. 17–18, 77.
24. See also D. L. Lewis, *W. E. B. Du Bois – The Fight for Equality and the American Century 1919–1963* (New York: Henry Holt, 2000), pp. 343 and 400 for additional examples.
25. W. E. B. Du Bois, *The World and Africa: An Inquiry into the Part Which Africa Has Played in World History* (1947; New York: International Publishers, 2003), p. 253.

7

AXEL R. SCHÄFER

Du Bois on Race: Economic and Cultural Perspectives

Introduction

For a generation of young, urbane, adventurous college graduates aspiring to an academic career, the late nineteenth century was a period of singular excitement and opportunity. America, struggling with the challenges of rapid urban and industrial growth, was open to foreign ideas and precedents, an intellectual sea-change challenged accepted dogmas and beliefs, the new social sciences came into their own, and transatlantic travel had become cheaper and easier than ever before. W. E. B. Du Bois's intellectual development and academic work owed much to his participation in the lively transatlantic exchange of ideas and atmosphere of experimentation which helped define the intellectual parameters of the fledgling social sciences and shaped the political ideas of a generation of progressive thinkers in the United States. In turn, Du Bois's historical and sociological research, from his student days at Fisk University, Harvard College, and the University of Berlin in the 1880s and 90s to his resignation as professor at Atlanta University in 1909, yielded a number of pioneering studies which advanced innovative research methods, opened up new fields of inquiry, and shattered old orthodoxies. Though encompassing only a small segment of his overall oeuvre, they provided crucial analytical underpinnings of his thought and activism throughout his career.

Generations of students have been inspired by Du Bois's work, yet his contemporaries paid little attention to his record as historian and social scientist. In his *Autobiography* (1968), he bitterly remarked that African American academics "remained unrecognized in learned societies and academic groups. We rated merely as Negroes studying Negroes, and after all, what had Negroes to do with America or science?"[1] Throughout his academic career, he experienced professional shunning, open discrimination, and deep-seated racial prejudice. What is more surprising, however, is that few modern studies of the social sciences in the United States include references to

Du Bois. Even those writers who explored him in detail and praise his emphasis on empirical research frequently charge that his European sojourn reinforced his elitism, authoritarian romanticism, and conservative notions of fixed racial attributes and hierarchies which limited his credentials as reformer. In the eyes of his most astute critic, David Levering Lewis, Du Bois remained "in the iron grip of an ideology of culture in which human progress was measured in terms of manners, the arts, great literature, and great ideals."[2]

Due to this regrettable myopia the radical subtexts of Du Bois's historical and sociological writings have often been ignored. Yet, his participation in the transatlantic intellectual exchange made him a crucial conduit for European social thought and methodology which had radical implications for his thinking on race, society, and culture. The power and poetic beauty of his oeuvre was to a large extent forged in the intellectually formative struggles of his student days and the insights imparted as a result of his academic work. A closer look at Du Bois's intellectual world, however, more than simply resuscitates the intellectual vitality and cosmopolitan breadth of progressive-era thought and reform. His journey of self-discovery and self-transcendence took him in a vastly different direction than many of his progressive wayfarers. While many of them, aided by their middle-class backgrounds and white Protestant heritage, settled into comfortable academic careers, Du Bois was denied permanent access to the scholarly life. While they grappled with the moral, political, and personal implications of the intellectual sea-change, his struggles with the same issues were infinitely more intense and sharpened by analytical acuity, a sense of alienation, proud self-assertion, a stronger feeling of moral outrage, and faith in cultural redemption. Du Bois's historical and sociological insights challenge the conceptual limitations and biases of early-twentieth-century social science. By the same token, his views illuminate the dilemmas and inner turmoil which accompany the sincere pursuit of knowledge torn between the demands of disinterested scholarship and the urge to work for social change.

Du Bois Abroad

The period when Du Bois was a student at Harvard and Berlin has long been recognized as an era of intense intellectual ferment. In many ways his experiences mirrored those of numerous other young American intellectuals who came of age in the heady days of the *fin-de-siècle* and who felt personally liberated through transatlantic study, alienated from their cultural and political roots, skeptical of traditional verities, and dedicated to the potentialities of social transformation. Attending a European university, preferably a German one, was *de rigueur* for any aspiring American intellectual prior to World

War I, and having excelled at Harvard, Du Bois was given the unique opportunity to go to Berlin. Setting sail in 1892, his diaries show him as becoming more easy-going, playful, and accessible with each week abroad. Sipping tea *Unter den Linden*, being a *flaneur* with gloves and walking stick on Berlin's *Kurfürstendamm*, traveling widely, getting entangled in amorous relations, and sporting a beard which was trimmed in the fashion of Emperor William II, he felt freer in these years than he would ever feel again. Germany offered a fresh perspective, a broadened horizon, a new way of thinking and feeling about himself. For the first time in his life, he felt treated as a peer and an equal.

Although Du Bois shared in his white compatriots' sense of elation at going abroad, a heightened sense of exile and self-transcendence, which became a wellspring of his writings, set him apart from his fellow students. On the one hand, his stay reinforced his conviction that European high culture contained within itself the potential to overcome racial stereotypes and that intellectuals were above color prejudice. Living in Germany allowed him to look "at the world as a man and not simply from a narrow racial and provincial outlook." "I was not less fanatically a Negro," he later reminisced, "but 'Negro' meant a greater, broader sense of humanity and world fellowship" (*Autobiography* 159, 157). On the other hand, Du Bois began to understand that the racial divide was rooted in historically developed economic structures and cultural conditioning, not in fixed biological or moral differences. His studies sharpened his sense that the race problems in the United States, the political development of Europe, and the fate of Asia and Africa could not be separated from each other. Following an invitation from a fellow student, Du Bois traveled through Eastern Europe and gained first-hand impressions of European ethnic conflicts. Witnessing the rise of German racism, the suffering of the poor, and the reality of class struggle made him sympathize with Marxism, to which he had been introduced at meetings of the German Social Democratic Party. He was also discriminated against in the region as either a Gypsy or a Jew. "It was an interesting visit and an old tale," he recalled, "tyranny in school and work; insult in home and on the street." Yet he noted a difference between the Eastern Europeans' situation and that of blacks. "Of course here, in contrast to America, there were the privileged Poles who escaped personal insult; there was the aristocracy who had some recognized rights. The whole mass of the oppressed were not reduced to one level" (*Autobiography* 174–5).

Race as an Economic Construct

Faith in cultural redemption, the awareness of race as a cultural and economic construct, and belief in the power of educated elites shaped Du Bois's outlook throughout his intellectual journey from academia to political advocacy and defined his specific contribution to historical and sociological scholarship. Rather than imparting cultural snobbism and elitist authoritarianism, his deep engagement with the main currents of late-nineteenth-century social thought helped him tie together the disparate components of his ideas in a radical reinterpretation of race and social change. Studying Kantian philosophy with George Santayana and ethics with William James at Harvard in the late 1880s had already started this process. A frequent visitor at James's house, Du Bois regarded him as one of his greatest influences in his life. James exposed Du Bois to the methods and ideas of pragmatism. He argued that truth was a social product, rather than a metaphysical absolute. He maintained that all meanings were contingent and provisional, rather than fixed and final. He rejected universal categories or totalizing theories in favor of cultural difference and historical specificity. And James insisted that in an open and uncertain universe man was a creative agent in the construction of political and social order, rather than just a passive object of the impersonal laws of biology or economics.

Building upon James's philosophical questioning of absolutes, Du Bois turned away from philosophy to the study of history and social problems. At this juncture, the teachings of the German historical school of economics helped him take his iconoclasm a step further by challenging the hallowed axioms of laissez-faire economics. In contrast to American economic thinkers such as William Graham Sumner and Frank W. Taussig, who had merged self-righteous Puritanism and social Darwinism to legitimize the laws of the market as the natural order of things, German scholars such as Gustav Schmoller, Adolf Wagner, Karl Knies, and Max Weber maintained that market capitalism was a social construct and that it had developed historically as an expression of a peculiar utilitarian spirit which located moral self-development in the actions of autonomous, self-disciplined, competitive-market individuals. Arguing that moral concepts manifested themselves in institutions, historicists viewed limited government, property rights, contract law, and notions of individual rights as specific expressions of nineteenth-century liberal ideology, rather than as grounded in universal truths.

Indebted to German idealism and its belief in the gradual unfolding of the ethical society, the historicists exhorted their students to understand the economic order of a society as time-bound and encouraged them to abandon the slavish devotion to allegedly immutable laws of economics in favor of finding ways of creating the good society. They argued that humans could neither be reduced to self-interested economic individuals, nor simply be seen as pawns of the environment, but needed to be understood as agents in their own and society's ethical self-realization in the context of social interaction. The social sciences were a crucial element in their social thought, because they viewed society not as an aggregation of autonomous individuals, but as an organism, where freedom, individuality, and morality were dependent on the institutional organization of groups and nations as ethical communities. Economics, Schmoller, Conrad, Knies, and others argued, was both about pure research and about establishing a science of reform. The close observation of actual conditions of production and exchange would not only enable scholars to understand the culture-specific laws of the development of social organisms, but also provide a solid ethical grounding for the formulation of interventionist economic policies.

Insisting that in Germany he "began to unite [his] economics and politics," Du Bois combined the normative basis and research methodology of the historical school in a number of empirical studies of the socioeconomic foundations of race in the United States (*Autobiography* 162). His doctoral thesis, published as *The Suppression of the African Slave-Trade to the United States of America, 1638–1870* (1896), systematically examined historical data to show that an unscrupulous North and a callous South conspired to undermine laws against the importation of slaves. Although flawed in specifics, namely its disregard of the role of the domestic slave trade in sustaining slavery, it was scrupulous in its documentation and offered a refreshing departure from the widespread neglect of race issues in American social science. The study also gave a first inkling that Du Bois was about to throw down the gauntlet to the broader racial consensus in American academia. Steeped in Darwinian evolutionism and Sumnerian belief in laissez-faire, most social scientists attributed black underclass status to biological inferiority, moral weakness, and misguided white philanthropy. Du Bois, however, asserted that racial hierarchies were the result of culturally constructed social and economic relations that used biological and moral concepts to legitimize exploitation.

He did this in his magisterial book *The Philadelphia Negro: A Social Study* (1899), a statistical and empirical study of African Americans based on painstaking research which he undertook during a one-year stint at the University of Pennsylvania. Instead of defining blacks as incapable of adjusting to the disciplinary rigors and work ethic required for industrial employment, as the sociology of the day did, Du Bois showed that industrial culture had kept blacks down by using racism to ensure a supply of cheap labor. In this "study in the art of cultural suasion through social science," Du Bois put his finger on one of the most powerful mechanisms which sustained American capitalism, namely the power of racism to pit blacks and poor whites against each other and divide the working class along racial and ethnic lines at the expense of class solidarity.[3] In the same vein, the study reflected Du Bois's growing outrage at white society educating and helping immigrants, while not rewarding blacks for their honest labor and talent.

Examining the restraints white society placed on black enterprise further in his *Atlanta University Studies*, Du Bois outlined his economic challenge to the teachings of the powerful advocate of black industrial education, Booker T. Washington. Du Bois exposed the paradox of Washington's "black capitalism," namely that individual economic success under the conditions of a racially tiered economic order created a vested interest in segregation on the part of wealthy blacks who themselves were facing discrimination. Black advancement along the lines of industrial education, Du Bois asserted, was based on the servant metaphor, in which blacks were allowed to rise to higher levels of service, but remained subordinate and inferior. It was a no-win situation, since an alliance with whites meant subservience, competition incited racism and prejudice, and the failure of black businesses reinforced notions of inferiority. Black capitalism, he maintained, kept the majority of blacks confined to degrading menial labor and helped sustain the traditional racial order. Therefore, Du Bois, in contrast to Washington, located real change in race relations not in inculcating the economic norms and values of market liberalism, but in an awareness that capitalism operated upon the premises of racial exploitation and was intimately tied to a conception of blacks as biologically inferior.

The climax of Du Bois's socioeconomic interpretation of black poverty, however, came almost forty years later with his influential *Black Reconstruction in America* (1935). While its main ideas had been long in the making, the book, written under the impression of the devastating effects of the Great Depression on African Americans, outlined most clearly that social and economic repression, not racial inferiority, caused black deprivation and disfranchisement. Depicting racism as part of class warfare, Du Bois exposed attempts by moneyed interests after the Civil War to stifle successful black self-government and industrial democracy. Although his own economic thinking remained more akin to the Fabians and the evolutionary views of Eduard Bernstein than to the revolutionary zeal of Marx, Du Bois regarded history and sociology as weapons for racial advancement, particularly after he had declared his Bolshevik sympathies in the wake of a visit to the Soviet Union in 1926.

The Cultural Reconceptualization of Race

Du Bois's achievements in his historical and sociological writings, however, were not confined to bringing empirical research and economic analysis to bear on the study of race. His social thought, nurtured in the fertile soil of

Harvard pragmatism and German higher education, reconceptualized race not only socioeconomically, but also culturally. He combined three views of culture in a fragile amalgam which broadly mirrored his personal experience of faith, exile, and self-transcendence: a classical humanist conception which regarded culture as embodying universal moral values beyond racial and class divisions; a romantic conception of culture which sought to uncover authentic cultural expressions and gifts of defined racial groupings; and a pragmatist-historicist conception which saw culture as a dynamic component in the contingent constructions of moral norms, socioeconomic structures, and political order. Together, they formed the leitmotif of his scholarship.

Surprisingly, although he subscribed to the relativistic teachings of pragmatism and historicism, Du Bois never lost faith in European high culture as embodying ultimate ideals and truths beyond cultural differences. On this basis he once again rejected Booker T. Washington's philosophy of self-help as an undue reduction of liberty to a matter of technical training, competitive achievement, and business success. Intimations of freedom through self-reflection, arts and letters, philosophy, poetry, sculpture, and knowledge of other cultures were, in his eyes, more important for the ethical advance of blacks from the legacy of slavery and serfdom. "We must give to our youth a training designed above all to make them men of power, of thought, of trained and cultivated taste," he declared.[4] In contrast to Washington's vision of a black economic elite which adopted the norms and practices of capitalism, Du Bois believed that the "accomplished moral intelligence" of the "talented tenth" would instilled a desire for freedom in the race.[5] This faith in cultural redemption sustained him throughout some of the darkest periods of racism. As a disillusioned Du Bois wrote after the riots and lynchings that followed the end of World War I, racism was not based on science or the "careful survey of the social development of men," but "is simply passionate, deep-seated heritage, and as such can be moved by neither argument nor fact. Only faith in humanity will lead the world to rise above its present color prejudice."[6]

While this faith cemented his adherence to European high culture, his sense of exile made him receptive to the teachings of German romantics such as Johann Gottfried Herder, Johann Gottlieb Fichte, and Friedrich Schleiermacher, who emphasized the need for authentic cultural self-expression against the alienating forces of cold and calculating civilization. Their belief in the distinct civilizational gift of each racial group and their search for social regeneration through a process of ethnographic recovery of cultural traditions left a deep imprint on Du Bois's social thought. In turn, he viewed social science research in terms of cultural archaeology, designed to uncover empirically the bedrock of organized African American mores, social structures, and ethical sentiments. This came to fruition in a number of studies commissioned by the Bureau of Labor Statistics and in the *Atlanta University Studies* volumes he wrote and edited between 1897 and 1913. The position at Atlanta University teaching economics, history, and sociology was Du Bois's first long-term academic employment. His years in this segregated city with an integrated campus, where the emphasis was both on industrial training and the liberal arts, were among his most scholarly productive. Not until funding for his position fell victim to resurgent racism, and the death of his child led to the gradual estrangement from his first wife, did Du Bois reconsider his career and choice of place. The encounter with black mass destitution and raw Southern racism – which at one point made him hurry home from a speaking engagement to defend his wife and baby from the threats of a brutal white mob – bolstered his faith in remedial social science, the moral heroism of simple black folk, and the inadequacy of Booker T. Washington's self-help ideology.

The *Atlanta University Studies*, particularly the volume on *The Negro Church* (1903), showed that slavery had not destroyed African American culture and ethnographically recovered the ethical foundations of black society dating from pre-slavery times. Likewise, Du Bois's famous speech, "The Conservation of Races" (1897), noted the spiritual and psychic differences between races and that each race had a "gift" to offer. He declared African Americans members of a vast historic race whose destiny was neither absorption into or servile imitation of Anglo-Saxon culture, but "stalwart originality which shall unswervingly follow Negro ideals."[7] Similarly, in "Strivings of the Negro People" (1897), Du Bois described the special beauty and humanity of blacks, their music, folk tales, and humor. He argued that the hardships of life had not broken the spirit of blacks, but had produced high standards of moral heroism in face of constant adversity, deeper affection for culture, and more profound insight into culture's power and beauty. Although Du Bois at times exhorted blacks to adjust to protestant middle-class norms and, particularly in *The Negro American Family* (1908), blamed the lack of civilization and morality on weak family structures, his main theme throughout these explorations of African American culture and life was to discover its uniqueness and beauty. By the same token, he presented black institutions and morals as containing both the germs of black ethical self-realization and of a broader moral vision for American society. In *Darkwater: Voices from within the Veil* (1920), his view that governments in African colonies after World War I should be based on indigenous black customs and local political traditions echoed the historicist belief in authentic cultural institutions as the basis for a moral society. Likewise, he declared that African American traditions were needed to humanize Euro-American civilization whose main achievements had been limited to technical and industrial progress, methods of political organization, and the nation-state.

If Du Bois's thinking had remained wedded to romantic beliefs in the unique civilizational gifts of fixed racial groups, his historical and sociological writings would have been inspiring, but could have easily been reworked into a rationale for racial and cultural exclusivism. However, Du Bois did not stop there. In the end, he suggested a new and radical perspective on race and racial formation which constituted his seminal contribution to American social thought. Influenced by the German idealist philosopher Georg Wilhelm Friedrich Hegel's ruminations on mastery and enslavement, Du Bois developed his famous concepts of "double-consciousness" and the "veil." Hegel had argued that what defined "master" and "slave" was not their distinct identities, but the fact that they could not exist independently of each other. The identities of both were a result of the consciousness of one mediated through that of the other. Ironically, both embodied the opposite of what defined them, since the "free" master understands dominance, while the "dependent" slave understands freedom.

The mutual construction of the identities of oppressor and oppressed, and the irony of their special insight into what defines their respective opposites, became central ideas in Du Bois's thought. They found their most potent and poetic expression in *The Souls of Black Folk* (1903) and its masterful phrase that whites created a world that yielded the black man no true self-consciousness "but only lets him see himself through the revelation of the other world."[8] Urging blacks to overcome their self-perception as caricatures, Du Bois developed this further in numerous essays which analyzed the role of mimicry, simulacra, cultivated deference, subterfuge, and masks, such as acting the clown and the "grinning Negro," in African American culture. Likewise, exhorting African Americans to fight their sense of being ashamed of the color of their skin, he showed that black society had tied status, respect, pride, and self-esteem to aping the behavior of whites and regarded insignia of whiteness, such as an Anglo accent or wearing the master's clothes, as sources of power.

In summation, Du Bois's cultural understanding of race advanced three profound insights which prefigured the "linguistic turn" in historical and sociological scholarship. First, he shifted the focus from totalizing theories and cultural essentialism toward the notion of race as a linguistic construct based on projections, fears, desires, and images of "the other." Secondly, he showed that American cultural identity could not be separated from the way Americans, Europeans, and Africans interacted with each other.

Conceptions of whiteness, for example, were only meaningful in relation to conceptualizations of blackness, since white culture was intimately tied to the legacy of black enslavement and its ideological legitimation. Finally, he maintained that the mutual construction of oppressor and oppressed implies its own subversion. Applying Hegelian dialectics, which asserted that everything contains within itself the seeds of its own overcoming, Du Bois's notion of double-consciousness linked social change to the recovery of the ethical dimension of African American culture and liberal arts education.

Race, Social Change, and Progressive Democracy

Du Bois found further intellectual support for these ideas when he discovered the teachings of Columbia anthropologist Franz Boas, who had come to Atlanta to deliver the 1906 commencement address. Boas attributed racial hierarchies to culturally rooted notions of superiority, not to skull shape, brain size, or other biological markers. He fuelled Du Bois's own ethnographic explorations into African history by hailing the glories of African culture and its relevance for black Americans. More importantly, his cultural relativism urged Du Bois to probe further the social and political potentialities of racial cross-fertilization. Merging economic analysis, romanticism, Hegelian dialectics, and pragmatist social thought with cultural relativism, Du Bois moved beyond the rigid racial categories of Herder and the metaphysical ruminations of Hegel toward a theory of political change which placed the "problem of the color-line" squarely at the center of a civilizational drama in which liberal democracy and the capitalist order would be replaced by progressive democracy and economic cooperation. In this scenario, the development of black consciousness and cultural participation, rather than being a way for African Americans to get ahead in liberal capitalist society, was part of developing society as an "organized community of attainment and endeavor."[9]

Du Bois's belief in progressive democracy mirrored that of John Dewey, the leading pragmatist social thinker of the period. Like Du Bois, Dewey defined democracy as "the effective embodiment of the moral ideal of a good which consists in the development of all the social capacities of every individual member."[10] While the utilitarian and individualistic ethics of laissez-faire liberalism had spawned a society that located freedom in limited government and the protection of private property rights, they argued, the interactionist ethics of progressivism would translate into a society that located liberty in economic interdependence and civic identity. In order to achieve this, a democratic society needed to create new non-commercial public institutions that enabled individuals to participate in political and economic decisions and to develop an inner sense that their freedom was tied to their social being. A true democratic government, Du Bois maintained, needed to recognize "not only the worth of the individual to himself, but the worth of his feelings and experiences to all." Shutting out a people on the basis of race was actually diminishing the progress of humanity, since "there is lost from the world an experience of untold value."[11] Both Dewey and Du Bois thus called on the state to use social science research to link industrial pursuits to the ethical development and welfare of the social organism via, for example, social insurance, city planning, state ownership of industries, redistributive tax policies, and housing cooperatives. Unlike many of his progressive wayfarers, Du Bois viewed reform not as a matter of magnifying the power of the state or of industrial efficiency, but of extending opportunities for all citizens to develop fully their social capacities.

Although Dewey and Du Bois shared a belief in progressive democracy, they differed in one crucial regard. Dewey, like his fellow sociologist George Herbert Mead, applauded the breakdown of customary morals and social ties through urbanization and industrialization. In his view, this loosened the stranglehold of small groups and exclusive loyalties and allowed a new consciousness of complex social interdependence to emerge. Du Bois, however, saw new social ethics emerging from the "double-consciousness" which characterized the historical experience of African Americans. For him, the awareness of the mutual construction of blackness and whiteness, and the ethnographic recovery of submerged cultural expressions among African Americans, was the ground upon which social reconstruction could take place. Hence, *The Souls of Black Folk* advanced not only the notion of the parity, but also the complementarity of blacks and whites. In the words of David Levering Lewis, its vision of "proud, enduring hyphenation" called on African Americans to cultivate "the moral and creative energies that lay hidden in the condition of [their] very alienation" and implored them to become "co-workers in the kingdom of culture."[12]

What appears to be a minor dispute indicates the larger tensions between Du Bois and the progressive mainstream. His transracial pluralism and radical interpretation of historicism and pragmatism continued to clash with white progressives' exclusion of blacks from the civilizational master narrative. Despite some notable exceptions, particularly Boas and the sociologists Lester Frank Ward, W. I. Thomas, and Robert Park, most American social scientists at best ignored the plight of blacks and at worst grouped them with subhuman species. Even progressive thinkers sympathetic to the plight of blacks found it difficult to free themselves from the entanglements of racial thought. Charles Horton Cooley, for example, morally rejected the idea of inferiority, but found no intellectual grounding for this attitude. Meanwhile, progressive sociologists such as Albion Small and Edward A. Ross, supported by the new biology of inheritance, affirmed the general consensus that blacks were inferior of their own making.

Racialism and Progressive Reform

It is deeply ironic that the high tide of progressivism coincided with some of the darkest moments of segregation, discrimination, and racial violence in the United States. Although some progressive reformers vigorously fought racism, most muckraking journalists and settlement-house workers categorized African Americans as backward people whose culture was incompatible with modern industrial society. Ray Stannard Baker's *Following the Color Line* (1908), one of the few books by a muckraker on the subject, concluded that blacks were "far inferior in education, intelligence, and efficiency to the white people as a class." As a result, they "must find their activities mostly in physical and more or less menial labour...before they can expect larger opportunities." Though noting the importance of Du Bois, Baker maintained that "the teaching of such men as Dr. Washington, emphasizing duties and responsibilities" was more needed.[13] Likewise, even among the most sympathetic settlement-house workers, such as Jane Addams, Louise de Koven Bowen, Frances Kellor, and Robert Woods, the notion prevailed that African Americans lacked inner moral restraint, that their family structures were weak, and that the black psyche had been degraded by slavery. Jane Addams's juxtaposition of the strong family sense of Italians with the lack of moral restraint among blacks, and Frances Kellor's critique of the absence of black domestic life excluded African Americans from the progressive scenario of social redemption. Despite significant efforts to attend to the needs of African Americans, for example by the settlement work of the National Urban League and Du Bois's friend Mary Ovington, most settlement houses eschewed integration. Many excluded blacks, conducted segregated activities, or followed their white ethnic clientele out of neighborhoods settled by African Americans who had migrated from the rural South to the urban North during and after World War I.

This racialist myopia of progressive social thought and reform contributed to the eventual abandonment of the radical cultural and socioeconomic dimension in progressivism in favor of concepts which saw the solution to overcoming the racial divide in economic growth and managed capitalism, rather than public ownership, industrial democracy, and economic redistribution. Du Bois's intellectual journey, however, took a distinctly different turn. The racialist consensus among social scientists and reformers, his sense that whenever he studied black workers he "had no meeting ground with the white laboring class," and Booker T. Washington's accommodationism drove him into the ranks of civil rights activists (*Autobiography* 233). He abandoned his academic position and began a long and often stormy career within the National Association for the Advancement of Colored People (NAACP), a fledgling civil rights organization founded in 1909 by settlement workers disillusioned with the hostile racial climate of progressive reform. In turn, Du Bois increasingly advocated the notion that blacks needed physical integration, but spiritual and cultural separation. While disenchanted with academic life and progressive reform, he never lost sight of the goal of transforming liberal capitalism into a cooperative commonwealth of public ownership and industrial democracy and of his commitment to politics as a search for ideals of justice in the struggle of communities to order themselves democratically. His embrace of Marxism needs to be seen in the context of this desire to preserve the humanitarian values, Hegelian outlook, and the rejection of laissez-faire economics which no longer found a home in progressivism.

With the exception of a brief interlude in the 1930s, Du Bois's move from academic to activist, editor, and author was permanent. The historical and sociological insights he had formed between the late 1880s and the early 1900s, however, as well as the unresolved tensions within these ideas, continued to shape his thinking and writing throughout his life and are still debated in scholarship today. On the one hand, Du Bois's search for authentic black roots was designed to create race consciousness, a sense of pride and belonging as a means of fighting defeatism and a sense of cultural inferiority internalized by blacks. Its holistic and organicist approach included elements of mythmaking and hero worship. On the other hand, his call for critical analysis sought to expose the artificiality and contingency of all notions of racial identity. It nurtured a skeptical and self-reflective mindset which sought to explode myths, reveal ambivalences, and question identities. Similarly, Du Bois's adulation of white high culture as a means of developing the inner freedom to transcend the racist cage clashed with his search for genuine black cultural expression as the basis of social reconstruction. Many of his critics have charged that his embrace of white high culture ignored the subversive components of black popular culture. By the same token, however, the question remains to what extent popular culture ultimately reaffirms the existing social order. Although popular culture was used by the underprivileged to legitimate their values, it neither challenged the maldistribution of wealth nor the class divide, and promoted consumer capitalism by idolizing celebrities, cultivating images of masculinity, seeing women as sexual objects, glorifying technology, and linking self-expression to consumption. Finally, Du Bois's writings continued to display the dilemma between separatism and integration. While his concept of the creative complementarity of races as "co-workers in the kingdom of culture" emphasized the integration of African Americans, his call to safeguard the distinctiveness of races and the voluntary segregation of black businesses and education suggests otherwise. Though he vigorously attacked racial exclusion and discrimination, Du Bois continued to fear that for blacks as a minority population, any kind of integration meant measuring themselves on the norms and standards defined by the dominant culture.

Conclusion

In summation, we can safely lay to rest criticism that Du Bois's European sojourn turned an "Afro-Saxon" patrician into a devotee of "romantic authoritarianism or incipient fascism."[14] In his social thought, Du Bois embraced white culture not in fawning sycophancy, but as a genuine part of a common humanity which allows blacks to live above the "veil." He promoted romantic notions of cultural recovery and authenticity not to assert fixed racial attributes, but to counter myths about black biological deficiencies and cultural inferiority. He adapted historicist and Hegelian teachings not to assert elitist conservatism, but to promote the cultural turn in the understanding of race. And he used pragmatist reasoning not to express the moral outrage of a Calvinist patrician, but to formulate a radical critique of the liberal capitalist order and its racialist undergirdings.

Revisiting Du Bois's historical and sociological writings thus means placing him back at the center of the radical intellectual sea-change in American social thought and the transatlantic exchange of ideas between 1870 and 1920. Blending American pragmatism, German historicism and romanticism, Hegelian philosophy, cultural anthropology, and Marxist economics, Du Bois not only pioneered methods of empirical research during the early period of professionalization of social sciences and studied African American life at a time when blacks were largely ignored by academics. He also profoundly challenged the racist consensus of the day which eschewed cultural cross-fertilization and regarded African Americans as incapable of civilizational advancement. Revealing the constructedness of racial categories, Du Bois contributed to the cognitive shift in the social sciences from a focus on biology to one on environment and culture in understanding race. Showing that Western civilization was culturally and economically bound up with colonization and slavery, he placed race relations and their study at the center of understanding the American experience. And recognizing that racist beliefs had shaped the very ideological and economic essence of laissez-faire capitalism and liberal democracy, he advocated a progressive model of democracy as an ethical community which combined the expansion of the public sphere of control with genuine cultural exchange and cross-fertilization.

In combining faith in the redemptive potential of cultural expression, a sense of alienation, and intellectual self-transcendence, Du Bois's historical and sociological imagination also raises issues that are basic to the scholarly endeavor. What is the relationship between scholarship and advocacy? Where does cultural analysis end and cultural pride begin? Does high culture or popular culture hold the key to cultural self-assertion? Is there a third way between integration and separation? However one is inclined to answer these questions, a glance at Du Bois's academic writings is essential in this quest.

Notes

1. W. E. B. Du Bois, *The Autobiography of W. E. B. Du Bois: A Soliloquy on Viewing My Life from the Last Decade of its First Century* (New York: International Publishers, 1968), p. 228. Hereafter cited in the text as *Autobiography*.

2. D. L. Lewis, *W. E. B. Du Bois: Biography of a Race, 1868–1919* (New York: Henry Holt, 1993), p. 144.

3. A. Rampersad, *The Art and Imagination of W. E. B. Du Bois* (New York: Schocken Books, 1990), p. 51. For a concise review of the impact of German life and scholarship on Du Bois's racial ideas, see B. S. Edwards, "W. E. B. Du Bois Between Worlds: Berlin, Empirical Social Research, and the Race Question," *Du Bois Review*, 3 (September 2006), pp. 395–424.

4. W. E. B. Du Bois, *The Education of Black People: Ten Critiques, 1906–1960*, ed. H. Aptheker (Amherst: University of Massachusetts Press, 1973), p. 14.

5. Rampersad, *Art and Imagination*, p. 67.

6. W. E. B. Du Bois, *Darkwater. Voices from within the Veil* (New York: Harcourt, Brace & Howe, 1920), p. 73.

7. *W. E. B. Du Bois Speaks: Speeches and Addresses, 1890–1919*, ed. P. S. Foner (New York: Pathfinder Press, 1970), pp. 73–85.

8. W. E. B. Du Bois, *The Souls of Black Folk* (Chicago: A. C. McClurg, 1903), p. 5.

9. J. Dewey and J. Tufts, *Ethics* (New York: Henry Holt and Co., 1908), p. 473.

10. *Ibid.*, p. 474.

11. Du Bois, *Darkwater*, p. 144.

12. Lewis, *Du Bois: Biography*, pp. 280–2.

13. R. S. Baker, *Following the Color Line: American Negro Citizenship in the Progressive Era* (New York: Doubleday, Page & Co., 1908), p. 304.

14. Rampersad, *Art and Imagination*, p. 45.

8

WILSON JEREMIAH MOSES

Africa and Pan-Africanism in the Thought of Du Bois

At every point in his career, Du Bois demonstrated a belief in the centrality of the African peoples in world history, and the interdependency of the continent of Africa with the rest of the world. He viewed this centrality and interdependence both in moral and in economic terms. He understood that Africa, no less than Europe, had been defined by and benefited from the cultures of the Mediterranean and the Atlantic, the Arabian Gulf, and the Indian Ocean. He also realized that Africa, Europe, the Near East, and the New World had mutually defined one another. To this, one must add that Du Bois also perceived the geographic centrality of Africa as both a doorway to and a barrier between the Atlantic, and the Indian Oceans. With his sensitivity to both elitist and grass-roots perspectives, Du Bois's insights are indispensable to a comprehension of any worldview that might currently be associated with terms such as "Africanity," "Afrocentrism," "Pan-Negroism," "Pan-Africanism," or "the black Atlantic."

Du Bois's earliest scholarly references to Africa made clear a desire to place African peoples at the center of history. These writings were equally imbued with racial romanticism, social scientific awareness, and a sense of political mission. He did not treat the issues of slavery, colonialism, and racism solely as moral issues, but as crucial elements of the global economy. He did not wish to view even such an obviously moral discourse as the African slave trade exclusively as a protest against victimization. Thus in *The Suppression of the African Slave-Trade to the United States of America, 1638–1870* (1896), the book of his doctoral dissertation, he perceived the collapse of the slave trade in terms of political economy as well as morality. And thus he introduced the Haitian revolution as a Pan-African event, a milestone in the histories of Africa, Europe, and the Americas. His dissertation was not informed by a profound knowledge of Africa, or of the role of Africans themselves either as agents or as opponents of the slave trade, but it did comprehend the emergence of a nascent Pan-Africanism in the struggle against slavery.

The role which the great Negro Toussaint, called L'Ouverture, played in the history of the United States has seldom been fully appreciated. Representing the age of revolution in America, he rose to leadership through a bloody terror, which contrived a Negro "problem" for the Western Hemisphere, intensified and defined the anti-slavery movement, became one of the causes, and probably the prime one, which led Napoleon to sell Louisiana for a song, and finally, through the interworking of all these effects, rendered more certain the final prohibition of the slave-trade by the United States in 1807.[1]

Du Bois's belief in the potency of Pan-Africanism was evident, not only in the foregoing allusions to the frustration of Napoleon and the opportunism of Jefferson, but also in his allusion to American fears of Pan-African revolt. Senator John Randolph of Virginia, as he noted, perceived that direct contact between the United States and Haiti might be a source of revolutionary infection for slaves elsewhere in the black world. This was an early expression of Du Bois's emerging awareness of Pan-Africanism as an element in the consciousness of New World "Africans." It was a theme that had appeared in the writings of the African Methodist Episcopal Bishop, Richard Allen as early as 1797, and this theme of unity with the Caribbean recurred in the antebellum Negro Convention movement. The term "African Movement" was used at a special meeting of the African Civilization Society in New York November 7, 1861, and by the mid-nineteenth century, the African Movement comprised two dreams: of Western Hemispheric revolutionary unity, and of an African center for Negro unity. Du Bois followed in the tradition of referring to "the African Movement" well into the 1920s. Thus, it can be seen that Du Bois's conception of the black struggle fell within the scope of a traditional "Pan-Africanism" that associated New World struggles such as the Haitian revolution, with the continual striving for Pan-African dignity and self-determination for the African continent.

Africa played, however, a more central role in Du Bois's "The Conservation of Races" (1897), delivered as an address to the American Negro Academy, the year after the publication of *The Suppression of the African Slave-Trade*. In this address Du Bois continued to view New World Africans, particularly African Americans as "the advance guard of the Negro people – the 8,000,000 people of Negro blood in the United States of America." Unlike his friend, the venerable Alexander Crummell, he continued to hope for the potential of African American leadership in Africa. Crummell, by 1895, had decided that indigenous African leadership was indispensable to African regeneration. Du Bois neither directly responded to, nor specifically rejected Crummell's idea, but nonetheless called on black Americans to "take their just place in the van of Pan-Negroism," as he then called it.[2]

Du Bois demonstrated a high regard, indeed an almost mystical veneration, for the history and destiny of African civilization in this address. He was, of course, speaking before a group of exceedingly distinguished older "race men," some of them having long records of involvement in "the African Movement," and others having championed the history and destiny of the African continent. The 28-year-old speaker was in his element as he addressed this group, and gave vent to a passion that had been somewhat more restrained in his dissertation. Crummell expressed pleasure with the speech, in which Du Bois asserted, with typically romantic rhetoric, "we are Negroes, members of a vast historic race that from the very dawn of creation has slept, but half awakening in the dark forests of its African fatherland."[3]

In his youthful works, Du Bois demonstrated an avoidance of extravagant claims for the past contributions of Black Africa to world history. In *The Negro* (1915) he wrote in the spirit of what Alexander Crummell had once called "the destined superiority of the Negro,"[4] and, like Crummell, he conceived the mission of the African peoples, as a message yet to be delivered. Yet it still seemed to him, as it had eighteen years earlier in "The Conservation of Races," that the African contribution to world civilization could not safely be connected with that of Egypt:

> I will not say that the Negro-race has yet given no message to the world, for it is still a mooted question among scientists as to just how far Egyptian civilization was Negro in its origin; if it was not wholly Negro, it was certainly very closely allied. Be that as it may, however, the fact still remains that the full, complete Negro message of the whole Negro race has not as yet been given to the world.[5]

This same semi-mystical, romantic approach to African history frequently surfaced in Du Bois's *The Souls of Black Folk* (1903): "After the Egyptian and Indian, the Greek and Roman, the Teuton and Mongolian, the Negro is a sort of seventh son, born with a veil, and gifted with second-sight in this American world, – a world which yields him no true self-consciousness, but only lets him see himself through the revelation of the other world."[6] What is curious about this rhetoric is not Du Bois's squeamishness about absolutely identifying the Negro destiny with the Egyptian past, but the arbitrary nature of his ethnology.

"Now, fancy Candace, Queen of Ethiopia, or Chephron, the Master of Egypt, being troubled with a double consciousness. Watch that symbolic, reposeful figure yonder, and you can but see one soul, one ideal, one striving, one line of a natural, rational progress. Look again, and you must agree that the idea of a double consciousness is absurd with these representative types...": so wrote West African nationalist J. E. Casley Hayford.[7] Other black thinkers as disparate as the Liberian patriot Edward Wilmot Blyden, a staunch "race man," and Frederick Douglass, an extreme assimilationist, were as convinced as Hayford of a racial connection between the modern Negro and the land of the Pharaohs.

The Negro reflected speculations on the geographical origins of the human species, prevalent at the time. Du Bois attributed the origins of mankind to Asia, rather than to Africa, in accord with what he believed to be the most accurate contemporary scholarship. Since the 1960s the majority of anthropologists seem to hold out for the African origins of the human species, and much of what Du Bois had to say in the second chapter of *The Negro*, entitled "The Coming of Black Men," now seems outdated and bizarre. In occasional chapters, however, we see the germination of ideas that are commonsensical and in accord with "modern science." Others reflect a tendency towards overly nice raciological distinctions, as in Du Bois's attempt to distinguish a variety of "Negro types."

> Three main Negro types early made their appearance: the lighter and smaller primitive stock; the larger forest Negro in the center and on the west coast, and the tall, black Nilotic Negro in the eastern Sudan. In the earliest times we find the Negroes in the valley of the Nile, pressing downward from the interior. Here they mingled with Semitic types, and after a lapse of millenniums there arose from this mingling the culture of Ethiopia and Egypt, probably the first of higher human cultures.[8]

By now Du Bois had arrived at a position similar to, if differently nuanced from, that which was promulgated by the nineteenth-century French racial theorist Joseph-Arthur de Gobineau, and which tied Egypt to the rest of the continent of Africa, through the mingling and mulaticization of Ancient Nilotic peoples. Gobineau has correctly been called a racist, but, irony of ironies, he occasionally endorsed racial amalgamation. As a devout Roman Catholic, he accepted the Christian doctrine that all humans were children of Adam and Eve, and the biblical proclamation of Acts 17:26 that God "hath made of one blood all nations of men."[9] Displaying a remarkable consistency, he thus rejected the "scientifically" fashionable theory of "polygenesis" which claimed that blacks and whites were different species.

In his *Essai sur l'inégalité des races humaines* (1853–5), Gobineau had pontificated that ancient kingdoms of the Nile and the Tigris-Euphrates, owed the creativity of their civilizations to the mingling of white and black "bloods." In *The Negro* Du Bois attributed to "the whole of Africa a distinct mulatto character. The primitive Negro stock was mulatto" (13). His purpose was to attack the idea that there was any such thing as a "true Negro," an idea that had been resisted by previous black authors, including Frederick Douglass. He was seeking to undermine the so-called Hamitic hypothesis: "Negro blood certainly appears in strong strain among the Semites, and the obvious mulatto groups in Africa, arising from ancient and modern mingling of Semitic and Negro, has given rise to the term 'Hamite,' under cover of which millions of Negroids have been characteristically transferred to the 'white' race by some eager scientists" (*The Negro* 9). Seemingly unaware, he sustained the theory of Gobineau that the cradles of civilization owed their artistic dynamism to the presence of the African or "Negroid" type, and that mulattoes had played an essential role in developing the ancient Egyptian civilization.

Gobineau had written, in Book II, chapter VII of his incoherent and rambling work, *Sur l'inegalite des races*: "Les arts et la poésie lyrique sont produits par le mélange des blancs avec les peuples noirs" (Art and lyric poetry are produced by the mixture of whites with the black peoples).[10] Du Bois was susceptible to this idea, for while categorically rejecting Gobineau's main thesis that black Africans were intellectually inferior, he accepted the idea that the children of Ethiopia had special gifts for "stories and songs." Consciously or unconsciously, in his early work he either paralleled or replicated Gobineau's mulatto/Hamitic hypothesis although to different ends. The raciological theories of both men were as empirically unfounded and logically inconsistent, as any other attempt to formulate a "scientific" theory of race. On the other hand, Du Bois and Gobineau agreed that Africans were neither an evolutionary dead-end, nor a threat to human progress, but that black people had been a vital force in the history of human progress (*The Negro* 30–46).

Nonetheless, regardless of how important the African presence might have been in the cradles of civilization, the question of the hour was what role black folk were to play in modern times. The question had been raised in the nineteenth century by Martin Delany, a Pan-Africanist, who toured both Africa and the American slave states, and who formulated a theory of African Redemption. Along with Henry Highland Garnet, it was Delany who had established the African Civilization Society, and begun using the term "African Movement." When Sylvester Williams, a Trinidad barrister, and Alexander Walters, a Methodist Bishop, called for a Pan-African Congress in London in 1900, and Du Bois joined them, they were revitalizing an extant tradition.

As Chairman of the Committee on Address at the Congress, Du Bois was responsible for the *Report of the Pan-African Conference*, which terminated with an appeal to "the Great Powers of the civilized world, trusting in the wide spirit of humanity, and the deep sense of justice of our age, for a generous recognition of the righteousness of our cause."[11] This statement reiterated themes that had dominated the ideology of the African movement during the preceding century, but the London rhetoric was far less militant than that of nineteenth-century black nationalists, like Garnet and Delany, who had admonished African peoples to self assertion.[12] The *Report* was, by contrast, an appeal to the colonial powers asking for greater fairness to the darker races, and calling on black folk "to prove to the world their incontestable right to be included among the brotherhood of man." Du Bois and the London delegates, whatever militant or revolutionary ideals they may have mulled in smoke-filled rooms, issued a relatively mild manifesto. They invoked the "Prince of Peace," and called on the "Nations of the world" to give to "Negroes and other dark men the largest and broadest opportunity for education and self-development."

The rhetoric was, in fact, similar to that developed by Booker T. Washington, who had famously argued at the Atlanta Exposition of 1895, that it was in the self-interest of the white Americans to uplift the black race. Hardly beyond the range of Washington's awareness, an African conference was also held at the Atlanta Exposition, which was twice addressed by Crummell on the subject of civilization and uplift. In 1912 Washington called an International Congress on the Negro at his Tuskegee Institute, which entertained at least two crusading nationalists, Casely Hayford of the Gold Coast and Bishop Henry McNeal Turner, the emigrationist firebrand, among its speakers. The Tuskegee conference, like the Atlanta Conference, was largely attended by whites, and centered on missionary and educational concerns. It could not be characterized as an expression of revolutionary nationalism, although on other occasions Tuskegee issued strong condemnations of both British and Belgian colonial abuses.[13]

Du Bois's Pan-African conferences also coincided with Marcus Garvey's rival Pan-African movement which held its annual meetings in New York. Garvey was a genius at media manipulation, with a conception of African redemption that was on some levels pragmatic and realistic. Garvey advocated a program of geopolitical separatism, but his cultural program was a throwback to Victorianism and the bourgeois, Christianizing, and assimilationist program of Alexander Crummell. The Jamaica-born activist described his goals as follows: "The Universal Negro Improvement Association is an organization among Negroes that is seeking to improve the condition of the race, with a view of establishing a nation in Africa where Negroes will be given the opportunity to develop by themselves..."[14] Garvey's often misrepresented and ridiculed project included a plan to take a contingent of New World Negroes to Africa. Thus his movement was easily dismissed as a harebrained scheme to expatriate all African Americans. Garvey denied that his movement was a simple back-to-Africa scheme, but on the other hand, in his attempts to gain the favor of American segregationists, he allowed himself to be interpreted in such a way as to indicate that he had abandoned all claims of African Americans to the rights of American citizenship.

Du Bois did not immediately oppose Garvey, recognizing that their commitments to African independence, to black economic power, and to a heroic interpretation of African history were similar. Nonetheless a conflict between two men with such powerful egos and theatrical temperaments was inevitable, as each desired to claim the Pan-African movement as his own invention. Du Bois correctly observed that Garvey's financial operations were not only recklessly ambitious, but dangerously mismanaged. He was not surprised that Garvey left himself open to trumped-up charges of mail fraud, which led to his imprisonment in 1925. Nonetheless, when Garvey's sentence was commuted two years later, Du Bois wrote, "He has a great and worthy dream. We wish him well. He is free; he has a following; he still has a chance to carry on his work in his own home and among his own people."[15]

One element that Garvey and Du Bois had in common with major African intellectuals was their understanding that World War I was inseparable from the European struggle over African colonies. Du Bois's article on "The African Roots of War," which appeared in *Atlantic Monthly* in May 1915, at the beginning of the war, when black troops were already involved in the usurpation of German colonies for the French and British empires, was a brilliant, if not unique analysis. If *The Negro* was an exercise in cultural Afrocentrism, "The African Roots of War" represented Afrocentrism in the most political sense of the term. Du Bois certainly made the case for the Afrocentric perspective, demonstrating the centrality of Africa to modern politics and economics. Well aware that Germany had been engaged in the struggle for status as a colonial power since the Berlin Conference of 1884, Du Bois recognized that the delegations of Congo to Belgium and of Southwest Africa to Germany were signs of Germany's desire for a status comparable to that of the other European world powers.

Germany's complicated relationship to Belgium culminating in the invasion of Belgium and the appropriation of its African colonies did not go unnoticed by Du Bois as a root cause of World War I. Despite his intellectual appreciation for German social science and his emotional affinity for German romanticism, he believed that German ambitions in Africa were more dangerous than those of Britain and France. This at least partially explains his appeals in *Crisis* to "close ranks," in the struggle against Germany.[16] Du Bois, in any case, became a fervent supporter of the war against Germany and linked this support with the idea of African independence. As were other African Americans, Du Bois was disappointed with the Paris Peace Conference and with the mandates system after the war, by which the former colonies of imperial Germany and the Ottoman Empire were not appropriated by the victor nations, but placed under an international administration overseen by the League of Nations. He issued a *Manifesto to the League of Nations* (Geneva, September 15, 1921) calling for a black representative to be appointed to the Mandates Commission. Although he was disappointed that the Commission continued to be made up entirely of Europeans, he did not contest the view that it was a distinct improvement over the colonial system.[17]

Building on the foundation of the London Conference of 1900, Du Bois organized a series of Pan-African Congresses in 1919, 1922, 1923, and 1925. His evaluation of post-war colonialism appeared in his essay, "Worlds of Color," published in *Foreign Affairs* (1925), and revised for inclusion in Alain Locke's *The New Negro* that same year. During the 1920s, certain contradictions in his position became glaringly evident. Du Bois was not certain whether he wished to confine himself to Pan-Africanism, or to support a much larger international movement, such as that represented by the Universal Races Congress of 1911, and celebrated in his novel *Dark Princess* (1928). Furthermore, his travels in Liberia in 1924, as American "Envoy Extraordinary and Minister Plenipotentary," and his, at that time, largely unknown dealings with the ruthless rubber baron Harvey Firestone, represented an accomodation to neocolonialism as Garvey balefully observed.

Du Bois centered his post-war appraisal of world history with his statement, "the problem of the twentieth century is the problem of the color line," an idea he had stubbornly insisted on since 1900, and was to repeat at various times in later years.[18] He understandably viewed the world in terms of the line of racial separation that existed in his own country, and of a color-line that encircled the world. Equally understandably, he viewed American segregation as part of a larger pattern of white supremacy in which European countries ruled darker peoples in Africa and Asia, without acknowledging any right to their participation in their own governance. The defeat of the Italian army at Adowa had offered a ray of hope for the darker races. Ethiopia remained independent, and Haiti, marginally so. By and large, however, with the exception of Japan, there was no nation of non-white people that commanded any respect from white people at all.

Du Bois's romantic conception of African civilization developed within the context of larger trends in Western thought. In the early years of the twentieth century, and increasingly after World War I, Western authors began to write of the failings of modern civilization. One of the first was Booker T. Washington's disciple, Robert E. Park, who famously drew a distinction between "culture," which he regarded as healthy and "civilization," which he regarded as decadent. After the war, the contrast between culture as positive and civilization as negative was most famously articulated in Oswald Spengler's influential *Der Untergang des Abendlandes* (1918–22), a title that is feebly mistranslated as *The Decline of the West*. Marcus Garvey contributed brilliantly to the discourse when he wrote, "We see a small percentage of the world's populace feeling happy and contented with this civilization that man has evolved and we see the masses of the human race on the other hand dissatisfied and discontented with the civilization of today."[19] Six years later, the title of Sigmund Freud's work *Das Unbehagen in der Kultur*, was inaccurately translated into English as *Civilization and its Discontents*.

Du Bois's essay, "What is Civilization? Africa's Answer" (1925) thus presented a conventional answer to what had become a conventional question. It echoed ideas presented in the Columbia University commencement address of Pixley Isaka Ka Seme (1906), sometimes quoted by Monroe Work, William H. Ferris, and other black intellectuals. Seme had recycled the views, and even the words, of the German scholar Leo Frobenius, whom Du Bois prominently footnoted in *The Negro*. It was with echoes of Gobineau and Frobenius that Du Bois wrote: "Three things Africa has given to the world, and they form the essence of African culture: Beginnings; the village unit; and Art in sculpture and music."[20]

Black Folk Then and Now (1939) was Du Bois's second book-length attempt to integrate the various problems of African history and current Pan-Africanism. It assumed a much more confident approach to the problem of race in ancient Egypt, on which he had postponed judgment in "The Conservation of Races." It included much material from its predecessor *The Negro*, but it was something more than a new edition. Du Bois was somewhat more systematic in his citations of works by earlier authors, including Melville Herskovits, Constantin Volney, Crummell, and Gobineau than he had been before. It is nonetheless difficult to tell from the scanty indexes, incomplete bibliographies, and sparse footnotes, exactly what Du Bois had read in the intervening quarter century, and how it had influenced him. Like its predecessor *Black Folk Then and Now* united the various worlds of Africa and the diaspora. The chapter on "Black Europe" was disappointing, for it did not really address the history of black people in Europe, as its title might have suggested, but rather Europe's colonial shadow in Africa. The history of Europeanized Africans was, of course among Du Bois's interests, as evidenced by the essay on the composer Samuel Coleridge-Taylor that had appeared earlier in *Darkwater* (1920). Unfortunately, however, very little was said about the significant African presence in contemporary Europe. Furthermore, with typical arrogance,

Du Bois failed to acknowledge the provenance of Afrocentric concepts in such African American forerunners as Douglass, Delany, and William Wells Brown. His neglect of the tradition in which *Black Folk Then and Now* was founded led to serious lapses in content and interpretation. Acknowledging the sturdy shoulders on which he stood would have strengthened Du Bois's position as a student of Pan-African thought, and strengthened his thesis respecting the cultural and intellectual endowments of African thinkers.

In the years immediately following the defeat of the Axis powers, African and Asian leaders, joined by New World black activists, were quick to point out the failures of the League of Nations and the contradictions of the Mandates system. After World War II, Du Bois published numerous works highlighting these obvious contradictions, most notably *Color and Democracy* (1945) and *The World and Africa* (1947). The United States, England, and France had rightly expressed their moral outrage at Nazi ambitions in Europe, while blandly tolerating the European domination of Africa and India by supposedly democratic powers. The Pan-African Conference, convened in Manchester in 1945 with Du Bois's active participation was an expression of the universal awareness of the hypocrisy represented by the democratic and egalitarian rhetoric of the victorious powers and their continuing domination over large portions of Asia and Africa.

The World and Africa was an attempt to synthesize Afrocentric experience. Du Bois still viewed the world in terms of color. But some of the walls seemed to be tumbling down, and he noted laconically, that several African American scientists had contributed to the development of the atomic bomb.[21] It is remarkable that he did not comment on the situational irony embedded within this statement. The involvement of black scientists in military research symbolized in a chilling context the blurring of the color line as "the problem of the twentieth century." The Frankenstein technology unleashed at Hiroshima seemed to forebode a final solution to all human problems.

The problem of colonialism that dominated so much of Du Bois's writing on Africa, as well the problem of American segregation has assumed newer and more subtle forms today, without replacing the older and more blatant ones. The overt preachment of black inferiority no longer seems to be either fashionable or necessary to the maintenance of white supremacy. The current balance of power in world economies seems to have little to do with Du Bois's predictions of progressive developments or realignments in *The World and Africa*. The rise of China in the world economy of the twentieth century seems to be firmly under the control of a party that is nominally communist, but dedicated to the interests of a nationalistic capitalistic elite.

But Du Bois's posthumous *Autobiography* (1968) and *The World and Africa* could hardly have anticipated these developments. With faith in a coming world revolution, he applied for membership in the Communist Party of the United States in 1961; then, at President Kwame Nkrumah's invitation, he took up residency in Ghana, where he believed: "socialism blossoms bold on Communism centuries old."[22] In his *Autobiography* he presented a view of Nkrumah's Ghana as representing the vanguard of a Pan-Africanism in league with China and the Soviet Union. But such a vision was becoming outmoded as the rift between China and the Soviet Union developed. The belief in an ancient African socialism represented the culmination of the idea that he had once referred to as "Pan-Negroism," the idea that the heritage and goals of black people transcended geographical limits. Du Bois's thinking on Africa was, however, significant in one undeniable respect: his appreciation of the role of Africa in history. In this regard his intellectual development was consistent and impressive. His message was not limited to sentimentalism regarding the African past, but represented a sophisticated appraisal of the importance of Africa to recent and contemporary world politics and economics. "Afrocentrism" is what we call this perspective today, and Du Bois was the originator of that term.[23]

In summary we may say that Du Bois entertained varying conceptions of Africa, Pan-Africanism, and Afrocentrism throughout his career. In earlier writings, such as "The Conservation of Races," he was tentative in his pronouncements concerning the African origins of civilization. By 1915 he entertained with increasing conviction a belief in the black African origins of Nilotic civilization. By the time *The Negro* had undergone its final revision as *The World and Africa*, he was vigorously asserting an Afrocentric conception of history and asserting the centrality of Africa to the past and to the future of the world. Such a global perspective was evident as early as 1896 when his dissertation explored the implications of the Haitian Revolt not only for African peoples but for the rest of the world.

Du Bois, like Garvey, heroically attempted to achieve a variety of cultural nationalism in connection with Africa, but the monumental version of African history and culture to which they aspired was "civilizationist." Like their predecessors in the movement, notably Blyden and Crummell, they tended to conceive Africa's worth in terms of its relationship to Western symbols of civilization, such as city building, architectural monuments, written languages, and those regions of Africa associated with such accomplishments. Thus, while Du Bois sincerely celebrated a *cultural* Afrocentrism, as represented in traditional village life, he seemed even more obsessed with a *civilizationist* Afrocentrism, represented by ancient Egypt and Ethiopia. Du Bois's appreciation of African culture, at least paid lip service to the West African Village, which he called "a perfect human thing." Influenced by Frobenius, Herskovits, and other modern anthropologists, Du Bois paid occasional homage to African village life, which he championed in such works as "The Negro Church" (1903) and "The Negro Family" (1907).

In 1911 Casely Hayford wrote in appraisal of *The Souls of Black Folk*: "It is apparent that Mr. Du Bois writes from an American standpoint, surrounded by an American atmosphere. And, of course, it is not his fault, for he knows no other."[24] Although Hayford was not entirely immune to accusations of Eurocentrism, there was some truth in his critique. Eventually, however, his appraisal became inadequate, if not completely incorrect, for shortly after publishing *The Souls of Black Folk*, Du Bois took the first steps to inventing an Afrocentrism in the broadest cultural, economic, and political sense. He eventually visited Africa, interacted vigorously with Africans, and died there in 1963. By the time of his last Pan-African Conference, which he addressed through his wife Shirley Graham, he had established his position within the international ranks of Pan-Africanism.[25] He abandoned, as Crummell had, the idea that African Americans could or should serve the role of civilizing missionaries. Thus with the publication of his *Autobiography*, he made clear that he no longer considered African Americans to have a significant role in Pan-African leadership.

As late as the Manchester Conference of 1945, Du Bois clearly viewed Pan-Africanism as an international connection among the peoples of the African diaspora. By the end of his life, however, he warned Africans against trusting Americans who sought to exploit sentimental ties for economic profit. He saw no future for a capitalism-based Pan-African unity. Inspired by apparent ties between Nkrumah's Ghana and Mao's China, he hoped to see a politically united Africa. This was a view that was not destined to fulfillment as the course of world events led to a transmogrification of the communism on which he placed his dying hopes. As the herald of communistic Pan-Africanism, his fate was to "continue in the direction of that promise which, like the horizon, recedes ever brightly and distantly beyond the hopeful traveller."[26]

Notes

1. W. E. B. Du Bois, *The Suppression of the African Slave-Trade to the United States of America, 1638–1870* (1896), in W. E. B. Du Bois, *Writings*, ed. N. Huggins (New York: Library of America, 1986), p. 74.
2. W. E. B. Du Bois, "The Conservation of the Races" (1897), in *Writings*, ed. Huggins, p. 820. Crummell's two Atlanta Exposition addresses are "Civilization a Collateral and Indispensable Instrumentality in Planting the Church in Africa"

and "The Absolute Need of an Indigenous Missionary Agency for Evangelization of Africa," republished in *Destiny and Race: Sermons and Addresses by Alexander Crummell, 1840–1898*, ed. W. J. Moses (Amherst: University of Massachusetts Press, 1992), pp. 269–88.

3. Du Bois, "Conservation of Races," p. 822.

4. Crummell, "The Destined Superiority of the Negro," in *Destiny and Race*, ed. Moses, pp. 194–206.

5. Du Bois, "Conservation of Races," pp. 819–20.

6. W. E. B. Du Bois, *The Souls of Black Folk* (1903), in *Writings*, ed. Huggins, p. 364.

7. J. E. Casely Hayford, *Ethiopia Unbound: Studies in Race Emancipation* (London: Phillips, 1911), p. 181.

8. W. E. B. Du Bois, *The Negro* (1915; New York: Oxford University Press, 1970), p. 13. Hereafter cited in the text as *The Negro*.

9. Du Bois, adapted this passage in his own "Credo" of 1904 and worded somewhat differently again in 1919: the latter reads: "I believe in God, was made of one blood, all nations that on earth do dwell" (*Darkwater: Voices from within the Veil* [New York: Harcourt, Brace and Howe, 1920], p. 3).

10. Arthur de Gobineau, *Essai sur l'inégalité des races humaines*, presentation de Hubert Juin (Paris: Editions Pierre Belford, 1967), Book 2, Ch. 7.

11. *Report of the Pan-African Conference, London, England* (1900), reprinted in *W. E. B. Du Bois: A Reader*, ed. D. L. Lewis (New York: Henry Holt, 1995). pp. 639–41. Also see Tony Martin's very useful work, *The Pan-African Connection: From Slavery to Garvey and Beyond* (Dover, MA: Majority Press, 1984).

12. *Report of the Pan-African Conference*, 640. Delany issued the call "Africa for the African race, and black men to rule them" in his *Official Report of the Niger Valley Exploring Party* (1861); reprinted in *Search for a Place: Black Separatism and Africa, 1860*, ed. H. H. Bell (Ann Arbor: University of Michigan Press, 1971), p. 121. Garnet was the author of *The Past and Present Condition, and the Destiny of the Colored Race* (1848) and of the militant David Walker's *Appeal in Four Articles; Together with a Preamble, to the Colored Citizens of the World, but in Particular, and Very Especially, to those of the United States of America* (1849).

13. For Washington's complicated and evolving attitudes respecting Africa, see V. Williams, *Rethinking Race: Franz Boas and his Contemporaries*, (Lexington: University Press of Kentucky, 1996), pp. 54–72.

14. Marcus Garvey, "Aims and Objectives of Movement for Solution of Negro Problems," in Garvey, *Philosophy and Opinions of Marcus Garvey*, ed. Amy Jacques-Garvey (London: Routledge, 1967), p. 37.

15. W. E. B. Du Bois, "Marcus Garvey," *Crisis* (December 1920, January 1921), in *Writings*, ed. Huggins, pp. 969–79. D. L. Lewis also discusses the rivalry between Du Bois's and Garvey's conferences and activities in *W. E. B. Du Bois: The Fight for Equality and the American Century 1919–1963* (New York: Henry Holt, 2000), pp. 37–84.

16. See, e.g., W. E. B. Du Bois, "Reconstruction and Africa" (1919), in *Writings*, ed. Huggins, pp. 1178–9.

17. See W. E. B. Du Bois, *Color and Democracy* (New York: Harcourt Brace, 1945).

18. Du Bois used the phrase "The Problem of the Twentieth Century is the Problem of the color-line," many times, e.g., in "To the Nations of the World," his address to the London Conference of 1900; reprinted in *The Oxford W. E. B. Du Bois Reader*, ed. E. J. Sundquist (New York: Oxford University Press, 1996), p. 625. He repeated the phrase at the beginning of chapter 2 of *The Souls of Black Folk*. He later published an article called "The Color Line Belts the World," *Colliers* (October 2, 1906); reprinted in *Du Bois: A Reader*, ed. Lewis, p. 42. After its inclusion in "Worlds of Color" and "The Negro Mind Reaches Out," he recycled it again in *Black Folk Then and Now* (1939).

19. Garvey, *Philosophy and Opinions*, p. 31.

20. W. E. B. Du Bois, "What is Civilization? Africa's Answer," in *Oxford Du Bois Reader*, ed. Sundquist, pp. 647–53.

21. W. E. B. Du Bois, *The World and Africa* (New York: Viking, 1946), p. 260.

22. See Du Bois's poem "Ghana Calls," *Freedomways* (First Quarter 1965), p. 100.

23. Du Bois employed "Afrocentrism," at least as early as 1962, in his "Provisional Draft: Not for General Distribution: Proposed Plans for an Encyclopedia Africana." The document is filed with Du Bois's letter to Daniel Walden, dated September 21, 1961, which Professor Walden generously donated to the Rare Books Room Pennsylvania State University, a fact brought to my attention by Professor Derek Alridge. The *Encyclopedia* was conceived by Du Bois as "unashamedly Afro-Centric, but not indifferent to the impact of the outside world upon Africa or to the impact of Africa upon the outside world." The term was used in the *Information Reports* issued by the Secretariat for an *Encyclopedia Africana* in Accra, Ghana (1962), under the Directorship of Du Bois. I thank the distinguished Africanist Adelaide Cromwell for bringing the document to my attention.

24. Casely Hayford, *Ethiopia Unbound*, p. 182.

25. The speech is reproduced in W. E. B. Du Bois, *The Autobiography of W. E. B. Du Bois: A Soliloquy on Viewing My Life from the Last Decade of its First Century*, ed. H. Aptheker (New York: International Publishers, 1968), pp. 405–8.

26. The prophetic quotation is from Dr. A. Herbert Bledsoe's letter to Mr. Emerson in Ralph Ellison's *Invisible Man* (New York: Signet, 1952), p. 168.

9

RICHARD H. KING

The Place of W. E. B. Du Bois in American and European Intellectual history

A protean figure such as W. E. B. Du Bois is difficult to place according to almost any criterion one can think of. Having been advised by his Harvard mentor William James to avoid philosophy because one could not make a living at it, Du Bois still felt the need to apply what he had learned as a student of philosophy to social problems.[1] Knowledge without application, theory without practice or policy implications, or, for that matter, art for art's sake made no sense to him. In this, he was clearly in the American grain, expressed in the overlap of pragmatic and Enlightenment traditions of thought, particularly of the progressive variety. Yet, Du Bois became less sanguine about the efficacy of knowledge in correcting social ills over the years. Not all prejudice responded to greater enlightenment. In this respect, he knew what Michel Foucault later emphasized – the inseparability of knowledge and power.

Because of his protean intellectual engagements, Du Bois is a rich but difficult subject for the intellectual historian. His extensive political journalism as editor of *Crisis* might be seen as a waste of his (intellectual) time, but it was a way for him to remain engaged with the everyday life of African Americans and their problems. His efforts on behalf, for instance, of Pan-Africanism and much of his writing about Africa lacked the intellectual complexity of first-rate philosophical or historical work. He was one of the "producer-directors" of the Harlem Renaissance in the 1920s rather than one of its major creative spirits. Not quite "theoretical" enough to be classified a social and cultural theorist, his work as an historian ranged from the iconoclastic to special pleading, while his literary style could be florid and unmodified by irony or self-criticism. Yet Du Bois was perhaps the best judge of how best to use his talents, and in the long run he may have done what was best for them.

Du Bois as Founder/Originator

As a way of establishing Du Bois's position in the intellectual history of Europe and America, it might be well to reflect on his position as an

African American thinker, a necessary starting point for his more cosmopolitan efforts. His reputation has waxed and waned over the years, but since the 1960s he has assumed the position of something like the "founding father" or, in less gendered terms, the "founder" of African American thought. This is not to say that Du Bois was the first African American to think about African American identity, to reflect on the scientific, moral, and philosophical dimensions of race and culture, or to turn his or her hand to fiction, poetry, or *belles lettres* about the African American experience. A sense of history as "providential" and black Americans as a "redeemer race" were common motifs in nineteenth-century African American thought. As Du Bois so clearly demonstrated in his own life, "romantic racialism" could appeal to subject as well as to dominant races.[2] All this reflected the African American effort to figure out how the historical experience endured by people of African descent could be understood and justified. Nor was Du Bois the first to note the enormous musical and spiritual power of the "Negro spirituals" or what he called the "sorrow songs" in *Souls*.[3] The point overall is that the African American world he spent his life trying to understand was culturally rich, if economically impoverished, and presented surprisingly rich intellectual opportunities.

Du Bois's special "founding" status can be seen in the way his own thinking encompassed most of the intellectual, literary, and cultural concerns preceding him and, in turn, established the intellectual and "spiritual" agenda for those who came after him. He was, and is, in Harold Bloom's terms, the "great poet" of the African American tradition, a unique composite of the visionary and the practical.[4] Alain Locke's introduction to *The New Negro* (1925) is perhaps the African American counterpart of Emerson's "American Scholar" address,[5] but Du Bois remains the great "precursor," against whom all African American thinkers and writers must measure themselves. In fact, Du Bois's thesis of black double-consciousness offers a more complex understanding of black American cultural identity than ones advocating simple rejection of, or untroubled assimilation into, the dominant white society. It recognized the ways that black and white Americans were linked, as well as separated, by more than conscious choice on either side.

To show the way Du Bois played this mediating and creative intellectual role, consider his view of history. He had one of the best educations of any American of the second half of the nineteenth century and developed a vision of history that drew both on the New World experience of people of African descent and upon European traditions of historical thinking. Clearly shaped by German history and thought, Du Bois reflected the nineteenth-century proclivity for thinking that history was imbued with a meaning or *telos*. For most of his life, he held to the view that what moved individuals and nations was "race" rather than economic desire or structures of production and consumption. All history is the history of racial conflict and progress. During the first third of his life, race was just coming into focus as a "scientific" concept, but still trailed meanings associated with "nation" or "ethnic group" or "people" as well as a group linked by common biological descent and sharing inherited characteristics. Clearly Hegel and Herder, as well as the emerging racial science of the late nineteenth century and even African concepts, suffuse Du Bois's own thinking about "folk" (*Volk*) and "soul" (*Geist, Seele*).[6] According to this view, every race had its own special talent or virtues which determined its crucial contribution to human perfection. Only at the end of history would race no longer be an important factor in individual or group self-consciousness. From this perspective, Du Bois was a typically optimistic, nineteenth-century Victorian with a rather benign view of the place of race in human history.

At the same time, his race-based vision of history had a hard-headed, realistic, and prospective cast, as reflected in his oft-cited dictum: "the problem of the twentieth century is the problem of the colour-line."[7] This was the key working hypothesis of Du Bois's history of the future and it proved to be remarkably prescient, if one takes "color" to signify race, ethnicity, and other inherited group characteristics. The venue where he first made this prophetic pronouncement – the Pan-African Conference in London in 1900 – also reflected the international (rather than just African American) context in which Du Bois increasingly worked from the late nineteenth century onwards. Thus his philosophy of history was forged on native grounds and with homegrown materials, drew upon European thought, and eventually was aimed at linking African Americans to their homeland, Africa.

Another example of Du Bois's ability to encompass a variety of different traditions can be seen in the sources of his most seminal idea – "double-consciousness" (or sense of "twoness"). Until fairly recently, most scholars of the subject have assumed that this concept derived from Ralph Waldo Emerson's thought, specifically the essay "The Transcendentalist" where he contrasts our concern for the mundane world with the spiritual dimension of existence. Another source was late-nineteenth-century psychiatry dealing with double or multiple centers of consciousness in certain individuals. William James also used the term, and placed the contrasting types of "healthy" and "sick" souls and "once" and "twice-born" individuals at the center of his psychology of religion. Indeed, the strong influence of Jamesian pragmatism on Du Bois has been one of the basic assumptions of Du Bois studies.[8]

However, in the first half of the 1990s, several intellectual historians challenged the explanation of double-consciousness. Shamoon Zamir contended that Du Bois's concept hardly fit very well with the high individualism of the New England tradition; nor did Emersonian double-consciousness have a dynamic social dimension to it. Zamir went on to suggest that Du Bois's influences "derived mainly from European and Euro-American intellectual traditions," specifically Hegel's dialectic analysis of the master-slave relationship. On this reading, Du Bois's concept of consciousness was of greater internal complexity and external dynamism than either Emerson's or James's. At roughly the same time, Richard C. Rath looked to Du Bois's increasing interest in Africa and Africans to illuminate key concerns such as "soul" and "veil" and the importance of African American music: a "pantheistic Afrocentric frame allowed him [Du Bois] to recombine and redefine elements of Euro-American philosophy." The African perspective allowed "black folk" to "maintain awareness of both simultaneously."[9] Overall, both Rath and Zamir found a much richer concept of the self in Du Bois than was suggested by the Emerson–James tradition of individualism, a point to which we will return later.

The point in locating the influences on Du Bois's concept of the African American "self" is to demonstrate the way intellectual historians have of contextualizing their subjects by unearthing, in archaeological fashion, the various traditions that have gone to make up a concept or an idea, in this case, the African American self. But no one of these sources alone nor all of them taken together in an additive fashion can explain Du Bois's concept of double-consciousness. Rather, the "genius" of Du Bois was to take one aspect of Hegel but not the philosophy of history or the absolute idealism. He was undoubtedly shaped by the New England tradition, but did not buy into its individualistic orientation; and while Africa supplied an enriching element to his central concerns, he knew that American Negroes *also* lived in the modern West. In sum, Du Bois created something, not out of whole cloth or purely from his own intuition and experience, but by reconfiguring various sources and his own experience in new ways. In short, he worked with the materials at hand.

Overall, tracing the genealogy of Du Bois's grand narrative of history or the origins of double-consciousness makes the point that no group's traditions are ever purely original or autonomous. Emerson's own declaration of cultural independence was deeply indebted to the philosophical and conceptual resources of German idealism and European and English romanticism. Similarly Du Bois, from his origins in New England, his experience in the South at Fisk in Nashville, his time at Harvard, his two years in Germany, and his increasing intellectual and political interest in Africa, *became* an original rather than being born one. He was first among equals in turning toward Africa in the 1910s and 1920s, while his work suggested that African American folk culture traced some of its elements back to Africa. This is not to suggest that all those who come after an "original" such as Du Bois agree with him. Rather, the initiator of a tradition serves as a standard point of reference, sometimes evoked ritualistically so as to guarantee one's pedigree and sometimes attacked with vehemence. Overall, intellectual and cultural originals provoke the strongest "counter statements" to use Albert Murray's phrase.[10]

The Du Boisian Presence

The ups and downs of Du Bois's reputation into the 1970s is frankly a surprise. Here it should be said that Du Bois has been pretty much neglected by (white) intellectual historians – as opposed to literary historians. He occasionally was mentioned in the context of the (by now overanalyzed) debate with Booker T. Washington, while his idea of the Talented Tenth and the concept of double-consciousness were referred to in passing.[11] One surprising exception to the general white neglect is Robert Penn Warren's *Who Speaks for the Negro?* (1964). In that collection of interviews and commentary, Warren returns repeatedly to the question about "splits in identity" and a "psychic split" among African Americans, thus demonstrating, by implication, the great pertinence Du Bois's ideas had in the emerging civil rights movement and black consciousness.[12] Yet, only since the late 1990s has a place been made for Du Bois and the black philosopher Alain Locke in the intellectual culture of pragmatism, primarily in connection with the idea of cultural pluralism.

But for African Americans, Du Bois has been "the man" for as long as most can remember, even when they disagreed with him – which has been quite often. Disagreements might have to do with political and aesthetic differences, arising from class, regional, and generational experiences, not to mention the power struggles within the black intellectual and cultural elite. As editor of the *Crisis*, Du Bois had a powerful mouthpiece for defending his ideas, but his was by no means the final word among the "New Negroes." His aesthetic views were conventionally Victorian. Art should be aimed at perpetuation of truth and beauty. Beyond that, art should have an explicit moral and, come to that, a political purpose. "All art is propaganda," he insisted in the mid-1920s, "and ever must be, despite the wailing of the purists."[13] Whether the idea of "double-consciousness" was the defining attribute of diasporic modernity, as Paul Gilroy has suggested in *The Black Atlantic* (1993), Du Bois was resolutely anti-modernist in his rejection of the autonomy of art and/or the artist, and his discomfort with transgressive themes and artistic experimentation was palpable. Thus he ran into strong opposition from the modernists among the Harlem Renaissance writers, such as Wallace Thurman or Zora Neale Hurston. Nor did Du Bois ever really "get" jazz or the blues. He was neither a devotee of the avant-garde nor a populist-folklorist either, though much in his work gave encouragement to exploration of the "souls" of black folk. That said, Du Bois encouraged new departures in African American visual culture by commissioning innovative graphics and illustrations in *Crisis*. He was largely responsible for painter Aaron Douglas's rise to prominence with his highly stylized, even "abstract" depiction of Africa and African Americans, a mode of representation far from conventional aesthetic realism, though it reflected a commitment to the uplift message Du Bois thought essential to African American art.

With the next generation of African American intellectuals, artists, and writers – Richard Wright (b. 1908), Romare Bearden (1911/12), Ralph Ellison (1914), Albert Murray (1916), and Harold Cruse (1916) – Du Bois assumed a somewhat different status. Though all of these figures lived in New York at one time or another, none was identified with the Renaissance nor with the so-called Talented Tenth as such, except perhaps for Bearden, who grew up and worked in Harlem as a social worker. Each was from the South and, except for Cruse, thematized the South (or Southwest in Ellison's case) in his work. The result was sometimes a kind of (black) southern "down home" pastoral ideal in sophisticated artistic form.[14] They wrote about or painted the "folk" from the inside and were acquainted both with rural and small-town life and big-city existence. Yet they also held to the most sophisticated of modernist assumptions and were influenced as much by white European as by black American artists. With the partial exception of Bearden, none was particularly interested in Africa as an inspiration or a source of images and themes. If anything united them, it was the experience of the Great Migration, a cultural, as well as geographical, transition from traditional folk life to the urban modernist experience. Like Du Bois, they placed music at the center of black creativity, but rather than the sorrow songs, the African American equivalent of the classical European "art song," they championed pre-1945 jazz, especially Armstrong and Ellington, and the blues.

But Du Bois seemed out of reach to them. According to Bearden, Du Bois was someone "everybody revered" but "he was hard to approach."[15] Of the group, Cruse was most powerfully drawn to the proto-nationalist-communalist of *Dusk of Dawn*, rather than the theorist of black subjectivity in *Souls*. Du Bois in particular was a shaping force in Cruse's late work *Plural but Equal* (1987), but in *The Crisis of the Negro Intellectual* (1967), he praised Du Bois's attempt to develop a specifically black cultural vision and philosophy and remarked on the way his ideas, as they developed in a complex three-cornered dialectic with those of Washington and Garvey, were still being debated.[16] Clearly, Du Bois was of direct political rather than only scholarly interest to Cruse Yet, two of the main objects of Cruse's wrath in *The Crisis of the Negro Intellectuals* were the Talented Tenth and the black Communist intellectuals, the former being the group whom Du Bois had picked out for leadership and the latter with whom Du Bois had come to identify in the last decade of his life.

If Du Bois had an alter ego among twentieth-century black intellectuals, it would be Richard Wright. Du Bois was a black New England Brahmin and *soi-disant aristo* – if not in social standing at least in his cultural preference and attitude – while Wright was Mississippi-born, impoverished, and without significant formal education. There was little love lost between the two. Wright was distinctly uncomfortable with the bourgeois high-mindedness of the Talented Tenth; nor did he later have any time for Du Bois's fellow-traveling apologetics for Stalin's Soviet Union or share Du Bois's visceral sense of kinship with Africa or with Pan-Africanism as a movement. Yet as a result of his trip to the Gold Coast in the mid-1950s and his support for decolonization, Wright also developed an international "take" on double-consciousness in which black American were caught between being Americans and having their roots in Africa, between being moderns and searching for traditional roots. While Du Bois theorized the notion of "doubleness," Wright's fictional characters, whether peasants or intellectuals, lived it out in their lives.[17]

Murray and Ellison seem to have had rather distant, if respectful, relationships to Du Bois. Significantly, there are no references to Du Bois in their correspondence from the 1950s, *Trading Twelves*. For Murray, Du Bois, one can surmise, was a monumental figure whom he respected but from whom one drew little artistic or intellectual sustenance. His *Omni-Americans* (1970) contains a few glancing references to Du Bois, while his attack on Claude Brown's *Manchild in the Promised Land* (1965) is headed "Soul for White Folks." Murray also refers to the way black intellectuals "may make vague references to Du Bois" but then turn to Malcolm X or Garvey for their polemical firepower. Unlike Du Bois, Murray was never tempted by Marxism, but seemed drawn to something like the Talented Tenth when he suggested that the key to black progress in America was the "so-called New Negro" as the "most fearsome revolutionary threat to the white status quo.[18] And like Du Bois, Murray's theory of culture derived from the romantic culturalism of Herder via the work of Constance

Rourke: "cultures begin on what I would call the folk level and develop upwards… It's all extension, elaboration, and refinement of the vernacular into a higher level."[19] Yet, as already mentioned, what most clearly separated him from Du Bois intellectually and aesthetically was the central place that the blues ethic/aesthetic assumed in Murray's thought.

With Ellison it was similar. In *Who Speaks for the Negro?* Warren asked what he thought of Du Bois's idea of the "split" psyche of American Negroes. Ellison's basic response was to question the notion of "twoness" or "double-consciousness" as an accurate reflection of black American identity. Taking the idea to refer to explicit values rather than complex psychological states, Ellison replied: "It is not whether I will accept or reject American values," but how "I can have the maximum influence upon those values." For Ellison, the difference between white and black Americans lay not in the values they accepted, since both were devoted to the ideals of a broadly democratic polity and culture. Rather it was in the degree to which white Americans acted on, rather than ignored, those ideals. Put another way, Ellison suggested that the split in American experience was between de facto cultural integration and segregation on the "socio-political level."[20] Interestingly Ellison's discomfort with the notion of double-consciousness – and hence dual black American allegiances – anticipated a 1996 article on Murray by black intellectual, Joe Wood. There Wood observes that Murray "insists on the essential sameness of all Americans…Du Bois's veil of 'double consciousness' doesn't exist." And yet, Wood continued, Murray "knows the two American audiences bring very different sensibilities" to their aesthetic, moral, and intellectual lives.[21] All this suggests that Du Bois's notion of double-consciousness remains a more complex and richer way to understand the relationship between white and black consciousness than the relatively "rational" views of Ellison and Murray, for whom white and black Americans mean largely the same thing when they praise democratic values.

With the 1960s Black Arts and Consciousness movement and then the emergence of a remarkable cadre of black women writers and intellectuals in the 1970s, Du Bois's direct influence seemed on the wane. Yet even though his ideas were often rejected by radical black intellectuals, they were seen as significant starting points and/or used as positions to reject even as an ideology of blackness was being forged. Largely male and resolutely masculine, the Black Arts movement differed drastically in class and cultural style from both Du Bois and Wright, to say the least. It projected an urban, self-styled ghetto image – loud, brash, and frequently obscene. Du Bois's dialectic of Negro and White or Wright's of the West and Africa was transformed into a Manichaean dualism where Black and White, the West and the Third World, stood over and against, rather than set in complex interaction with, one another. To the militant intellectuals of the Black Arts movement such as Amiri Baraka, the point was not to re-affirm double-consciousness, but to overcome it. "We must," wrote Larry Neal, "integrate with ourselves."[22] By doing so, the white world would be reduced in importance, even nullified. In its place, they sought to reconstruct a purely black culture and consciousness. As an answer to "alienation" from self and others, "wholeness" was proposed. Black group autonomy and political unity – and more pertinently black "soul" – were the remedies for the sickness perpetrated by the white soul of America. The (re)discovery of Africa did not divide, as Wright seemed to suggest, but would heal the alienated black psyche.

Yet even in questioning double-consciousness, the acceptance of "soul" as perhaps its central concept testified to the persistence of the Du Boisian rhetoric in black American thought. In the tradition of romantic culturalism, the dominant way of charactering a people was "soul" or "spirit" rather than "mind" or "character." In fact, of course, Du Bois's championing of Pan-Africanism over the years also showed one of the ways in which he was a precursor as much as an opponent. For 1960s black radicals the white West had "minds," while black people of Africa and the diaspora had "souls." Nor did the Black Arts movement disagree with Du Bois's emphasis upon music as the key mode of black expression, but it was a secular (avant-garde jazz) or non-theologically spiritual ("soul" music) rather than the religious "sorrow songs" that they apotheosized.

With women writers and intellectuals, the stance toward Du Bois was harder to figure out. Obligatory references to him as part of the black literary and intellectual tradition were frequent. Typically he had become "Dr. Du Bois." At the same time, Alice Walker's quest for spiritual and literary ances-tors in the late 1960s led her to Zora Neale Hurston not W. E. B. Du Bois. From the South like Walker, Hurston's literary gifts and high spirits were a far cry from his aristocratic hauteur and what seemed his arch-bourgeois respectability. She was and remained a highly talented and eccentric outsider rather than the establishment figure Du Bois often seemed to be. In a later collection *Black Literature and Literary Theory* (1984), critical theorist Barbara Johnson astutely observed what was obvious once she mentioned it – that double-consciousness was always rendered as male, from Du Bois down through other black male intellectuals such as James Weldon Johnson and Richard Wright.[23]

More generally, this "womanist" line of interrogation of Du Bois was as important a perspective on double-consciousness as anything the Black Arts/Consciousness movement proposed about the political and cultural inadequacy of black "twoness." Not only did black women wonder whether double-consciousness might be primarily a male construal of race relations, they also insisted that black women were not only split between the black and white values; they were internally divided by male and female conceptions of the world. Indeed, Walker, Toni Morrison, and others suggested that black male writers and intellectuals were, as James Baldwin once suggested about Richard Wright, too obsessed with the white world of power and influence. In protesting against white domination, the notion of the self that black male writers proposed mirrored rather than transcended white-imposed domination. And, for younger black literary critics such as Henry Louis Gates, Jr., the eccentric rather than strident black consciousness of Hurston, the comic-tragic vision of Ellison, and the extravagantly parodic vision of Ishmael Reed were important revoicings of and tropes of Du Boisian double-consciousness.[24] They had a playful aspect to them that paid homage to, but went beyond, the essentially humourless Du Bois.

The Enduring Intellectual Legacy and Questions

Numerous aspects of Du Bois's intellectual legacy are in the process of being re-assessed. A fuller account here would discuss the way Du Bois, along with C. L. R. James and Richard Wright, stand at the center of the intellectual history of Black Marxism. Pan-Africanism and its domestic Black Nationalist cousin can not be understood without factoring in the dominant role of Du Bois. During the last decade, his "The Conservation of Races" (1897) has been the starting point for a passionate debate among African American and black diasporic philosophers over viability of the concept of race as a biological as well as an historical, linguistic, cultural, and sociological entity.[25] Since these issues receive attention elsewhere in this volume, I want to focus on three specific issues that illustrate Du Bois's importance in the intellectual history of our time.

The first concerns his relationship to the tradition of American pragmatism. Recently, Wilson J. Moses has wondered how convincing a case can be made for Du Bois's position as a pragmatist. Speaking in favor has been Cornel West who identified Du Bois as a "Jamesean organic intellectual," devoted to the perpetuation (restoration) of democratic culture, engaged in philosophy as "cultural criticism," and committed to "self-creation and individuality."[26] In a similar vein Ross Posnock makes a strong case for Du Bois's place in the party of "pragmatist pluralism," a position which Posnock distinguishes from "cultural pluralism." Like West's, Posnock's pragmatism is very much a cultural-aesthetic rather than a calculating, utilitarian activity. It challenges the status quo rather than emphasizing the adaptive nature of thought. But Posnock, contra West, sees Du Bois as belonging more to the category of "cosmopolitan" than "organic" intellectuals.[27]

Certainly, the version of pragmatism presented by both men is an appealing one. But there are two problems. First, pragmatism seems more a mood or orientation than a coherent philosophical position. That is, neither man offers a coherent, comprehensive examination of what pragmatism was and is. Second is whether Du Bois belongs to the tradition of pragmatism, however construed. As already mentioned, Du Bois believed that knowledge and art have concrete implications and should, in that sense, be practical. But that hardly distinguishes pragmatism from any number of other positions, including Marxism. Du Bois would hardly qualify as a pragmatist if we use it to describe a position aimed at compromise, even trimming, of values and beliefs. Personally he could be overbearing and authoritarian. His political instincts were hardly (small "d") democratic at all. Though it is difficult not to find the pragmatism presented by Posnock and West appealing, Du Bois doesn't somehow *feel* like a pragmatist of this sort, however much his early career was shaped by James. Perhaps a fuller development of the idea of a *culture*, rather than a *philosophy*, of pragmatism might help to resolve this issue.

Second, there is an on-going debate about the positive and negative implications of double-consciousness, the idea upon which Du Bois's status as a major thinker depends. Aside from its sources which we have already examined, what did the term mean for Du Bois and what might it mean for us? One source of the power of double-consciousness is the range of meanings it takes in. First, as Dickson Bruce has suggested, it can be seen as the result of the imposition of hostile stereotypes and images of African Americans, including, as some have noted, the idea of black Americans as a "problem," even by their liberal and radical friends. This is double-consciousness as a form of alienation. Secondly, double-consciousness alludes to the fact that African Americans are both Americans and African Americans (if the "African" part is taken seriously), something which has positive as well as negative effects. Thirdly, double-consciousness also refers to the contrast Du Bois drew between black spirituality and white materialism, a contrast that hearkens back to Emerson's contrast between "understanding" and "soul."[28]

But beyond that, double-consciousness is the outcome of the symbolic "fall" of black Americans into racial self-consciousness. Du Bois explains and then unpacks the social ontology of the African American self, as it emerged in a power-driven, racially discriminatory social order. It is about becoming human but in a particular, historically inflected way. Part of the power of Du Bois's account derives from the allusive richness of Hegel's original analysis of the master-slave relationship. It is not just about the creation of masterly and slavish consciousness, but about the creation of human self-consciousness itself. Du Bois's "genius" was to see how the specific nature of the African American experience could be illuminated by the Hegelian model of human interaction, without being unduly limited by it.

Yet not without reason, critics have wondered about various aspects of the idea of double-consciousness. Some have suggested that it is a particular problem of middle-class blacks and/or light-skinned blacks; that is, it was a problem experienced primarily by Du Bois and the Talented Tenth. A more important objection stresses the negative connotations of double-consciousness. It can sound like a euphemism for the black pathological self, a nervous and febrile form of self-consciousness. Nationalists have been particularly suspicious of double-consciousness for this reason. In addition, Adolph Reed has suggested that by overemphasizing it in Du Bois's thought, contemporary black intellectuals have shifted the terrain of resistance from economics and politics to the expressive culture.[29] As a result they are more interested in black subjectivity than solidarity and prefer textual performance to political action. Finally, one might wonder whether at this historical juncture racial self-consciousness and black subjectivity can still fit into the rather specialized theoretical framework which Du Bois brought to them, one that, as we have already seen, privileges a "male" version of the self.

A final issue has to do with the most appropriate geographical-culture milieu for taking Du Bois's measure as a thinker and assessing his broad intellectual significance. Much of his appeal lies in his engagement with the crucial issues of his time, place, and people. Yet the neglect of Du Bois by mainstream American intellectual historians (as opposed to literary scholars and historians) makes one wonder if Du Bois will ever get his due there. The European, especially German, provenance of the formative stages of his intellectual development is beyond question, but no longer of great importance in itself. But Paul Gilroy's selection of Du Bois as one of the presiding presences over the modern black diaspora marks out, I think, the most appropriate context within which to locate Du Bois as a thinker.[30] That context is not Euro-American intellectual history as such. Rather he belongs most clearly to the rich intellectual and cultural history of the Black Atlantic, one which includes twentieth-century figures such as C. L. R. James, Frantz Fanon, Aimé Césaire, and Léopold Sédar Senghor among others. It is a setting that encompasses the international and the local, the cosmopolitan and the provincial; and includes the West Indies and West Africa rather than being confined to the United States and Europe. Perhaps this was the destination Du Bois intended for us all along.

Notes

1. S. Sullivan, "W E B Du Bois, 1868–1963," in *The Blackwell Guide to American Philosophy*, ed. A. T. Marsoobian and J. Ryder (Malden and Oxford: Blackwell, 2004), p. 199.

2. See M. Bay, *The White Image in the Black Mind* (New York: Oxford University Press, 2000); J. Earnest, *Liberation Historiography: African American Writers and the Challenge of History* (Chapel Hill: University of North Carolina Press, 2003); and G. M. Fredrickson, *The Black Image in the White mind: The Debate on Afro-American Character and Destiny, 1817–1914* (1971; Wesleyan, CN: Wesleyan University Press, 1978).

3. W. E. B Du Bois, *The Souls of Black Folk* (New York: Fawcett Books, 1961).

4. See H. Bloom, *The Anxiety of Influence: A Theory of Poetry*, 2nd edn. (New York: Oxford University Press, 1997).

5. D. L. Lewis, *W. E. B. Du Bois: Biography of a Race, 1868–1919* (New York: Henry Holt, 1993), p. 166.

6. See Bay, *White Image*, and R. H. King, *Race, Culture and the Intellectuals, 1940–1970* (Washington, D.C. and Baltimore: Wilson Center Press and Johns Hopkins University Press, 2004), pp. 37–48.

7. Cited in B. H. Edwards, *The Practice of Diaspora: Literature, Translation, and the Rise of Black Internationalism* (Cambridge: Harvard University Press, 2003), p. 1.

8. D. D. Bruce, Jr., "W. E. B. Du Bois and the Idea of Double Consciousness," *American Literature*, 64, no. 2 (1992), pp. 299–309.

9. S. Zamir, *Dark Voices: W. E. B. Du Bois and American Thought, 1888–1903* (Chicago: University of Chicago Press, 1995), pp. 2, 12–13; R. C. Rath, "Echo and Narcissus: The Afrocentric Pragmatism of W. E. B. Du Bois," *Journal of American History*, 84 (September 1997), pp. 476, 483.

10. A. Murray, *From the Briarpatch File: On Context, Procedure, and American Identity* (New York: Pantheon, 2003), p. 189.

11. Exceptions here are A. Meier, *Negro Thought in America, 1880–1915: Racial Ideologies in the Age of Booker T. Washington* (Ann Arbor: University of Michigan Press, 1965); and D. Tallack, *Twentieth-Century America: The Intellectual and Cultural Context* (London and New York: Longman, 1991), pp. 253–81.

12. R. Penn Warren, *Who Speaks for the Negro?* (New York: Random House, 1965): See also R. Posnock, *Color and Culture: Black writers and the Making of the Modern Intellectual* (Cambridge: Harvard University Press, 1998); and L. Menand, *The Metaphysical Club* (New York: Farrar, Straus and Giroux, 2001) for discussion of Du Bois as part of the tradition of pragmatism.

13. Lewis, *Du Bois: Biography*, p. 175.

14. J. G. Watts, *Heroism and the Black Intellectual* (Chapel Hill: University of North Carolina Press, 1994), p. 104.

15. Quoted in *Conversations with Albert Murray*, ed. Roberta S. Maguire (Jackson: University Press of Mississippi, 1997), p. 41.

16. H. Cruse, *The Crisis of the Negro Intellectual* (1967; New York: New York Review of Books Classics, 2005), pp. 39, 334.

17. King, *Race, Culture*, pp. 202–15.
18. A. Murray, *The Omni-Americans* (New York: Avon Books, 1970), pp. 143, 270, 133.
19. *Conversations*, ed. Maguire, p. 146.
20. Quoted in Warren, *Who Speaks*, p. 327.
21. Quoted in *Conversations*, ed. Maguire, p. 104.
22. Quoted in King, *Race, Culture*, p. 279.
23. B. Johnson, "Metaphor and Metonymy in *Their Eyes Were Watching God*," in *Black Literature and Literary Theory*, ed. H. L. Gates, Jr. (New York and London, Methuen, 1984), pp. 214–16.
24. See H. L. Gates, Jr., "The Blackness of Blackness: A Critique of the Sign and the Signifying Monkey," in *Black Literary Theory*, ed. Gates, pp. 286–321.
25. C. J. Robinson, *Black Marxism: The Making of the Black Radical Tradition* (1983; Chapel Hill: University of North Carolina Press, 2000); W. E. B. Du Bois, "The Conservation of Races" (1897), in *W. E. B. Du Bois: A Reader*, ed. D. L. Lewis (New York: Henry Holt, 1995).
26. See W. J. Moses, *Creative Conflict in African American Thought* (Cambridge: Cambridge University Press, 2004); and C. West, *The American Evasion of Philosophy: A Genealogy of Pragmatism* (Madison: University of Wisconsin Press, 1989), pp. 138, 1, 143.
27. Posnock, *Color and Culture*, pp. 6, 305, 48–9.
28. See Bruce, "Du Bois and the Idea of Double Consciousness."
29. A. Reed, Jr., *W. E. B. Du Bois and American Political Thought: Fabianism and the Color Line* (New York: Oxford University Press, 1997).
30. P. Gilroy, *The Black Atlantic: Modernity and Double Consciousness* (London: Verso, 1993).

10

MICHAEL STONE-RICHARDS

Race, Marxism, and Colonial Experience: Du Bois and Fanon

All of existence lived as a masked form leads thereby to a grotesque and caricatural world in which man never for long feels himself at ease...: it is a world in which man does not feel sheltered from danger.

Roland Kuhn, *Phénoménologie du masque*[1]

I

It is characteristic of twentieth-century black radical intellectual culture that, moving toward Marxism, it comes to discover its difference from Marxism. Canonically, this was stated by the Martiniquan poet and thinker Aimé Césaire in his *Lettre à Maurice Thorez*, his letter of resignation from the Parti Communiste français in 1956. Césaire does not dismiss the revolutionary project to which he had devoted his life since his student days at the Ecole Normale in Paris, his encounters with Surrealism and André Breton, his formative friendship with Léopold Sédar Senghor and the collective formation of Negritude, rather he asserts an issue of singularity, what he terms a "fact of capital importance":

> Singularity of our "situation in the world," which can be mistaken for no other. Singularity of our problems, which can be subsumed under no other problem. Singularity of our history, interrupted terrible transformations that belong to it alone. Singularity of our culture, which we intend to quicken in ever more real ways...[2]

There are variations on this position and Cedric J. Robinson's important book on *Black Marxism* (1983) is a study motivated by the way in which the encounter with and difference from Marxism by black radical thought has been a means of self-definition. Both W. E. B Du Bois and Frantz Fanon (the latter in a French context shaped early on by Surrealism and Negritude, by World War II, the collapse of colonialism, and the early signs of an emergent neocolonialism) would move toward the language of

Marxist analysis before, each in his different manner, pulling back to affirm the distinctiveness of black experience, though something would remain or persist, and often the structure of Marxian thought would remain with the terms changed. So, for example, though Fanon rejects the proletariat as the subject of historical movement, he will accept the principal of such a historical, cultural, and political subject and declare the peasant the bearer of this privilege. Like C. L. R. James, though without James's rigorous rationalism, Fanon will develop a version of post-Leninist thought which comprehends the Party and its fetishism of Organization as the enemy of Revolution and so, in common with James, will espouse a form of spontaneism. The problematic of spontaneity developed by James is not so far from Du Bois's concern with internal organization – or *the colored world within* – as might first seem to be the case, for the critique of the Party – that is, of bureaucratic capitalism – and organization, based upon an articulation of movement and spontaneity, goes hand-in-hand with a mode of thinking centered upon the experience. Furthermore, this thinking centered upon experience is implicitly a social phenomenology of alienation which in no way denies, rejects or transcends Marx because, in a profound sense, James, Fanon, and Du Bois, all recoup the Marx of Young (Left) Hegelianism, in short, the philosophical anthropology of alienation articulated from Hegel to Marx and of which the *Economic MSS of 1844* since their recovery in 1920s have long since, with Lukcas's *History of Class Consciousness* (1923), become the *locus classicus*. For Du Bois there are partly biographical and partly intellectual reasons for this convergence, stemming from his studies in Germany and the role of German Idealist thought in his own formation (*Bildung*).[3] For Fanon this particular mode of thought comes partly through his adoption of Sartrean anthropology, and partly from his own reading of Hegel's *Phänomenologie des Geistes* in Hyppolite's translation.[4] For James this mode of thought is arrived at partly through original and collective analysis (the Johnson-Forester tendency of ex-members of the Socialist Workers Party) and partly through his own engagement with Hegel's *Science of Logic* precisely where it had been understood for some time that Hegel's *Logic* was the middle term between the *Phenomenology of Spirit* and *World-Spirit*. Within the development, then, of these thinkers, Marxism is approached always in terms of experience – for Du Bois and Fanon the differential experience of blackness – and in terms, too, of the problem of organization which is often conceived differentially as movement outside the Party. (When finally Du Bois joins the Party three years before his death, it is as a sign of hope if not faith.) Underlying all is the dimension of alienation, for it is the Hegelian dimension of Marx's thought that makes it available to thinkers who accept the singularity of blackness but cannot eschew universality of thought.

II

It is in preparation for his study *Black Reconstruction in America* (1935) that Du Bois will begin a sustained engagement with Marxist thought, by which we will here understand an approach to social knowledge in terms of which agency is recognized in the relations of production and certain forms assumed by these relations, such as The Black Worker, The White Worker, The General Strike, productive of a new kind of historical dramaturgy. In "Karl Marx and the Negro" (1933), Du Bois considered that "Without doubt the greatest figure in the science of modern industry" is Karl Marx.[5] Marx, we are told, "knew something about American Negroes," but it was only indirectly; however, Marx realized, for his method made it possible, that the Civil War was to be understood structurally as a tension between two forms of social system, namely, those of slavery and free labor. In another one of his early essays on "Marxism and the Negro Problem" (1933), Du Bois would say that "There are certain books in the world which every searcher for truth must know: the *Bible, Critique of Pure Reason, Origin of Species,* and Karl Marx's *Capital.*"[6] In short, engagement with Marx is not presented as a question first and foremost of revolutionary violence, but of cultural literacy, a theme that would slowly develop in the radical socialist tradition of *Socialism ou barbarie,* namely, the idea that the modes of diagnoses of Marxist thought are the minimal requirements to stave off cultural barbarism. Du Bois would then continue, in the same essay, in a way that makes it clear that he can be understood as addressing himself, that: "The task which Karl Marx set himself was to study and inter-pret the organization of industry in the modern world" ("Marxism" 539). This having been stated Du Bois then quotes a passage from *The Communist Manifesto* that makes clear that Marxism provides a method – of analysis, of comprehension – that furthermore introduces the element of *class struggle* and hence the problem of exploitation. This, says Du Bois, is the fundamental proposition that had been laid down by *The Communist Manifesto* prior to the revolutions of 1848:

> That in every historical epoch the prevailing mode of economic production and exchange, and the social organization necessarily following from it, form the basis upon which is built up, and from which alone can be explained, the political and intellectual history of that epoch; that consequently the whole history of mankind...has been a history of class struggles, contests between exploiting and exploited, ruling and oppressed classes; that the history of these class struggles forms a series of evolution in which, now-a-days, a stage has been reached where the exploited and oppressed class (the proletariat) cannot attain its emancipation from the sway of the exploiting and ruling class

(the bourgeoisie) without, at the same time, and once and for all, emancipating society at large from all exploitation, oppression, class-distinction and class-struggles. ("Marxism" 539)

He recognizes that the method of analysis offered by Marxism is one that is co-incident with the development of modernity as structural modernization, and as such he accepts a characterization of capitalism in terms of a convergence thesis of modernity, namely, the argument that says that modernity is precisely where the forces and relations of capitalism structure commodity production: "[The] large development of a petty bourgeoisie within the American laboring class is a post-Marxian phenomenon [Du Bois clearly means by this post-Marx himself] and the result of the tremendous worldwide development of capitalism in the twentieth-century. The market of capitalistic production has gained an effective world-wide organization" ("Marxism" 541). This perception of the structural dimension of a convergence thesis of modernity makes it possible, then, for Du Bois to recognize the analytic capacity of Marxist thought, above all its diagnostic powers, while at the same time feeling the need for an adaptation to the cultural specificities of first the United States and then the black experience. Whence it can be seen that if he accepts the Marxian diagnosis of modern capitalism, it is, as such, he writes, "it must be modified in the United States of America and especially so far as the Negro group is concerned" ("Marxism" 543). Even in the opening chapter of Black Reconstruction, that devoted to "The Black Worker," Du Bois was quite clear that in 1863: "there was real meaning to slavery different from that we may apply to the laborer today. It was in part psychological, the enforced personal feeling of inferiority, the calling of another Master; the standing with hat in hand. It was the helplessness. It was the defenselessness of family life."[7] He will be consistent, in his approach to Marxism, in emphasizing the moment and structure of racial difference continuous with the psychological dimension. The way in which he signals this modification is precisely in terms of a form of experience that continues the marginalization of black labor, for such is the degree of the Negro's exploitation: "His only defense is such internal organization as will protect him from both parties, and such practical economic insight as will prevent inside the race group any large development of capitalistic exploitation" ("Marxism" 543). Much will hinge on the construal of this expression internal organization: it can be interpreted to mean both internal psychic organization – mechanisms, then, of psychic defense – as well as the mechanisms of defense available to and deployed by a group at the level of a community whether in terms of economic or social solidarity. This ambiguity is important for not only do we see Du

Bois stressing Marxism as a method of analysis, nowhere does he recant his earlier refusal of the violent revolutionary posture that many of his contemporaries saw as the logical conclusion of the 1917 Russian revolution,[8] and this is so even when, in 1960, not long before his departure to Ghana, he declares his commitment to Communism "in every honest way...without deceit or hurt and in any way possible, without war";[9] and nowhere in his "Application for membership in the Communist Party of the United States of America" does he mention or make allusion to revolutionary violence as part of a political practice.[10] Yet with the composition of *Dusk of Dawn* (1940) he will deepen and exploit the structural ambiguity of *internal organization* in the chapter dealing with "The Colored World Within" – itself an extension at the structural level of the conception of double-consciousness first articulated in *The Souls of Black Folk* in 1903 – where we learn that "The Communist philosophy was a program for a majority, not for a relatively small minority," that, indeed, an "imported Russian Communism" could not address the issues resultant from the vertical – rather than merely horizontal – fissure, "a complete *separation* of classes by race, cutting square across the economic layers" (my emphasis).[11] The irony is that even at the very moment that Du Bois recognizes the analytic power of Marxian thought in the composition of *Black Reconstruction*, he comes upon its limitations in a way that *surprises* him, when, that is, Revolution – or at the very least, a form of Liberation in "The Coming of the Lord"[12] – comes outside of system, outside of theory, and which will soon be recuperated by the forces of reaction.

III

That *Souls* is a work that explores spectrality, and the status of an intermediate existence for the black soul has received much comment as part of the discussion of its central concept of double-consciousness. It is by now also well established that this work draws upon the dramaturgy of Hegel's *Phenomenology of Spirit* for the articulation of selfhood and double-consciousness.[13] Here I should like to consider how an aspect of double-consciousness is further developed in terms of the concept of double environment in *Dusk of Dawn*, a work which may be seen as a corrective pendant to *Black Reconstruction* in its presentation of the social phenomenology of alienated experience. Such categories, such types as The Black Worker, The Black Proletariat in South Carolina, etc., from *Black Reconstruction*, are in *Dusk of Dawn* recalibrated in terms of "The White World" and "The Colored World Within," and thereby offer a different kind of analysis that recognizes and addresses "subconscious trains of reasoning and unconscious nervous reflexes" to reach a truer self (*Dusk* 679). This truer self is subject to a double environment of which even the Negro is said to be unaware, namely, that to the surrounding white environment there is also "the environment furnished by his own colored group" (*Dusk* 681), *the colored world within*, within the outer environment of the contiguous white environment and within his own psychic and material structurations. At every point in Du Bois's presentation the terms "inner," "interiority," "degradation," "segregation," "inner economy" refer simultaneously to material and psychic circumstances, an inner economy of affect: there is an inner world of the Negro, for which the example given is a "group of Negroes, say, in Harlem [i.e. an educated group], not in their role of agitation and reform, but in their daily intercourse and *play*" (*Dusk* 682, my emphasis). Even in such a grouping, with no white person present, discussion of the color-line cannot be avoided, and soon they come upon the idea that in order to live in a certain way, a way not possible among whites, it may be necessary to live apart from less educated people of color. For Du Bois, however, this is not merely a sociological but "an *inner problem* of the Negro group itself" (*Dusk* 686, my emphasis), the means by which is posed questions of the "inner problems of contact with their own lower classes," and the question "why does not the Negro race build up a class structure of its own, parallel to that of the whites, but separate...?" (*Dusk*, 689–90, 691). From this point Du Bois's language takes on a life of its own shadowing, "The inner contradiction and frustration which this involves" (*Dusk* 690), as though the archaic psychic experience of the race, whose concept he seeks, is sedimented in terms the syntax of which he would find: separation, which is to say here, segregation, leads inevitably to degradation which as "social degradation is intensified and emphasized *by* discrimination" (*Dusk* 687, my emphasis) – and then the language seems like a cross between a curious experiment in chemistry (Brownian motion) and thermodynamics (conservation of energy). It is said, for example, of the previously mentioned Harlem group that

They form a self-segregated culture group. They have come to know each other partly by *chance*, partly by *design*, but form a small *integrated clique* because of similar likes and dislikes and ideas, because of *corresponding* culture. This is happening all over the land... It is not a matter yet of a few broad super-imposed social classes, but rather smaller cliques and groups gradually *integrating and extending* out of their neighborhoods into neighboring districts and cities.

...

Is cultural *separation* in *the same territory* feasible? To force a group of various levels of culture to *segregate itself*, will certainly *retard* its advance, since it must put *energy* not simply into social advance, but in the vast and intricate *effort* to *duplicate, evolve,* and *contrive* new social institutions to *maintain* their advance and guard against *retrogression.* (*Dusk* 692, my emphases)

And this, it turns out, is the abiding fear: the risk of retrogression attendant upon the dissipation of energy in "duplicating white development" (*Dusk* 693). It is clear that the metaphors of energy, conservation, development work both in material terms (social and economic solidarity) as well as in psychic terms, and as such the metaphorics reduplicate the processes of defense mechanisms against splitting in unconscious fantasy and anxiety, for Du Bois will quickly associate retrogression with a *spiritual* retrogression (*Dusk* 696) that may come about in the act of *waiting* for development.

Underlying Du Bois's thought here is the long-held belief from *Souls* – in the remarkable chapter "Of the Training of Black Men" – that black social experience has been conditioned at the level of the unconscious by a "tangle of thought and after-thought" (*Souls* 146) that takes on psycho-pathological colors: the primal memory of the slave ship (*the death ship*), the fear that the white perception of the Negro might be "true." Education – in the sense of German *Bildung* (spiritual development, formation, education, and training) rather than the Tuskegee project – was there thought the way out of this social alienation, of breaking this tangle of thought and afterthought "streaming from [the time of] the death-ship" (*Souls* 146). It is here that Du Bois joins Fanon and James in the recognition of the pathological dimension to modern social experience in which, following Marxism, capitalism will be understood as the mechanism of reproduction at the level of the planet for, as Fanon would put it: "There exists an objective complicity of capitalism with the violent forces which break out [*éclatent*] in colonial territory."[14]

IV

Following on from the account of the social phenomenology of alienation in *the colored world within* with its structure of double environment, I will look at the way in which Fanon naturalizes the psychopathological vocabulary of his psychiatric training. This naturalization of the psychopathogical vocabulary is undertaken in order to present an account of the lived phenomenology of the distortion of temporality brought about by alienation, division, and radical separation in the double environment in which black racial identity is formed, not only in a *de jure* colonial experience, but within black experience as a minority mode; forever within this minority mode there is marginalization within its own cultural geography, a cultural geography constrained within a nation-state formation the privileges of which do not extend to the

subjects of the field of double environment. Here we will explore the profound continuity between Du Bois and Fanon on the psychopathologization
of experience inherent to double-consciousness, the lived-experience of
twoness: "two souls, two thoughts, two unreconciled strivings; two
warring ideals in one dark body" (*Souls* 102). For the Fanon of *Peau noir,
masques blancs* (1952) writing on the *lived experience of the black man*,
where, working through the categories of phenomenological psychiatry, it
is, not transference, but the encounter (*la rencontre*) that is the operant
category, the experience is given thus:

> And then it was given to us to affront the white gaze. An unaccustomed weight
> oppressed us. The truly existing world challenged our contribution. In the white
> world, the person of color encounters difficulties in the elaboration of his body
> schema [*schema corporel*]. The knowledge of the body is a uniquely negative
> activity. It is a knowledge in the third person.[15]

For as is only too clear to Fanon, the elements of double-consciousness –
second-sight, seeing oneself only through *another* consciousness, "this
sense of always looking at one's self [not oneself] through the eyes of
another" (*Souls* 102) – are structurally the conditions of psychosis. Fanon
not only places this moment in the confrontation with the gaze of the
other, he situates it in the skin as surface and contact with the surrounding
world, for it is the skin that registers what in another chapter he will call
"Le Nègre et la psychopathologie" (The Negro and Psychopathology):
"Then the body schema [*schema corporel*], attacked on many points, col-
lapses, giving place to a racial epidermic schema" (*Peau noir* 90). And
later, Fanon will observe that where "the psychic structure is shown
fragile, one is participating at a collapse of the self [*Moi*]" (*Peau noir* 125).
For Fanon, these are near psychotic conditions that can be triggered by the
gaze dissolving the contact between self and world into one of dangerous
porosity, and it was because he believed that black existential experience
belonged to the dynamics (and object relations) of psychosis (or, one
might say today: border-line pathology) that Fanon, in a lifelong ambivalence toward Freudian thought, felt at certain moments that psychoanalysis
could not help clarify the inner world of black experience since the bedrock
of psychoanalysis, he accepted, was the terrain of the transferential neuroses
(cf. *Peau noir* 123). Instead, the sense of constitutive division as an existential mark is the mode of black identity characterized by violence and terror.
For Fanon, not twoness but Manichaeanism is the name for this doubleness,
this social ontology under capitalism – for, it is said, colonialism *bears upon
being and modifies it fundamentally* (*Damnés* 26). It is a social ontology
that belongs not only to *de jure* colonialism but *de facto* to any sphere

where the commodity forms of capitalism prevail,[16] for it is the claim of Fanon, the Fanon of "De la violence," that "The colonial context is characterized by the dichotomy [division] that it inflicts upon the world... The colonial world is a compartmentalized world... The colonial world is a world cut in two" (*Damnés* 32). He will also say that

> This compartmentalized world, this world cut in two is inhabited by different species. The originality of the colonial context is that the economic realities, the inequalities, the enormous difference of styles of life, never manage to mask such human realities. When one sees the colonial context in its immediacy, it is clear that what partitions the world is at first the fact of belonging or not to such a species, to such a race. (*Damnés* 28)

Throughout, this organization – *arrangement* is Fanon's French – of the world is one presided over by violence, a violence which, following and re-inforcing the Manichaeanism of the colonial world, leads to a freezing of movement and temporality for *the zone of the colonized*, the colonized *de facto* as well as *de jure*: leading to the loss of agency and movement on the part of the colonized (cf. *Damnés* 36). Immobility is the loss of time and with this loss goes the ability to be an agent, an actor in history: "The colonizer makes history and knows that he has made it," while the colonized is condemned to a zone of immobility in a Manichaean world: "[A world] compartmentalized, Manichaean, immobile, a world of statues" (*Damnés* 36). We have from Fanon a remarkable description of the phenomenology of loss of temporality, of this fall into (spiritual) immobility – so close to the negative phenomenology of a Maurice Blanchot, equally anticipatory of the conception of slavery as social death in the work of Claude Meillassoux and Orlando Patterson – in a situation where psychopathology and fundamental anthropology coincide, where, that is, the situatedness of the person finds itself in question, both person and situation, both person and framework of intelligibility, whence Fanon begins his report on "Le 'syndrome nord african'" with the phenomenological truism: "It is freely said that man is unceasingly in question for himself, and that he denies himself when he affects [*prétend*] no longer to be [a being in question]."[17] We might here think of the opening of *Souls* which speaks of the self as problem, where, the self being put in question by its *situation* becomes an *enigma* to itself: "And yet, being a problem is a strange experience, – peculiar even for one who has never been anything else" (*Souls* 101). Precisely, then, Fanon's phenomenologically medical aim, following Karl Jasper's, is to place the person as being in situation, for when this is done it becomes unmistakable the way in which the situation affects both doctor and patient – the situation, that is, is an active agent of subjection in relation to which subjectivity is passive recognition – such that for the patient, the colonized patient, to recount the evolution and history of his life *it would be better to say the history of his death*, what Fanon characterizes and presents as:

> An everyday death.
> A death on the tram,
> a death in the consultation process,
> a death with prostitutes,
> a death in the workplace [*chantier*],
> a death at the cinema,
> a multiple death in the newspapers,
> a death in the fear of all the honest people coming out after midnight.
> A death,
> yes a DEATH.[18]

This is the work of repressing temporality and self-movement, whence Alexandre Kojève's lapidary statement from his anthropological reading of Hegel so important to Sartre and Fanon: "To suppress time is therefore also to suppress Man,"[19] and without this temporality there can be no authenticity or historicity, hence the perpetual play of masks and masking resultant of a divided world with subjects constitutively divided, whence Fanon can say that the process of decolonization "will unify this world in a radical act [decision] by lifting its heterogeneity from it, unifying it [instead] on the basis of the nation, sometimes that of race" (*Damnés* 32).

In their search to overcome psychic damage, Fanon and Du Bois recognize the role of capitalism – through a convergence thesis of modernity – as the framework for the spread of neocolonialism, that is, the spread of violence as constitutive of the social subject on the model of the violence of slave subjects perfected in the economic development of the United States. They also agree upon, if not the uniqueness, the distinctiveness of the role of violence and inveterate terror in the formation of the black subject under modernity, and here one must agree with Paul Gilroy – if not the analysis of Hegel's master-slave narrative in which his account is embedded – that at the core of Du Bois's account of modernity is "his positioning of slavery in relation to modern civilization, and in his emphasis upon the constitutive role of that terror in configuring modern black political cultures."[20] Gilroy dramatizes Du Bois's perception of the inaugural violence characteristic of every point of contact between European force and non-European cultures. Césaire had also spoken of such contact and went further in seeing in it an equation: "*colonization* = *thingification*."[21] This is the equation that Du Bois and Fanon sought to undo.

V

> Organization is at an end. The task is to abolish organization. The task today is to call for, to teach, to illustrate, to develop *spontaneity*.
>
> C. L. R. James, *Notes on Dialectics*[22]

How, though, this equation between thing and colonization spread by capitalism could be undone takes us to the question of organization. For Du Bois there was always the question of fit between the self and organization – the NAACP – between organization and society which necessitated the need: to be international (the five Pan-African Congresses between 1919 [Paris] and 1945 [Manchester]), to be tactical (the Niagara Movement), or to separate culture from politics (membership of the Socialist Party). At issue is in part the question of organization in terms of defense: the Party, the Peasant, the Black Worker – and before that the talented tenth or even the NAACP – are so many figures for this issue of internal and communitarian organization, for always the issue is concomitantly one of experience, or, to be more precise with James, it is a question of *movement*, the interruption of continuity, self-movement, "This movement, activity, spontaneous, internally necessary,"[23] which statement is itself a near repeating of Lenin from his reading of Hegel's *Science of Logic*:

> Movement and "self-movement" (NB this. An independent [*eigenmachtige*] spontaneous, *internally necessary* movement), "alteration," "movement and life," principle of every self-movement," "impulse," (drive) to "movement" and to "activity" – opposite of "dead being" – who would believe that this is the core of "Hegelianism"…[24]

Movement, though, requires a frame if spontaneous, self-movement is to be creative, and this issue was clearly posed by Aimé Césaire in his discourse pronounced at the historic First International Congress of Black Writers and Artists held in the Sorbonne, Paris, in 1956. There, alluding to the Lenin of the *Philosophical Notebook* on the relation of politics to culture, the same Lenin that is the basis of James's *Notes on Dialectics*, Césaire spoke on *the death of culture* wrought by an expanding capitalism which in its expansion creates a neocolonial subject everywhere in its train, for where self-determination and self-movement are suppressed the creative potency of that culture is thereby killed. "Every culture," says Césaire, "in order to blossom has need of a frame [*cadre*], a structure. Now, it is certain that the elements which structure the cultural life of a colonized people, disappear or become debased [*s'abartadissent*] from the very presence of the colonial regime."[25] This, he argues, is the first result of a particular form of political organization, an effect which constitutes the theft through parasitism of the temporality of a culture, and through this loss of movement constituted by this divestiture of temporality, the conditions for a sustained form of self-alienation are given. Organization, then, is not separate from internally necessary movement, self-movement, but the two are dialectically implicated one in the other, and both Fanon and James, in a more lucid manner than Du Bois, albeit in different contexts, opted for the radical refusal of party organization as the enemy of the realization of internally necessary movement. Alone of the three thinkers considered here, James remained a committed self-declared Marxist and post-Trotskyite thinker motivated by the need to salvage Lenin's thought from the moral abortion called Stalinism. For James, Lenin had realized after 1914: "That organization had become the enemy of the very thing it had been formed to develop – the revolutionary creative activity of the workers."[26] If the Stalinization of the Party after the death of Lenin in 1924 was the historical occasion of James's rethinking of the role of organization, the theoretical centre of his view can be directly stated: Hegel's *Science of Logic* identifies movement with life, and contradiction is the motive and cause of social and intellectual movement by which quantity can be changed into quality and content and form held in the tension that makes possible difference within identity and identity in difference. The Party as embodied organization, for James, is a negation of this dialectic, and above all a negation of the need for *processes of transition*. Increasingly, James came to feel from his reading of the *Science of Logic* with Lenin's *Philosophical Notebook* that authentic revolutionary activity should be aimed at the abolition of any party and that "the vanguard can only organize itself on the basis of the destruction of the stranglehold that the existing organizations have on the proletariat by means of which it is suffering such ghastly defeats."[27]

Fanon devotes an extended reflection to the issue of spontaneity as means of challenging the role of elites in revolutionary politics and especially the fetishism of organization (*Damnés* 79). Where, however, James dwells on the critique of the Party, Fanon develops an almost mystical account of spontaneity as he sees in this mechanisms and occasions of fusion. He rejects wholesale the nationalist parties and their importation of modern forms and political practices which would seek to modernize the peasant and instead valorizes those moments that not only escape control, but predictability; hence he valorizes what is outside theory and system. The two pages of "Grandeur et faiblesses de la spontanéité" dealing with this aspect of the refusal of organization make for astonishing reading. First, the identification of agency: "The lumpen-proletariat, this cohort of detribalized, clanless hungry types, constitutes one of the most spontaneous and the most radically revolutionary forces of a colonized people" (*Damnés* 93). It is, furthermore, these "useless [*désoeuvrés*], classless types [who], by the means of militant and decisive action, are going to recover the path of the nation" (*Damnés* 94). They are not (Nietzschean) over-men, but under-men (*sous-hommes*) who will be joined by prostitutes and "all those men and women who move between madness and suicide" (*Damnés* 94). This spontaneously activated body will lead to the "ensemble of the colony entering into a trance" as they become possessed (*le people enthousiaste*); indeed, there will be a veritable triumph of the cult of spontaneity, where the spontaneous will be king (*Damnés* 95), and where "In a veritable collective ecstasy once opposing families will [spontaneously] forget everything, wipe the slate clean," as old, deep enmities surface in order to be cathartically and definitively purified. In this state, the authentic people will discover themselves *sovereign*, and social death will be undone as, again in an image of fusion: "Each point thus awakened from the colonial sleep lives at an insupportable temperature" of creative heat (*Damnés* 96). It is an extraordinary scene, this image of what Fanon himself admits is a "spectacular voluntarism" (*Damnés* 99). That Fanon should mention sovereignty in this context makes clear the seriousness of his intention, and it is in principle the price that he is willing to pay to avoid the fetishism of Organization, the control of the Party.

This way of thinking is not available to Du Bois. That the question of organization was important to him is only too clear from his biography. Having not accepted the role of the revolutionary cadre of a James, he could not reject wholesale organization, just as not being part of a vanguard party in conditions of war, like Fanon in Algeria, the dream of fusion, of unmediated oneness in the sovereign nation is not one that he could entertain – though assuredly the dream of union is part of his sensibility. So if there is not a theory and practice of organization as such in Du Bois, there is ample recognition of it and its problems above all in *Black Reconstruction in America* where he addresses revolutionary consciousness. He touches on the role of organization in the chapter called "The Price of Disaster":

> As the Negro laborers organized separately, there came slowly to realization the fact that here was not only separate organization but a separation in leading ideas; because among Negroes, and particularly in the South, there was being put into force one of the most extraordinary experiments of Marxism that the world, before the Russian revolution, had seen. That is, backed by the military power of the United States, a dictatorship of labor was to be attempted. (*Reconstruction* 358)

At the very same moment that this revolutionary possibility is envisaged, the (white) labor movement is going in another, purely *economic*, direction which will result in seeing the newly liberated blacks as threat; thus

Du Bois comments: "Not a word was said of Negro suffrage and the need of the labor vote, black and white, if the demands of labor were to be realized" (*Reconstruction* 358). With the increasing separation of black and white labor, the problem of organization cannot be conceived as merely an economic one (*pace* Tuskegee), and there is a glimpse of this in Du Bois which brings him close to James's conception of free self-movement, movement free of organization. There is a moment at the heart of *Black Reconstruction in America* which seems to catch Du Bois by surprise, and that is his recognition that though his researches suggest that historical and economic factors favored the collapse of the South in the context of what he held to be a general strike – though others would question the accuracy of this term "general strike" here – he writes that freedom for the slave "was the logical result of a crazy attempt to wage war in the midst of four million black slaves, and trying the while sublimely to ignore the interests of those slaves in the outcome of the fighting. Yet these slaves had enormous power in their hands. Simply by stopping work, they could threaten the Confederacy with starvation" (*Reconstruction* 121). There may, though, have been other less quantifiable factors at play, for to the economic and military factors must be added that the freedom to act on the part of the slaves, that is, the description under which they themselves acted, seemed motivated by…prayer and belief. That Du Bois characterizes the condition of the slaves, "even the more intelligent ones, [as caught] in religious and hysterical fervor" (*Reconstruction* 102) – what for Fanon would be the high temperature of creative fusion and *enthusiasm* – suggests that he may have missed the significance of the absence of organization in the realization of a space – a moment – of spontaneous movement which he describes so beautifully, as though in free movement one could touch time: "for the first time in their life, they could travel; they could see; they could change the dead level of their labor; they could talk to friends and sit at sundown and in moonlight, listening and imparting wonder-tales" (*Reconstruction* 122). And the mark of the authenticity of this felt movement: its *suddenness*, that it "was a sudden beginning of an entirely new era" (*Reconstruction* 122).

Notes

1. R. Kuhn, "L'esthétique dans l'existence masquée," *Phénoménologie du masque* (Paris: Desclée de Brouwer, 1957), p. 156. All translations are by the author, unless otherwise indicated.
2. A. Césaire, *Lettre à Maurice Thorez* (Paris: Présence Africaine, 1956), p. 8; quoted in A. J. Arnold, *Modernism and Negritude: The Poetry and Poetics of Aimé Césaire* (Cambridge: Harvard University Press, 1981), pp. 171–2.

3. Cf. C. J. Robinson, *Black Marxism: The Making of the Black Radical Tradition* (Chapel Hill: University of North Carolina Press, 2000); P. Gilroy, "'Cheer the Weary Traveller': W. E. B. Du Bois, Germany, and the Politics of (Dis)placement," *The Black Atlantic: Modernity and Double Consciousness* (London: Verso, 1993); but especially S. Zamir, *Dark Voices: W. E. B. Du Bois and American Thought, 1888–1903* (Chicago: University of Chicago Press, 1995).

4. G. W. F. Hegel, *La Phénoménologie de l'esprit*, trans. J. Hyppolite 2 vols, (Paris: Aubier-Montaigne, 1951).

5. W. E. B. Du Bois, "Karl Marx and the Negro," *Crisis*, 40, no. 2 (March 1933), p. 55.

6. W. E. B. Du Bois, "Marxism and the Negro Problem," in *W. E. B. Du Bois: A Reader*, ed. D. L. Lewis (New York: Henry Holt, 1995), p. 538. Hereafter cited in the text as "Marxism."

7. W. E. B. Du Bois, *Black Reconstruction in America* (1935; New York: Free Press, 1992), p. 9. Hereafter cited in the text as *Reconstruction*.

8. Cf. W. E. B. Du Bois, "The Negro and Radical Thought" (1921), his reply to Claude McKay as well as "The Negro and Communism" (1931), in *Du Bois: A Reader*, ed. Lewis.

9. W. E. B. Du Bois, "Socialism and the American Negro" (May 1960), cited in M. Marable, *W. E. B. Du Bois: Black Radical Democrat* (1986; Boulder and London: Paradigm Publishers, 2005), p. 206.

10. Cf. W. E. B. Du Bois, "Application for membership in the Communist Party of the United States of America," in *Du Bois: A Reader*, ed. Lewis, pp. 631–3.

11. W. E. B. Du Bois, *Dusk of Dawn: An Essay toward an Autobiography of a Race Concept (1940)*, in *W. E. B. Du Bois: Writings*, ed. N. Huggins (New York: Library of America, 1986), p. 704. My emphasis. Hereafter cited in the text as *Dusk*.

12. Cf. Du Bois, *Reconstruction*, pp. 122–3.

13. Of course no reading of consciousness in terms of dramaturgy can avoid Hegel. No one has done more to bring out the evasion of Hegel in Du Bois scholarship than S. Zamir, "'Double Consciousness': Locating the Self," in *Dark Voices*.

14. F. Fanon, *Les Damnés de la terre* (1961; Paris: Editions de la Découverte, 1987), p. 46. Hereafter cited in the text as *Damnés*.

15. F. Fanon, "L'Expérience vécue du noir," *Peau noir, masques blancs* (1952; Paris: Seuil, 1992), p. 89. Hereafter cited in the text as *Peau noir*.

16. Cf. G. Debord, *Oeuvres cinématographiques complètes, 1952–1978* (1978; Paris: Gallimard, 1994), p. 196.

17. F. Fanon, "Le 'syndrome nord africain,'" *Pour la revolution africaine* (1964; Paris: La Découverte, 2001), p. 13.

18. *Ibid.*, p. 23.

19. A. Kojève, *Introduction à la lecture de Hegel* (Paris: Gallimard, 1947), p. 384.

20. Gilroy, *Black Atlantic*, p. 118.

21. A. Césaire, *Discours sur le colonialisme* (Paris: Présence Africaine, 1955), p. 22.

22. Cf. C. L. R. James, "Dialectical Materialism and the Fate of Humanity," in *The C. L. R. Reader*, ed. A. Grimshaw (Oxford: Basil Blackwell, 1997), p. 154.

23. Cf. C. L. R. James, "Dialectical Materialism and the Fate of Humanity," p. 154.

24. V. Lenin, *Philosophical Notebook (1929–30)*, quoted in James, *Notes on Dialectics* (London: Allison and Busby, 1980), p. 101.

25. A. Césaire, "Culture et colonization," in *Le Premier Congrès International des écrivains et artistes noirs* (Paris: Présence Africaine, 1956), p. 194.

26. James, *Notes on Dialectics*, p. 116.

27. *Ibid.*, p. 117.

1. Works by Du Bois

(a) Principal Books

The Suppression of the African Slave-Trade to the United States of America, 1638–1870. New York: Longmans, Green, 1896.

Atlanta University Publications on the Study of Negro Problems. Publications of the Atlanta University Conferences, ed. Du Bois (Atlanta, 1898–1913).

The Philadelphia Negro: A Social Study. Boston: Ginn and Company, 1899.

The Souls of Black Folk: Essays and Sketches. Chicago: A. C. McClurg, 1903.

John Brown. Philadelphia: George W. Jacobs, 1909.

The Quest of the Silver Fleece: A Novel. Chicago: A. C. McClurg, 1911.

The Negro. New York: Henry Holt, 1915.

Darkwater: Voices from within the Veil. New York: Harcourt, Brace & Howe, 1920.

The Gift of Black Folk: Negroes in the Making of America. Boston: Stratford, 1924.

Dark Princess: A Romance. New York: Harcourt, Brace, 1928.

Africa – Its Place in Modern History. Girard, KS: Haldeman-Julius, 1930.

Africa – Its Geography, People and Products. Girard, KS: Haldeman-Julius, 1930.

Black Reconstruction in America: An Essay toward a History of the Part Which Black Folk Played in the Attempt to Reconstruct Democracy in America, 1860–1880. New York: Harcourt, Brace, 1935.

Black Folk Then and Now: An Essay in the History and Sociology of the Negro Race. New York: Henry Holt, 1939.

Dusk of Dawn: An Essay toward an Autobiography of a Race Concept. New York: Harcourt, Brace, 1940.

Color and Democracy: Colonies and Peace. New York: Harcourt, Brace, 1945.

The World and Africa: An Inquiry into the Part Which Africa Has Played in World History. New York: Viking, 1947.

In Battle for Peace: The Story of My 83rd Birthday. With Comment by Shirley Graham. New York: Masses & Mainstream, 1952.

The Black Flame Trilogy

  Mansart Builds a School. New York: Mainstream, 1959.

  The Ordeal of Mansart. New York: Mainstream, 1957.

  Worlds of Color. New York: Mainstream, 1961.

An ABC of Color: Selections from over a Half Century of the Writings of W. E. B. Du Bois. Berlin: Seven Seas, 1963.

The Autobiography of W. E. B. Du Bois: A Soliloquy on Viewing My Life from the Last Decade of its First Century, ed. H. Aptheker. New York: International Publishers, 1968.
W. E. B. Du Bois. *The Atlanta University Publications*, Nos. 1, 2, 4, 8, 9, 11, 13–18. New York: Arno Press and New York Times, 1968.

(b) Essays

Du Bois remained a prolific essayist and journalist throughout his long career. Among the short works most relevant to the discussions in the present volume are "The Conservation of Races" (1897), "The Talented Tenth" (1903), "The Damnation of Women" (1920), and "Criteria of Negro Art" (1926). These, as well as a substantial selection of editorials from the *Crisis*, can be found in *Writings* (ed. N. Huggins, 1986). Equally useful selections can be found in the readers edited by D. L. Lewis and E. J. Sundquist. Details of all three volumes are provided in the "Collections" section below.

(c) Collections

Aptheker, H (ed.). *Against Racism: Unpublished Essays, Papers, Addresses, 1887–1961. W. E. B. Du Bois.* Amherst: University of Massachusetts Press, 1985.
—. (ed.). *The Complete Published Works of W. E. B. Du Bois.* 35 vols. Millwood, NY: Kraus-Thomson, 1973.
—. (ed.). *The Correspondence of W. E. B. Du Bois.* 3 vols. Amherst: University of Massachusetts Press, 1973–8.
—. (ed.). *The Education of Black People: Ten Critiques, 1906–1960*, ed. Amherst: University of Massachusetts Press, 1973.
—. (ed.). *Newspaper Columns by W. E. B. Du Bois.* White Plains, NY: Kraus-Thomson Organization, 1986.
—. (ed.). *Writings by W. E. B. Du Bois in Periodicals Edited by Others.* 4 vols. Millwood, NY: Kraus-Thomson, 1982.
Foner, P. S. (ed.). *W. E. B. Du Bois Speaks: Speeches and Addresses 1890–1919.* New York: Pathfinder Press, 1970.
Huggins, N. (ed.). *W. E. B. Du Bois: Writings.* New York: Library of America, 1986.
Lewis, D. L. (ed.). *W. E. B. Du Bois: A Reader.* New York: Henry Holt, 1995.
Sundquist, E. J. (ed.). *The Oxford W. E. B. Du Bois Reader.* New York: Oxford University Press, 1996.

(d) A note on Editions of The Souls of Black Folk

The volume edited by D. W. Blight and R. Gooding-Williams (Boston: Bedford Book, 1997) is the most thoroughly annotated edition available and also contains other essays by Du Bois as well as some correspondence and photographs. The edition by H. L. Gates, Jr., and T. H. Oliver (New York: Norton, 1999) contains very helpful annotations and is especially useful for its inclusion of contextual and critical readings.

2. Works on Du Bois

Aldridge, D. "Conceptualizing a Du Boisian Philosophy of Education: Toward a Model for African-American Education," *Educational Theory* 49, no. 3 (1999), pp. 359–80.

Allen, E., Jr. "'Ever Feeling One's Twoness': 'Double Ideals' and 'Double Consciousness' in *The Souls of Black Folk*," *Critique of Anthropology*, 12, no. 3 (1992), pp. 261–75.

Appiah, K. A. "Ethics in a World of Strangers: W. E. B. Du Bois and the Spirit of Cosmopolitanism," *Berlin Journal*, 11 (2005), pp. 23–6.

—. "The Uncompleted Argument: Du Bois and the Illusion of Race," *Critical Inquiry*, 12, no. 1 (Autumn 1985), pp. 21–37.

Aptheker, H. *The Literary Legacy of W. E. B. Du Bois*. White Plains, NY: Kraus International, 1989.

—. "*The Souls of Black Folk*: A Comparison of the 1903 and 1952 Editions," *Negro History Bulletin*, 34, no. 1 (January 1971), pp. 15–17.

Baker, H. A., Jr. "The Black Man of Culture: W. E. B. Du Bois and *The Souls of Black Folk*," in *Long Black Song*. Charlottesville: University of Virginia Press, 1972.

Banks, W. *Black Intellectuals: Race and Responsibility in American Life*. New York: Norton, 1996.

Bay, M. *The White Image in the Black Mind*. New York: Oxford University Press, 2000.

Bell, B. "W. E. B. Du Bois's Struggle to Reconcile Folk and High Art," in *Critical Essays on W. E. B. Du Bois*, ed. W. L. Andrews. Boston: G. K. Hall, 1985, pp. 106–22.

—., E. Grosholz, and J. Stewart (eds). *W. E. B. Du Bois on Race and Culture: Philosophy, Politics, and Poetics*. New York: Routledge, Chapman, and Hall, 1996.

Berman, R. A. "Du Bois and Wagner: Race, Nation and Culture between the United States and Germany," *German Quarterly*, 70, no. 2 (1997), pp. 123–35.

Blight, D. W. "W. E. B. Du Bois and the Struggle for American Historical Memory," in *History and Memory in African-American Culture*, ed. G. Fabre and R. O'Meally. New York: Oxford University Press, 1994.

Boxhill, B. R. "Du Bois's Dilemma," in *Blacks and Social Justice*. Otowa, NJ: Rowman and Allanheld, 1984.

Bremen, B. A. "Du Bois, Emerson, and the 'Fate' of Black Folk," *American Literary Realism*, 24 (Spring 1992), pp. 80–8.

Brint, S. and J. LaValle. "DuBois Ascendant! And Other Results from the Brint – LaValle Theory Sections Survey," *Perspectives*, 22, no. 1 (2000), p. 1.

Broderick, F. L. "German Influence on the Scholarship of W. E. B. Du Bois," *Phylon*, 19, no. 4 (Winter 1958), pp. 367–71.

—. *W. E. B. Du Bois: Negro Leader in a Time of Crisis*. Stanford: Stanford University Press, 1959.

Brodwin, S. "The Veil Transcended: Form and Meaning in W. E. B. Du Bois' *The Souls of Black Folk*," *Journal of Black Studies*, 2 (March 1972), pp. 303–21.

Bruce, D. D., Jr. "W. E. B. Du Bois and the Idea of Double Consciousness," *American Literature*, 64, no. 2 (1992), pp. 299–309.

Byerman, K. *Seizing the Word: History, Art, and the Self in the Work of W. E. B. Du Bois*. Athens: University of Georgia Press, 1994.

Carby, H. V. *Race Men*. Cambridge: Harvard University Press, 1998.

Coser, L. A. *Masters of Sociological Thought: Ideas in Historical and Social Context*. 2nd edition. New York: Harcourt Brace Jovanovich, 1977.

Coviello, P. "Intimacy and Affliction: Du Bois, Race, and Psychoanalysis," *Modern Language Quarterly*, 64, no. 1 (2003), pp. 1–32.

Cruse, H. *The Crisis of the Negro Intellectual: A Historical Analysis of the Failure of Black Leadership* (1967). New York: New York Review of Books Classics, 2005.

—. *Plural but Equal: A Critical Study of Blacks and Minorities and America's Plural Society*. New York: William Morrow, 1987.

De Marco, J. *The Social Thought of W. E. B. Du Bois*. Lanham, MD: University Press of America, 1983.

Early, G. (ed.). *Lure and Loathing: Essays on Race, Identity, and the Ambivalence Assimilation*. New York: Allen Lane, 1993.

Earnest, J. *Liberation Historiography: African American Writers and the Challenge of History*. Chapel Hill: University of North Carolina Press, 2003.

Edwards, B. H. *The Practice of Diaspora: Literature, Translation, and the Rise of Black Internationalism*. Cambridge: Harvard University Press, 2003.

Edwards, B. S. "W. E. B. Du Bois Between Worlds: Berlin, Empirical Social Research, and the Race Question," *Du Bois Review*, 3 (September 2006), pp. 395–424.

Fontenot, C. J., Jr. "Du Bois's 'Of the Coming of John,' Toomer's 'Kabnis,' and the Dilemma of Self-Representation," in *The Souls of Black Folk One Hundred Years Later*, ed. D. Hubbard. Columbia: University of Missouri Press, 2003, pp. 130–60.

Frederickson, G. M. *The Black Image in the White Mind: The Debate on Afro-American Character and Destiny, 1817–1914*. New York: Harper and Row, 1971.

Gates, H. L., Jr. "The Trope of a New Negro and the Reconstruction of the Image of the Black," *Representations*, 24 (1988), pp. 129–55.

Giles, P. *Virtual Americas: Transnational Fictions and the Transatlantic Imaginary*. Durham, NC: Duke University Press, 2002.

Gillman, S., and A. E. Weinbaum. *Next to the Color Line: Gender, Sexuality and W. E. B. Du Bois*. Minneapolis: University of Minnesota Press, 2007.

Gilroy, P. *The Black Atlantic: Modernity and Double Consciousness*. London: Verso, 1993.

Gooding-Williams, R. "Du Bois's Counter-Sublime," *Massachusetts Review: A Quarterly of Literature, the Arts and Public Affairs*, 35, no. 2 (Summer 1994), pp. 202–24.

—. "Philosophy of History and Social Critique in *The Souls of Black Folk*," *Social Science Information*, 26, no. 1 (1987), pp. 99–114.

Gordon, L. R. "Du Bois's Humanistic Philosophy of Human Sciences," *Annals of the American Academy of Political and Social Science*, 568 (2000), pp. 265–80.

Green, D. S., and E. D. Driver. "W. E. B. Du Bois: A Case in the Sociology of Sociological Negation," *Phylon*, 37, no. 4 (1976), 308–33.

Griffin, F. J. "Black Feminists and Du Bois: Respectability, Protection and Beyond," *Annals of the American Academy of Political and Social Science*, 568 (2000), pp. 28–40.

Hancock, A.-M. "W. E. B. Du Bois: Intellectual Forefather of Intersectionality?," *SOULS: A Critical Journal of Black Politics, Culture and Society*, 7 (2005), pp. 74–84.

Harrison, F. V. "The Du Boisian Legacy in Anthropology," *Critique of Anthropology*, 12, no. 3 (1993), pp. 239–60.

Herring, S. "Du Bois and the Minstrels," *MELUS*, 22 (Summer 1997), pp. 3–18.

Holt, T. C. "The Political Uses of Alienation: W. E. B. Du Bois on Politics, Race and Culture, 1903–1940," *American Quarterly*, 42, no. 2 (1990), pp. 301–23.

Jones, G. "'Whose Line Is It Anyway?' W. E. B. Du Bois and the Language of the Color-Line," in *Race Consciousness: African-American Studies for the New Century*, ed. J. J. Fossett and Jeffrey A. Tucker. New York: New York University Press, 1997.

Katz, M. B. "Race, Poverty and Welfare: Du Bois' Legacy for Policy," *Annals of the American Academy of Political and Social Science*, 568 (2000), pp. 111–27.

—, and T. J. Sugrue (eds.). *W. E. B. Du Bois, Race, and the City: The Philadelphia Negro and its Legacy*. Philadelphia: University of Pennsylvania Press, 1998.

Kilson, M. "The Washington and Du Bois Leadership Paradigms Reconsidered," *Annals of the American Academy of Political and Social Science*, 568 (2000), pp. 298–313.

Kim, D. H. "Modern Order and the Promise of Anarchy: From the 'Writhing Age' of *Souls* to World Reconstruction," *Hamline Review*, 28 (2004), pp. 22–71.

King, R. H. *Race, Culture and the Intellectuals, 1940–1970*, Washington, D.C. and Baltimore: Wilson Center Press and Johns Hopkins University Press, 2004.

Kirkland, F. M. "Modernity and Intellectual Life in Black," *Philosophical Forum*, 24, nos. 1–3 (1992–3), pp. 136–65.

Krell, D. F. "The Bodies of Black Folk: From Kant and Hegel to Du Bois and Baldwin," *boundary*, 27 (2000), pp. 103–34.

Lange, W. "W. E. B. Du Bois and the First Scientific Study of Afro-America," *Phylon*, 44, no. 2 (1983), pp. 135–46.

Lemke, S. "Berlin and Boundaries," *boundary 2*, 27, 3 (2000), pp. 45–78.

—. *Primitivist Modernism: Black Culture and the Origins of Transatlantic Modernism*. New York: Oxford University Press, 1998.

Lewis, D. L. *W. E. B. Du Bois: Biography of a Race, 1868–1919*. New York: Henry Holt, 1993.

—. *W. E. B. Du Bois: The Fight for Equality and the American Century 1919–1963*. New York: Henry Holt, 2000.

Logan, R. W. *The Negro in American Life and Thought: The Nadir, 1877–1901*. New York: Dial Press, 1954.

Lott, T. L. "Du Bois on the Invention of Race," *Philosophical Forum*, 24, nos. 1–3 (1992–3), pp. 116–87.

Marable, M. *W. E. B. Du Bois: Black Radical Democrat*. Boston: Twayne, 1986.

Maxwell, W. J. *New Negro, Old Left: African-American Writing and Communism Between the Wars*. New York: Columbia University Press, 1999.

McKay, Nellie. "W. E. B. Du Bois: The Black Women in His Writings – Selected Fictional and Autobiographical Portraits," in *Critical Essays on W. E. B. Du Bois*, ed. W. L. Andrews. Boston: G. K. Hall, 1985.

Meier, A. *Negro Thought in America, 1880–1915: Racial Ideologies in the Age of Booker T. Washington*. Ann Arbor: University of Michigan Press, 1965.

Menand, L. *The Metaphysical Club*. New York: Farrar, Straus and Giroux, 2001.

Milligan, N. M. "W. E. B. Du Bois' American Pragmatism," *Journal of American Culture*, 8 (1985), pp. 31–7.

Mizruchi, S. "Neighbors, Strangers, Corpses: Death and Sympathy in the Early Writings of W. E. B. Du Bois," in *The Souls of Black Folk*, ed. H. L. Gates, Jr., and T. H. Oliver (New York: Norton, 1999), pp. 286–95.

Monteiro, A., "Being an African in the World: The Du Boisian Epistemology," *Annals of the American Academy of Political and Social Science*, 568 (2000), pp. 220–34.

Moore, J. B. *W. E. B. Du Bois*. Boston: Twayne, 1981.

Moses, W. J. *Alexander Crummell: A Study of Civilisation and Discontent*. New York: Oxford University Press, 1989.

—. *Creative Conflict in African American Thought: Frederick Douglass, Alexander Crummell, Booker T. Washington, W. E. B. Du Bois, and Marcus Garvey*. Cambridge: Cambridge University Press, 2004.

—. *The Golden Age of Black Nationalism, 1850–1925*. Hamden, CN: Archon Books, 1978.

Moss, A. A., Jr. *The American Negro Academy: Voice of the Talented Tenth*. Baton Rouge: Louisiana State University Press, 1981.

Muller, N. L. "Du Boisian Pragmatism and 'The Problem of the Twentieth Century,'" *Critique of Anthropology*, 12, no. 3 (1992), pp. 319–37.

North, M. *The Dialect of Modernism: Race, Language and Twentieth-Century Literature*. New York: Oxford University Press, 1994.

Olson, J. "W. E. B. Du Bois and the Race Concept," *SOULS: A Critical Journal of Black Politics, Culture and Society*, 7 (2005), pp. 118–28.

Outlaw, L. T. "W. E. B. Du Bois on the Study of Social Problems," *Annals of the American Academy of Political and Social Science*, 568 (2000), pp. 281–97.

Peterson, D. "Notes from the Underworld: Dostoyevsky, Du Bois, and the Discovery of the Ethnic Soul," *Massachusetts Review*, 35 (Summer 1994), pp. 225–47.

Posnock, R. *Color and Culture: Black Writers and the Making of the Modern Intellectual*. Cambridge: Harvard University Press, 1998.

Pratt Guterl, M. *The Color of Race in America 1900–1940*. Cambridge: Harvard University Press, 2001.

Provenzo, E. F., Jr. *Du Bois on Education*. Walnut Creek, CA: Alta Mira Press, 2002.

Rampersad, A. *The Art and Imagination of W. E. B. Du Bois*. Cambridge: Harvard University Press, 1976.

—. "Slavery and the Literary Imagination: Du Bois's *The Souls of Black Folk*," in *Slavery and the Literary Imagination*, ed. D. McDowell and A. Rampersad. Baltimore: Johns Hopkins University Press, 1989, pp. 104–24.

Rath, R. C. "Echo and Narcissus: The Afrocentric Pragmatism of W. E. B. Du Bois," *Journal of American History*, 84 (September 1997), pp. 461–95.

Reed, A., Jr. "W. E. B. Du Bois: A Perspective on the Bases of His Political Thought," *Political Theory*, 13 (August 1985), pp. 431–56.

—. *W. E. B. Du Bois and American Political Thought: Fabianism and the Color Line*. New York, Oxford University Press, 1997.

Robinson, C. J. *Black Marxism: The Making of the Black Radical Tradition* (1983), Foreword by Robin D. G. Kelley; new preface by the author. Chapel Hill: University of North Carolina Press, 2000.

Rowe. J. C. (ed.). *Post-Nationalist American Studies*. Berkeley: University of California Press, 2000.

Rudwick, E. M. "Notes on a Forgotten Black Sociologist: W. E. B. Du Bois and the Sociological Profession," *American Sociologist*, 4 (November 1969), pp. 303–6.

—. *W. E. B. Du Bois: A Study in Minority Group Leadership*. Philadelphia: University of Pennsylvania Press, 1960.

—. "W. E. B. Du Bois as Sociologist," in *Black Sociologists: Historical and Contemporary Perspectives*, ed. J. E. Blackwell and M. Janowitz. Chicago: University of Chicago Press, 1974, pp. 25–55.

Santori, G. "Probation of the Races," *SOULS: A Critical Journal of Black Politics, Culture and Society*, 7 (2005), pp. 96–117.

Sawyer, M. Q. "Du Bois's Double Consciousness versus Latin American Exceptionalism: Joe Arroyo, Salsa, and Negritude," *SOULS: A Critical Journal of Black Politics, Culture and Society*, 7 (2005), pp. 85–95.

Schrager, C. D. "Both Sides of the Veil: Race, Science, and Mysticism in W. E. B. Du Bois," *American Quarterly*, 48 (December 1996), pp. 551–87.

Shelby, T. *We Who Are Dark: The Philosophical Foundations of Black Solidarity*. Cambridge: Harvard University Press, 2005.

Siemerling, W. *The New North American Studies: Culture, Writing and the Politics of Re/cognition*. London: Routledge, 2005.

Stepto, R. *From Behind the Veil: A Study of Afro-American Narrative*. Urbana: University of Illinois Press, 1979.

Sundquist, E. J. *To Wake the Nations: Race in the Making of American Literature*. Cambridge: Harvard University Press, 1993.

Taylor, P. C. "Appiah's Uncontested Argument: W. E. B. Du Bois and the Reality of Race," *Social Theory and Practice*, 26, no. 1 (Spring 2000), pp. 103–28.

Townsend, K. "'Manhood' at Harvard: W. E. B. Du Bois," *Raritan*, 15 (Spring 1996), pp. 70–82.

Wald, P. *Constituting Americans: Cultural Anxiety and Narrative Form*. Durham, NC: Duke University Press, 1995.

Walker, C. D. B. "'Of the Coming of John [and Jane]': African American Intellectuals in Europe, 1888–1938," *Amerikastudien/American Studies*, 47, no. 1 (2002), pp. 7–22.

Warren, K. W. *Black and White Strangers: Race and American Literary Realism*. Chicago: University of Chicago Press, 1993.

—. "Delimiting America: The Legacy of Du Bois," *American Literary History* (Spring 1989), pp. 172–89.

—. "Troubled Black Humanity in *The Souls of Black Folk* and *The Autobiography of an Ex-Colored Man*," in *The Cambridge Companion to American Realism and Naturalism: Howells to London*, ed. Donald Pizer. Cambridge: Cambridge University Press, 1995.

West, C. *The American Evasion of Philosophy: A Genealogy of Pragmatism*. Madison: University of Wisconsin Press, 1989.

Williams, E. "Why the Music 'Put [Him] All A-Tun': Wagner's Lohengrin and the Politics of Cultural Segregation in Du Bois's 'Of the Coming of John,'" draft. 23.8.2006. http//216.239.59.104/search?q=cache:3Ytfji82cQJ:institute. emerson. edu/wip/williams

Williamson, J. *The Crucible of Race: Black-White Relations in the American South since Emancipation*. New York: Oxford University Press, 1984.

Wolfenstein, E. V. "Recognition and *The Souls of Black Folks*," *SOULS: A Critical Journal of Black Politics, Culture and Society*, 7 (2005), pp. 129–39.

Zamir, S. *Dark Voices: W. E. B. Du Bois and American Thought, 1888–1903*. Chicago: University of Chicago Press, 1995.

—. "'The Sorrow Songs'/'Song of Myself': Du Bois, the Crisis of Leadership, and Prophetic Imagination," in *The Black Columbiad: Defining Moments in African American Literature and Culture*, ed. W. Sollors and M. Dietrich. Cambridge: Harvard University Press, 1994, pp. 145–66.

Zuckerman, P. (ed.). *The Social Theory of W. E. B. Du Bois*. Thousand Oaks, CA: Pine Forge Press, 2004.

INDEX